Open access edition supported by the National Endowment for the Humanities /
Andrew W. Mellon Foundation Humanities Open Book Program.

Johns Hopkins University Press
2715 North Charles Street
Baltimore, Maryland 21218-4363
www.press.jhu.edu

ISBN-13: 978-1-4214-2991-5 (open access)
ISBN-10: 1-4214-2991-8 (open access)

ISBN-13: 978-1-4214-3032-4 (pbk. : alk. paper)
ISBN-10: 1-4214-3032-0 (pbk. : alk. paper)

ISBN-13: 978-1-4214-3073-7 (electronic)
ISBN-10: 1-4214-3073-8 (electronic)

This page supersedes the copyright page included in the original publication of this work.

BOSSES, MACHINES,
AND URBAN VOTERS

REVISED EDITION

Bosses, Machines, and Urban Voters

JOHN M. ALLSWANG

THE JOHNS HOPKINS UNIVERSITY PRESS
Baltimore and London

The Johns Hopkins University Press
701 West 40th Street
Baltimore, Maryland 21211
The Johns Hopkins Press Ltd., London

Library of Congress Cataloging in Publication Data

Allswang, John M.
  Bosses, machines, and urban voters.

  Bibliography: p.
  Includes index.
  1. Municipal government—United States—History.
2. Politicians—United States—History. I. Title.
JS309.A37   1986   320.8'0973   85-24042
ISBN 0-8018-3323-X
ISBN 0-8018-3312-4 (pbk.)

for
SUZANNE, EDEN, AND YAEL
—one more time

CONTENTS

PREFACE TO THE
1986 EDITION

Ten years ago, Americans were deeply involved in the celebration of their bicentennial year. At that time, we became well acquainted, once again, with our colonial predecessors, the revolutionary generation, and even the hardy pioneers of the nineteenth century. We learned less, however, about our urban pioneers, and particularly about the Boss Tweeds, the Tony Cermaks, and their little-remembered but numerous counterparts. This was unfortunate, because urbanization, its concomitant industrialization and immigration, and the politics that emanated from them are very important aspects of our country's second century.

That was why I wrote the first edition of this book, in 1977. And it is because the phenomenon it studies continues to be both interesting and important, with its dynamic not quite spent in the early years of the nation's third century, that I have now revised it, carrying it on to the present day.

Henry Adams and George Washington Plunkitt were contemporaries; that Plunkitt is less well remembered is regrettable, not because he was more or less "important," but because his education was as illustrative of the milieu of millions of newer Americans as Adams's was of thousands of older ones. New York Commissioner Charles Francis Murphy and President Theodore Roosevelt were also contemporaries, and to some degree direct opponents; as far as the lives of many New Yorkers were concerned, the commissioner may well have been a more towering figure than the president.

The urban political machine and its more or less absolute leader, the boss, have been matters of heightened scholarly interest in recent decades largely because of an increased desire to understand our urban past. As an urban nation, we naturally try to understand the development of urban politics, the clearest expression of the social and economic development of the city. The study of the city's political development provides a path for understanding the dynamics of its growth, its interpersonal and group relationships, and its role, generally, in our nation's development. And for many of our cities, particularly the larger ones, one or another variety of what is generally called "machine politics" was, for varying periods of time, characteristic.

In the pages that follow I try to suggest the whys and the ways of the bosses and the machines, particularly in terms of their internal dynamics and of the people who supported and opposed them. If the boss has been characteristic of the city, it can equally be said that the city has been characteristic of the boss. Each has required the other. The reasons for this lie in the social, cultural, and economic complexity of the modern city, and most especially in the kinds of people who have lived there and the kinds of problems they have faced. Thus my inquiry involves much more than politics in some sterile sense—it gets us into an understanding of what American cities have been all about to those who have lived in them.

This is largely a historical problem, a function of the past. But not entirely so. The factors that led to the rise of the boss and the machine are not yet gone, and some factors seem likely to survive this century. But both seem nearly gone, and the reasons for this are central to the inquiry of this book.

In the first chapter I deal with the concepts of the boss and the machine and with their development over time. In surveying a century's writing on bosses, I hope not only to develop the concept itself but also to suggest the ways in which scholars and the public at large have been interested in and troubled by "the problem" of the machine. Bosses and machines, after all, have not only been important aspects of urbanization; they have been major issues, as well.

I hope that the first chapter will provide the reader with the necessary grounding for a more sophisticated understanding of particulars. These particulars are provided in the next four chapters, which consider in some detail five different bosses and machines, at various times. Through these case studies the reader can see the principles outlined in Chapter 1 in action and can also draw some individual conclusions about the significance of what I am describing. In addition to trying carefully to develop the careers of the bosses themselves, I want to put those careers in the context of the other side of the picture—the voters: who they were and why they seem to have made the choices they did. To accomplish the latter task I have made use of some simple statistical techniques and have tried to show how they can be useful.

Chapter 6 deals with the present, with some of the major social and demographic issues with which contemporary urban politics—machine or not—must contend. This chapter and the Epilogue also confront more directly the question of the overall effect of machines and some of the reasons for their decline. To some degree, they suggest that the "machine/reform" dichotomy is often overstressed—that the form of urban government has been of less importance than one might imagine.

In the first edition of this book, where its central questions and theses were developed, I benefited considerably from the help of colleagues and friends. I am particularly indebted to Profs. Bruce M. Stave and Samuel T. McSeveney, and to Laurance P. Nathan, Esq., for their suggestions and corrections. The second edition reflects some years of rethinking these matters, plus a continuing fascination with the development of Chicago politics as a laboratory *par excellence* for viewing the contemporary American city. Everything in the book, fact and interpretation, is my own responsiblility, and I hereby exonerate colleagues named and unnamed of any shared burden for what the reader may not like.

As usual when I am writing books, my wife and daughters viewed the process with an affectionate and supportive lack of interest, which has always seemed to me entirely appropriate. And so I lovingly dedicate one more book to them, in thanks for their not being any more obstructionist than is their custom.

BOSSES, MACHINES, AND URBAN VOTERS

1

OF CITY BOSSES AND COLLEGE GRADUATES

George Washington Plunkitt, New York district leader and Tammany Hall apologist, in defending political bossism, asked pointedly: "Have you ever thought what would become of the country if the bosses were put out of business, and their places were taken by a lot of cart-tail orators and college graduates? It would be chaos." It is a question worth pondering, and will be developed further below. But it also suggests one of the problems which has plagued the popular understanding of bossism from the time of Tweed to our own day.

Writers on bosses and bossism have been what Plunkitt would see as "college graduates," i.e., people of some education, who looked at the political machine from the outside. Whether they romanticized and glamorized the boss or saw him as the epitome of urban evil, such writers, particularly in the early twentieth century, did look at him from another world, and did seek common themes that probably did not exist. And they have looked for effects from bossism that also may well not have existed: one of the most striking things about American urban government in modern times is that basic human problems have been dealt with in about the same way in one city after another regardless of the form of city government.

This book is another approach by a "college graduate" to the phenomenon of the urban boss, one whose author is as convinced of his ability to see "reality" as were the earlier authors whose errors he will be only too ready to point out. Perhaps time and the incremental growth of understanding do permit the contemporary to understand things better; only additional time will make that clear, however.

Certainly the urban boss is one of the enduring themes of popular and scholarly literature in the United States. It is a fascination as old as the modern city and, if the current spate of texts, readers, and popular studies is any indication, seems to strike a no less responsive chord today than it did one hundred years ago. This is partly due to a certain aura of romance attached to the boss, as seen in such popular works as the novel and film of Edwin O'Connor's *The Last Hurrah*. Partly, also, it is due to the aura of scandal and corruption that has seemed attendant upon bosses and urban politics in general, which has made them exciting to read about. And partly, too, it is because urban politics has been so important in modern life, and those referred to as bosses so often central therein, that it has been very logical for college graduates to write about them and for the public to follow along.

I hope in the pages to follow to introduce the general topic in such a way as to shed some light on what bossism may have been all about, or is all about; and at the same time to try to understand why people have been so aroused by it. Central to this is the question of who supported the people who were called bosses—why, in a democratic polity, have they been so often, if decreasingly, successful? And as a corollary of that—who opposed the bosses, and why? and what has been the measure of their success?

Richard J. Daley of Chicago was frequently referred to as the "last" big city boss, heading the last of the big city political machines. Indeed, his colorful and controversial career in our own day played no small part in the current wave of interest in bossism. And I shall look directly at Daley, as well as several of his predecessors, in the hope of finding what, if anything, there is in common in bosses and bossing. Why did a boss continue to rule in Chicago while, as is common knowledge, this phenomenon had died out everywhere else? Was it due to Daley, or Chicago, or something else entirely? That is a question, and a theme, that might well be our focus, for in it is the whole concept of bossism, its dimensions and reality.

A number of terms have been nearly universal in over a century's attention to urban politics—*boss, bossism, machine, ring*. But one might well ask whether they have any precise meaning. They do not—which is precisely why there is so much disagreement over these phenomena, when and where they have existed, and whether they have been good or evil. I shall try to make some sense of this as we go along, but, essentially, the differences between a boss and a leader, between a machine and an organization, are normative, and exist primarily in the mind of the speaker.

There are, to be sure, certain things which we shall see as fairly common in what has been called "boss politics"; it is a system hierarchical in structure, highly responsive to immediate needs of the electorate, strongly focussed on political control as an end in itself, and generally very partisan. But these characteristics permit tremendous variety of form and content. And they can be as characteristic of urban "reform politics"—a construct even less unambiguous, rhetorically and really, than "machine politics"—as of that politics deplored by those who labeled themselves reformers.

Among the most important variables influencing the politics of any city is the city itself—its demographic composition, geography, economic and class characteristics, and the system of law, especially state law, within which it exists. It is these variables which most students of bossism—pro, con, or somewhere in between—have insufficiently dealt with. That is a major error because it has led to oversimplification and overgeneralization; and, I think, it has led to a great deal of misunderstanding. In any city at any particular time, these characteristics are central in determining which among the governmental options open to it happen to be chosen. That political party, or organization, or candidate(s) which seem most likely to most voters to deal with what they comprehend as their urban needs tends to win. Beneath this generalization, of course there are many specific factors. But it is nonetheless a crucial generalization; very often scholars and popular writers—those "college graduates" again—seek complexities and conspiracies only because they ignore the obvious.

For my own purposes, I shall make no distinction between a *machine* and an *organization,* and will use the terms interchangeably. Likewise I make no distinction between *boss* and *leader,* although I will not use the latter term very often. Since there is inevitably, as a result of usage, a certain pejorative sense to the words *boss* and *machine,* I am thus trying to neutralize them in order to render them more useful. The terms have been by no means neutral to many who have used them in the past, as we shall see; but the ultimate decision about whether the terms have any real meaning at all must be made a bit later. And the ultimate decision about whether or not, if bosses and machines are real, they are good or bad, has to remain interpretive and personal.

One of the ideas most intimately associated with the concept of bossism has been that of control. The general view has been that a boss, or a machine, is a political entity that controls blocs of votes—often seen in terms of ethnic or economic groups in the city (or state, since a boss can be more than a citywide figure, although such will not be of central concern here). And I think it is important to put this idea aside at the outset, both because it is a presumption that is misleading until proven, and because I think it is, in fact, inaccurate. It is very important to remember that American urban politics exists within a democratic polity—people do vote for their officeholders. One can find vote stealing in American cities, under Tweed and probably also under Daley, as well as in between; one can find intimidation and misdirection of voters; and one can find a hundred other associated evils at various times and in various places. But, in boss-run cities as well as those receiving more favorable appellations, most people most of the time voted free from duress and without illusions. Voting is a rational act, a choice among alternatives; the alternatives were sometimes great and sometimes small, but the vast majority of voters have always made choices on the basis of their own rational appraisal of the alternatives in terms of their own lives.

Thus to talk of a boss or machine controlling voters is quite an over-simplification: it generally accords too much power to the boss and too little attention to the voter. I shall try not to fall into that trap here. Indeed, most bosses who have lost power, and most machines that have ground to a halt, have done so less because of reform pressure per se than because they have lost the support of too many voters. The reasons for this loss of support have been highly various and were often not those the so-called reformers believed.

For this reason I shall pay less attention to reform and reformers as such, and more to the kinds of alternatives that seemed available to voters as they saw them. Voters, as individuals or as members of social, cultural, or economic groups, were aware of what middle-class and upper-class reformers offered them, and were aware of what the machine—or sometimes rival machines—offered them. Their decision-making process determined the shape of modern American politics, and I shall therefore focus on the bosses and the voters, and their interrelationship, as key factors in the development of machine politics in America.

But the boss has been not only a major phenomenon in urban politics, he (there have been, to my knowledge, no women to whom the term has been applied) has also been a major issue therein. For this reason, and also to expand our understanding of bossism and of the popular and scholarly interest in bossism over a hundred years, I want to look in some detail at what has been said about bosses from Tweed to Daley. It is neither possible nor necessary to attempt an encyclopedic survey of the literature of bossism. Rather, I want to show the variety of approaches taken in the scholarly and popular literature and especially to devote some time to those works which have been most influential in shaping popular and scholarly attitudes toward and understanding of bosses and machines.

Some have suggested that the first American boss was Aaron Burr; others opt for Martin Van Buren and his "Albany Regency." But we can safely ignore those powerful political figures who flourished before the rise of the modern city and settle, with most scholars, on William Marcy Tweed of New York. New York in the 1860s was the first place, and the first time, that the constituent elementary requirements of the modern urban political machine really existed. And it is testimony to this that the first popular exposés of the evils of bossism arose with Tweed.

Tweed's case was somewhat unusual, since contemporary writings about the Tweed Ring did play a central role in that machine's downfall. In most cases, publicity has had less effect. Nonetheless, the ideas and the stereotypes developed in opposition to Tweed anticipated much that would characterize the appraisal of bossism for a hundred years. This was particularly true with the famous political cartoons of Thomas Nast in *Harper's Weekly*, which, with the exposé in the *New York Times*, were of the greatest significance.

Nast's cartoons, which combined a strong intellectual message with even stronger emotional and humorous appeal, pictured Tweed and his minions as gross, coarse, vulgar, and entirely self-serving. The bosses pictured by Nast were in public life only for their own material gain, and they dealt with the public from a position of profound cynicism. At first the impact of the cartoons was only general, but as other sources began to build a solid factual case against the Tweed Ring, the cartoons served as telling reiterations of those charges.

The *New York Times*, also, became increasingly effective. Its view of the Ring was equally negative and equally emotional, at first. And it was not followed by the rest of the press in 1870, when it appeared that the paper's own partisanship was as much the source of its views as anything else. But by the summer of 1871, when the *Times* was able to begin publication of hard data on the Ring's thefts, it became more influential, especially as reinforced by Nast's cartoons. Many other newspapers then took up the crusade, which led to Tweed's defeat in the 1871 elections and his ultimate trial and conviction.

The general picture of bossism in Tweed's New York was focussed entirely on its evils, with little attention to the function it served. The bosses were corrupt and greedy men, maladministering the city for their own private gain. The exposé received strong middle- and upper-class support since those were the groups least served by the Tweed Ring. And what social interest the crusade had was typical of much of the battle against bossism from that time forward—nativism, in terms of anti-Irish Catholicism, was very much present.

The exposers of Tweed did not consider the ways in which his machine, playing an important social role, served the immigrants. Rather, they focussed on the power the machine in effect gave to unassimilated, dangerous classes in New York. If they were hardly analytic in their understanding of the relationship between the boss and the urban masses, the "reformers" of New York at least realized that such a relationship did exist and was crucial to the existence of the machine. Their solution was to replace the machine with a government responsive to other groups in the society—not to try to deal with the problems of those groups which had turned to the machine for support. This, too, would be a standard approach, and limitation, of urban reformers, as we shall see below.

The concern with bossism expanded, as the institution itself did, during the remainder of the nineteenth century. Journalists in many cities, rising nonmachine politicians like Theodore Roosevelt, and middle- and upper-class business groups whose interests became increasingly contrary to those of the mass-based machine, were the major foci of written and active opposition. As industry and immigration developed together and the number and size of American cities increased immensely between the time of Tweed and the First World War, the number of places amenable to machine politics likewise increased. And so, too, did the study and exposure of bossism.

The picture of the boss and the machine in the late nineteenth century remained pretty consistent. The machine politician was corrupt, immoral, and entirely self-serving. Moreover, his power derived from an alliance with the most untrustworthy and disreputable elements in the urban society, thus posing the threat not only of bad government but also of social danger. It was a contemporary evil requiring excision.

Not surprisingly, the European commentators who were so interested in America, and especially the American industrial city, also focussed on bossism. And in so doing, they provided probably the first "scholarly" literature on this phenomenon. The first significant approach came in 1888 with the publication of James Bryce's famous and widely read two-volume study of American government, *The American Commonwealth*. Bryce was an attorney and member of the House of Commons who had visited the United States several times, starting in 1870; he was later British ambassador to the United States (1907-13) and was made a viscount (hence the common appellation Lord Bryce) in 1913.

Bryce's volumes form one of the classic studies of American government and society—not so profound as de Tocqueville's, but, along with that by Ostrogorski, of the next rank. Most of his second volume concentrated on the nature of the American party system, which led to considerable attention to what he called "the machine" at all governmental levels. He was impressed with the centrality of the full-time, permanent party managers, well organized at every level of activity, who, it seemed to him, had an entirely different motivation from officeholders, participants at nominating conventions, or the public at large. It was this self-serving group, oriented to its own narrow interest, that he labeled "the machine." Certain tendencies in American politics, such as the great frequency of elections and the great number of offices voted for, created the need for such a professional intermediary group. Thus, he felt, the very representativeness of American politics, compared with that of Europe (via the primary, Americans even chose their candidates, which greatly impressed Bryce), combined with the less ideological nature of American politics, created the special role filled by the machine. He seemed to feel that the American alternative to an aristocracy was the party apparatus, with the professional politician providing the stability and permanency provided in Europe by a distinct class.

Like other commentators, Bryce was fascinated with the American city, which did seem a microcosm of the political nature and problems of the whole society. The city, he said, was distinctive because, in addition to generally having elections more frequently, having a great number of offices, lacking issues, and having universal suffrage, it also had "a very large population of ignorant immigrants" and a situation wherein "the leading men are all intensely occupied with business." Moreover, the population was so large and complex that "the interest of each individual in good government is comparatively small." It was this set of circumstances which permitted the development of generally unadmirable city machines.

Bryce saw the immigrants as ignorant but shrewd; they had an implicit sense of the strength of group voting and of alliance with party organizations. Moreover, urban populations were impermanent and lacked a tradition of leadership. Thus there derived a purely partisan group politics, devoid of issues or even of commitment to quality individuals. It was a situation facilitating corruption and misgovernment generally.

Again and again Bryce went back to the mass base of the machine, the role of the "ignorant masses." The urban masses were not the same as the "working class," the latter being a group for which he had respect. It was the amorphous mass—"largely Irish and Germans, together with Poles and Russians, Bohemians, negroes, Frenchmen, Italians, and such native Americans as have fallen from their first estate into drink or penury" —that concerned him. On the one hand, these groups were well organized and powerful, and on the other, they possessed "neither national patriotism nor a sense of civic duty." Unfortunately, he concluded, "the pity is that they have been allowed civic power." To have enfranchised such a group was politically dangerous, Bryce argued; their political loyalties derived from a base contrary to good government. They were loyal to the party which had welcomed them on their arrival in America or to the party which seemed best to represent their own "race"; they were often moved by Roman Catholic "religious sympathy," by "protection of the liquor traffic," or by narrow ethnic hatreds, as the Irish were in supporting the party most opposed to England.

In all of this Bryce was indeed perceptive, and very close to the truth.

His understanding of the structure of American urban politics was quite accurate; but his ideas about its content and effects now seem unpersuasive. I shall try to return again and again to the question of whether definitive and general conclusions about the content and merit of government can be derived from the study of its structure or form. Certainly most of the early literature on machines and bosses agreed with Bryce—indeed, was influenced by him.

Although Bryce was very much impressed by the popular base of urban misgovernment, that was not his only focus. His conclusion that American government suffered greatly from the tendency of the "best men" to turn to business rather than to public life was very persuasive in the late nineteenth century. And he argued that businessmen were also directly culpable, in that they often supported corrupt government if it served their pecuniary ends. This, too, was one of the main themes of writing on the machine for the next fifty years.

In looking at the boss, separate from the machine, Bryce saw many of the same forces in operation. The boss was a consummate expression of the professional politician's "desire for office, and for office as a means of gain." Once again, on top of facile overgeneralization, Bryce went on to a perceptive description of the ways in which a boss developed. And he again stressed the social context: bossism was more likely in the large city, where there existed "the largest masses of manageable voters as well as numerous offices and plentiful opportunities for jobbing." The boss was a man who was able to build a base for himself, in his own neighborhood, or in a "grog-shop or beer-saloon, which perhaps he keeps himself," and use it to rise in the party machine. If he was shrewd enough, he could rise to the top of the machine and become the boss of the whole city, or even a wider area than that.

Thus Bryce articulated, without actually using the words, the hierarchical nature of machine politics, culminating some of the time in an individual who sat astride the whole thing and thus "bossed" it. The boss, in himself and as an institution, was not innately evil. Rather, he was "a leader to whom certain peculiar social and political conditions have given a character dissimilar from the party leaders whom Europe knows." What was evil, Bryce felt, was that bossism was part of a politics that existed irrespective of issues, or even of focus on high quality personnel. And for this reason at least (and, I think, because of Bryce's feeling, in spite of what he may have said before, that the boss was indeed evil as an individual), Bryce advocated a "war against bossism."

The good citizens of boss- and machine-ruled cities were not passive, they were just outnumbered. Reform was under way and took several paths: (1) active involvement by the "good citizens," who should be more involved in politics at all levels, especially in the primaries; (2) reform lists of candidates in general elections, offering an alternative to corrupt parties; (3) abstention from voting, which could sometimes at least topple the party in power from its control.

But, Bryce concluded, one victory by reformers did not change things. He realized that the social context produced the machine; but he could only offer reforms which took no cognizance of the social system itself. While he bemoaned "apathy or short-sightedness in the upper classes," he also realized that the United States, as compared with Europe, was truly an example of "government by public opinion." The people really did rule, and their representatives were indeed very much like them.

Thus Bryce was caught in a quandary emanating partly from his own European, class-bound conception of government and politics, but coming more from the realities of the situation. The boss and the machine derived from a democratic polity and a given social situation; he did not really want to change the polity and apparently had no conception of the possibility of changing the social situation. He, and those who followed him, would consequently tend to focus on symptoms of the situation they disparaged (the individuals who won elections, for example) and would never understand that only through changing the social context could meaningful change in the political system itself actually be implemented.

We must be careful of taking a commentator like Bryce out of his chronological setting. He shared, for example, the quasi-scientific racist beliefs of his times, which had a considerable effect on his view of the urban masses. And he shared, with many Americans as well as Europeans, the common view that men of means and substance did have a less selfish relationship to the societies—urban or otherwise—in which they lived. That these assumptions were incorrect is certainly true; but it would be unfair for us to expect many nineteenth-century people to see that.

Two things are important in Bryce's work: (1) one can find a clear presentation of the ideas about machine politics that were common among interested middle- and upper-class people in the United States at the end of the nineteenth century, and (2) this analysis was very influential in shaping the development of urban "reform" activities at least down to the time of the First World War.

The second of the two great scholarly works on American politics of this period was Moisei Ostrogorski's *Democracy and the Organization of Political Parties*. This two-volume work, one volume of which focussed on England and the other on the United States, was first published in 1902, with a preface by Lord Bryce. Ostrogorski had a more academic background—in both Russia and France—than Bryce, when he wrote his work, and was generally more interested in theory and structure. It is a much less descriptive work in its devotion to theory; this makes it perhaps more intellectually enduring than Bryce, but also explains why it was less influential in its own time outside of academic circles. But the extent to which Ostrogorski, writing almost fifteen years later, agrees or disagrees with Bryce is a matter of some interest. His book takes us right into the Progressive Era in America and offers insight into the assumptions motivating those who called themselves reformers at that time.

Despite his concern with building a theory of democratic politics, Ostrogorski, on the whole, tended to agree with Bryce. He was, from the standpoint of the early twentieth century, somewhat broader in his approach, being more concerned than his predecessor with the role of those at the top of society, especially businessmen, in the problems of government. More important, his normative conclusions were almost identical to those of Bryce.

As a good turn-of-the-century social Darwinist, Ostrogorski saw the politician as one who rose to power via "natural selection." Political leaders came from all ranks of society and based their careers on their followings, first neighborhood, and then broader. Ostrogorski saw the importance of gangs and clubs, which did indeed serve as the original source of power of leaders like his own contemporary Charles Francis Murphy of New York. Youthful gangs grew into young adult social clubs, and "this merry crew is a latent political force; when the elections come round it may furnish a compact band of voters. The small politician therefore has but to lay his hand on it." Similarly, he said, foreign stock was a usable base—one could organize his "fellow countrymen" into a viable group for political purposes.

Ostrogorski agreed with Bryce that it was difficult to get good men into politics; employment was uncertain, the pay was poor, and so on. Thus the more able stayed in business, and the end effect was to facilitate party control of urban government. And the machine was a less than ideal form for democratic government because, by its very nature, it required at least majority support and thus tended "to offend no one, to please everyone," by avoiding the issues. Too often, moreover, the machine politician "gained his ends by corruption and seduction," devices that were less offensive to the voters than firm positions on the issues might be.

Ostrogorski recognized the role of patronage in machine politics, and he saw the machine in essentially feudal terms, as composed of greater and lesser leaders, each with his own set of tenants: "each Machine being in reality composed of a number of smaller and smaller Machines which form so many microcosms within it." He saw the machine, then, as a hierarchical structure which rested on the relationship between the machine politician and the urban masses. Like Bryce, he was impressed with the role that the "lower orders" of society played therein, often "under the auspices of the saloon-keeper, who is their guide, the director of their conscience." In the rapidly growing industrial metropolis, which epitomized the physical, social, and other needs of modern times, the machine filled a void which no other agency seemed equipped for, especially for the masses.

But Ostrogorski was also impressed with the way there seemed to be a mutuality of interest between the machine and business interests, an idea of increasing popularity at that time. The capitalists, according to this view, supported and financed the machine in return for its support of their economic ambitions, through such things as favorable tax rates, franchises for the provision of urban services, and so on. If capitalism had not created the machine or the boss, it had certainly raised their stature and enhanced their powers.

Thus, to Ostrogorski, pecuniary and social needs of different groups combined to facilitate the rise of the machine, accompanied almost always by bribery and chicanery in general:

The rapid growth of the cities, inevitably accompanied by the rise of a poverty-stricken and semi-criminal class, the arrival of wretched emigrants from Europe, and the extension of the suffrage to the besotted Negroes, had, in their turn, swelled the venal contingents. The appearance, on the political stage, of the rich corporations, and, in general, of the big industrial and financial concerns . . . helped to supply the funds for buying voters. . . . The electors who deliberately sell themselves belong, in the cities, mostly to the dregs of the population.

This was hardly a very optimistic view of American urban democracy. But it can be seen as rather typically "progressive," very much a part of its time.

The boss, to Ostrogorski, was simply that man who, by dint of his success, rose to the top of this hierarchical structure: "the extraordinary powers, unparalleled under the regime of free institutions, which the Machine exercises, centre eventually in a single man—the boss." And the boss, particularly the city boss, tended to be coarse, insensitive, a "vulgar demagogue"; he was often intelligent, but almost never moral. In him one sees a microcosm of the machine—the lack of concern for issues, the positive opposition to "high class candidates," the basic cynicism and drive for power and gain alone.

Ostrogorski had a clearer sense of the structure of the machine, and of its functional strength, than had Bryce before him—although the difference can be easily overstated—but his general conclusions were pretty much the same. Americans, he felt, were too optimistic and too easy-going; in a democratic polity this was a danger and had led, in the city, to the machine. He felt the answer lay primarily in the minimization of party and maximization of issues: "Down with 'party,' Up with 'League' "—the league being an *ad hoc* grouping focussed on issues as its main concern. It can be said that although he understood the distinctiveness of American politics, he was like Bryce unable, in his prescriptions for melioration, to avoid European approaches, which were, in the final analysis, inapplicable.

Ostrogorski, looking back from 1902, did feel that there had been a considerable rise in "reform" spirit in recent years. He was impressed by civil service reform, and the Australian (secret) ballot. But he felt that the interest that many reformers evinced in centralization (e.g., an all-powerful mayor) had not worked. The reformers were too often more interested in form than they were in substance, and spent too much time fighting one another over it. Here Ostrogorski was playing around with the concept of the "latent functions of the machine" but did not really see its theoretical implications at that time. It was for this reason that he himself really focussed more on form than on function in his own prescriptions for reform. As a theorist of sorts he must have been frustrated by his inability to formulate a real theory of municipal politics, to devise other than *ad hoc* reforms; like all of us he was trapped in the thinking of his own time, and could move outside of it only to a limited extent.

The writings of Bryce and Ostrogorski were important because they hit upon one of the central concerns of the Progressive Era. This period of roughly 1890 to 1915 is one about which scholars and others have written a great deal, much of it in too general terms. One thing, at least, seems clear: it was a time when more and more groups—economic, social, cultural—turned to government to deal with their problems. At local, state, and national levels there was a tendency for Americans to put aside their traditional suspicions of active government out of necessity; the rapid changes in American society attendant upon industrialization simply made voluntary action inadequate to deal with the wants of too many Americans.

But within this generalization there is room for much variety. Different groups of Americans simply did not all seek the same things, whether in purely economic terms or in political ones. It is this which much of the writing on progressivism has failed to come to terms with. Early twentieth century writers and most of the historians who followed them have tended too readily to adopt the viewpoint of some middle-class groups of the period and to see it in those groups' terms. Thus they have accepted the idea of "reform" as articulated by those groups, largely ignoring the fact that one man's reform may well be another's reaction. We shall see below that historians have in recent years moved to new levels of analysis. But this point is important as it relates to our own concern, since middle- and upper-class opposition to machine politics was often phrased as a part of the "reform" effort of the Progressive Era and indeed was one of the central foci thereof.

Consequently, popularizers of the ideas of observers like Bryce and Ostrogorski were generally read, and they were also sometimes effective in mobilizing opposition to bosses and machines. The major defenders of these institutions, apart from the professional urban politicians themselves, were primarily the less articulate and certainly less powerful lower-class masses upon whose support the machines were built. Thus, down at least to the 1950s, the general American view of machine politics was one which stressed its moral failings and its overall inefficiency, with little concern for the role in urban society that those machines were actually playing.

Among the popular writers of the Progressive Era who concerned themselves with urban politics, Lincoln Steffens was one of the most famous and most influential. Steffens was a man of many talents and many enthusiasms, but his first real fame came as a journalist, from the series of articles he wrote for *McClure's Magazine* in 1902 and 1903, which were then put together in book form as *The Shame of the Cities* (1904). With this series Steffens emerged as one of the foremost "muckrakers" of the time—one who sought to reform evils by exposing them, so that concerned citizens would be confronted with the evils of their society that cried out for correction.

Among the muckrakers, Steffens is one of the more perceptive and less emotional. He cast a broader net and looked in more directions than many of his contemporaries; he was also more evenhanded in dealing with the various elements of urban society. Recent scholarship has shown his basic generalizations to have been wrong, or at least far too broad; but this does not gainsay the effect he had upon his readers generally, and in terms of specific action.

Following the suggestions of his publisher, Steffens went out to the cities to find what was going on in urban America, particularly in terms of rumors of great misgovernment therein. He was shocked by what he found, and wrote his articles, as he put it, "as a reporter of the shame of American cities. They were written with a purpose . . . to sound for the civic pride of an apparently shameless citizenship."

What most affected him was that urban misgovernment was not the fault exclusively of corrupt politicians and the immigrant masses, as earlier writers had argued. Rather, in typical progressive fashion, Steffens also found respectable middle-class and business interests equally culpable. He did not dismiss the importance of a mass of unassimilated voters as a support of the machines, but concluded that the problem was a good deal deeper and more general: "no one class is at fault, nor any one breed, nor any particular interest or group of interests." Indeed, as he saw it, the focus of some reformers on immigrants was "one of the hypocritical lies that save us from the clear sight of ourselves."

We tend, Steffens argued, to criticize the politician and praise the businessman. But the small businessman is a "poor citizen," since he tends to ignore public affairs. And the big businessman is worse; he does not ignore politics, but on the contrary is "busy with politics"—bribing, corrupting, and colluding. "He is a self-righteous fraud, this big business man. He is the chief source of corruption." He is corrupt as an officeholder himself, and also in his corrupting of others who hold office. If profit is the end, Steffens argued, good government cannot be the means: "The commercial spirit is the spirit of profit, not patriotism; of credit, not honor; . . . of trade and dickering, not principle."

The politicians, on the other hand, were only "political merchants," with few scruples of their own; they give us what we want, what sells. They are no better and no worse than the nonpoliticians, but are after their own gain and provide no leadership. Thus a corrupt alliance of sorts, including the politicians and the big businessmen, and based on the apathy of the rest of the population, had been the key to urban corruption.

In his individual essays on various cities (St. Louis, Minneapolis, Pittsburgh, Philadelphia, Chicago, New York) Steffens developed his theory of municipal corruption. St. Louis most impressed him, as "the worst-governed city in the land," and one wherein corruption came "from the top." He seemed to find some distinction—not clear to the reader—between good and bad businessmen, since he argued that before about 1890 the city had been well led by "merchants and businessmen." But after that date, the lure of lucrative franchises and other illicit wealth resulted in "the riffraff" taking over the city council (Steffens is always weak on process), and the city went to the dogs. In all of St. Louis's public affairs Steffens could find only one honest man, the circuit (district) attorney, Joseph W. Folk, whom he turned into a national hero of sorts. The businessmen and their profit motive, on the other hand, were the primary culprits, something which he first found in St. Louis and then discovered as well in other cities.

Five months after his first visit, Steffens returned to St. Louis. He found that his article had not been without effect, in that fourteen men had been tried. However, the system remained, and thus even the "conviction of the boodlers" had no long-term significance. So long as the system remained the same, he felt, just removing corrupt men would avail little—new ones would inevitably replace them. And what was true for St. Louis was equally true for his other cities: "The Shame of Minneapolis," "Pittsburg [sic]: A City Ashamed," "Philadelphia: Corrupt and Contented." Only in Chicago ("Half Free and Fighting On") and New York ("Good Government to the Test") did he find signs of a new civic responsibility and potential guidelines for the rest of the country.

The way to fight bad government, Steffens argued, was to look at cities which were relatively well governed. Chicago was useful both because of what had been accomplished there and what remained to be done. The "real reform" accomplished in Chicago had been done by the people, rather than some small aristocratic group. And what they had done was to defeat "boodling," the hardest of all urban evils to overcome. It had been done, as Steffens saw it, through one agency, the Municipal Voters League, and largely through one man, its head, George E. Cole. The league, created by the Civic Federation in 1895, had strong business and professional support and functioned by publicizing the records of boodling city councilmen, exposing them to the public and thereby defeating them at the polls. By 1898, he said, the Municipal Voters League "had nominated a majority of the City Council."

This was an important step toward reform, Steffens said, but by itself it could not last. The nonpoliticians who were elected to office in 1898 soon lost their seats. Moreover, the league never got the support of the big corporations, the railroads, or big business generally. The league did recoup its position in 1900, under Walter L. Fisher, whom Steffens characterized as "a reform boss," whose power came from the willing support of the people. So there was hope for Chicago, and Steffens was optimistic. But this optimism was tempered with his feeling that the reformers would have to hold onto the support of "the people" long enough to persuade the professional politicians that reform was other than a transitory phenomenon.

The trouble with Steffens's analysis of Chicago was that it was superficial, and in a way apolitical. He assumed certain kinds of behavior—especially the absence of bribery—as the key ends of municipal government, and entirely ignored the social context of the city's politics. What middle-class people who thought as he did saw as reform, was reform; the rest was unadmirable. Certainly Steffens would be unhappy with the course of Chicago politics after 1902.

This is seen perhaps more clearly in his analysis of New York, a city where "the honest men are in," and good government is in control. In Chicago, it had been a case of a watchdog agency monitoring politics; but New York was better—it had moved a step beyond that, to where the good government forces actually ruled. His focus was on the Seth Low administration, in Steffens's view a paradigm of reform, especially as compared with its alternative, Tammany Hall. "Tammany is bad government; not inefficient, but dishonest . . . the embodiment of corruption." He realized that Tammany involved "democratic corruption," that it was "a grafting system in which more individuals share than any I have studied." But it was nonetheless corrupt, and in relative terms the people got little. So the hope of New York was the continuation of Seth Low over Tammany in the 1903 election.

As we shall see in Chapter 3, Steffens's hopes were unavailing: Tammany beat Low in 1903, for essentially popular reasons. But Steffens, in a "Post Scriptum" to the book version of his article, said this was because the "local corporations contributed heavily to the Tammany campaign fund." There was little evidence to support this conclusion; but once he had his theory, Steffens tended to bend actual behavior to fit it.

To Steffens, municipal misgovernment was a function of a general malaise; it was "not merely political; it was financial, commercial, social." Moreover, it was the responsibility of everyone, of people who separated public from private morality. He had great faith in the power of exposé— that ordinary people, who were essentially good, would react responsibly once the evils of their communities were known. Like opponents of the machine at all times, he also felt that partisanship was an evil, an impediment to responsible politics. The parties were used by the bosses as "nothing but a means to corrupt ends. . . . If we would leave the parties to the politicians, and would vote not for the party, not even for men, but for the city, and the State, and the nation, we should rule parties, and cities, and States, and nation." It was an optimistic conclusion, and too facile by far. Like many progressives, Steffens added to earlier assumptions about the root of urban evil the new one of the role of evil big business. He was not entirely incorrect, in a narrow political sense, since the economic growth of the city was very much a part of the overall situation that conditioned the development of urban politics and government. But, if business interests in some times and some places supported machines, they more often opposed them, for reasons just as economically self-serving, as we shall see. More to the point, Steffens, like so many progressives, had a set of blinders which limited his view almost exclusively to the more superficial political and economic characteristics of his time. He ignored the basic social nexus in which urban politics operated, and his understanding of what was going on was extremely limited by his approach. The reformers who followed Steffens's prescription tended to fail for this reason; they were focussing on matters of only tangential or secondary concern to most of the voters of American cities at the time.

That Steffens and other progressive critics added the evil businessman to the sources of municipal misgovernment should not suggest that there was a lessening concern with the role of the urban masses therein in the early twentieth century. On the contrary, the rising nativism, economic competition, and issue divisions of the time tended to reinforce the feeling that the largely immigrant urban masses were a key source of the machine and of bad government generally. This kind of reasoning played an important role in the ultimate success of legislation to restrict immigration during and after the First World War.

A convenient summary of the progressive view of the machine can be seen in the writings in 1919 and 1920 of Samuel P. Orth. Orth wrote two volumes in the multi-volume Chronicles of America series, one *Our Foreigners* and the other *The Boss and the Machine*. It is of course suggestive that the editors of the series should assign both of these popular history volumes to the same man. But Orth was in fact less nativistic than many academicians of the time, and his interpretation in general was balanced and relatively unemotional.

In writing on America's immigrant groups, Orth dealt with them non-politically and in a generally supportive fashion. But he was typical of his time in tending to see groups in simplistic social and cultural stereotypes (Bohemians were social radicals, Jews were radical and materialistic, etc.). On the whole, he maintained an entire separation of theme in his two books, even though they were published within a year of one another.

He shared the general progressive concern about the potential evils of party. As he put it, a party had two aspects: "as an agency of the electorate" and "as an organization, an army determined to achieve certain conquests." Moreover, each aspect of party attracted a "different type of person." The latter aspect of party, and the self-serving type of person it attracted, were the dangers seen in the boss and the machine. And the city was the root of this evil; even national machines had their sources in the cities. The cities provided the sources of corruption upon which machine politics—the wrong kind of partisanship—flourished, and thus bad government had grown.

Orth did see the in-migrants to the cities, both from rural America and from abroad, as a force facilitating bossism. The European immigrants, he argued, had no sense of democracy, nor any natural understanding of American institutions; they were "easily influenced and easily led" and provided a buttress for the machine. But equally culpable were the businessmen, "the alliance between business and politics," of which Steffens had written.

While Orth acknowledged that the machine served some ends, as in giving "work, or food, or shelter" to the immigrant, this was not really basic to its strength. Rather, it was "the scientific efficiency of the organization." Indeed, both in terms of the social base of the machine, and in terms of the role of business behind it, Orth is very general and unconvincing. Like many progressives, he took his generalizations more on faith than on evidence, and was not very discriminating. Tammany, for example, seemed to him exactly the same under Murphy as it had been under Tweed; we shall see in the next two chapters that this was hardly the case.

His conclusions were as typical as his analysis. The key to political reform, Orth argued, was an aware and informed electorate, which would lead to better regulation of balloting, of lobbying, and of the kind of people who held office. He was a great believer in things like initiative and referendum, which permitted an aware electorate to circumvent or override "the evils of state legislatures." And his final chapter, "The Expert at Last," expressed the profound progressive faith in apolitical expertise. An expanded civil service system and an electorate convinced of the validity of experts would provide the crucial advantage of removing essential services from politics, from the "spoilsman and his minions." This, at city, state, and national levels, to Orth and to most progressives, was a key element in reform, in their almost unconscious equation of party with political evil.

I have now surveyed about fifty years of writing on the urban political machine, and one thing at least appears evident: that this writing was uniformly critical of the bosses and the machines at the same time that both seem to have flourished. In the case studies of the ensuing chapters we shall, I hope, see why this was so. But here one might logically ask: if the bosses and machines had so many voting defenders in the cities, did they not also have intellectual defenders in books or the press? Where, indeed, are the writings which defended the partisan urban political organization? The answer is that such writings did not emerge; neither the urban politician nor his constituent was prone to theorizing or to writing generally. That field remained the province of the middle and upper classes, within which there was almost no open defense of the machine. Those who wrote about the political evils of bossism either ignored its social context or wrote about it only in generally pejorative terms—of the role the ignorant immigrant played in the triumph of the machine. And even those who wrote sympathetically of the plight of the urban masses, like Jacob Riis in the 1890s, never concluded that the urban political organization was a viable means of dealing with their problems. On the contrary, if such critics dealt with political aspects at all, they tended to argue that reform from above—progressive-type reform—was the only answer.

The most famous defense of the machine before the 1920s came, very colorfully, from an articulate, if ungrammatical, machine politician himself. The informal lectures of George Washington Plunkitt of Tammany Hall, delivered from his seat on the bootblack stand at the New York county courthouse and transcribed by the newspaperman William L. Riordan, are as famous for their audacity and humor as for their ideas. But, in his own vivid fashion, Plunkitt did, at the very beginning of the twentieth century, articulate most of the themes that scholars and others since have seen as, if not justifications of machine politics, at least explanations of its flourishing at that time and after.

Plunkitt (1842-1924) was a professional politician and Tammany district leader who enjoyed talking about his career. In Riordan he found an ideal Boswell, and his lectures were published first in the press and in 1905 in book form. They were widely read and alluded to at the time, primarily for their humor and for what they seemed to reveal of the extent to which the machine was as corrupt and as evil as many middle-class people believed. Some critics also saw in the system portrayed by Plunkitt a clear explanation of why Tammany fared as well as it did.

Plunkitt was quite frank about how he had personally profited from his political position. He made his famous distinction between "honest graft and dishonest graft," defending the former and condemning the latter. Honest graft included things like the party activist's learning of land the city was thinking of buying, buying it ahead of time at a low price, and selling it to the city dear; or, conniving with others to keep bids way down on used granite blocks the city was selling, getting them for a song, and making a handsome profit on the transaction. These kinds of graft were honest because "they didn't steal a dollar from the city treasury" or from any individual directly. To be sure, Plunkitt's reasoning stopped at a convenient level, but it was to him logical; and he did not defend outright stealing or bribery. As he put it in one of his most quoted remarks, "I seen my opportunities and I took 'em."

To Plunkitt the professional politician was the true "statesman," and in describing "How to Become a Statesman" he began to illustrate how Tammany functioned. The last thing one needed was education; those who "cram their heads with all sorts of college rot" are almost inevitably doomed to failure in politics. Likewise oratory was useless: "You never heard of Charlie Murphy delivering a speech, did you?" Rather, one rose in politics through the "marketable commodity" of votes—one's own, and then any others one could get committed to him. Starting with his family, and then his neighborhood, the would-be politician builds a base which the party respects; and success creates greater opportunity to expand this base and move, slowly but steadily, up the ladder. Once in, the politician remains in power and rises in the hierarchy by understanding and serving his district. As Plunkitt put it, "Study human nature and act accordin'." The politician works constantly to know his people and to relate to them in their own terms. If a resident likes to sing, or to play baseball, the alert district leader invites him to join the district glee club or team. If the people are poor, the leader gives them help, especially in time of tragedy like a fire, or even during unemployment. "The poor," Plunkitt argued, "are the most grateful people in the world."

Plunkitt lived up to his own precepts about the district leader's active involvement with his constituents, as illustrated by Riordan's own observations of his daily labors. He was known by everyone, and his help was solicited by everyone, especially the poor. He was very much at home in his district, and with its people; and he was actively working at politics, or on call for such work, twenty-four hours a day. If there was a fire, he appeared and was ready to assist the dispossessed; if a saloon keeper or any other constituent was jailed for one violation or another, Plunkitt arrived with bail money; indeed, he spent a great deal of time at the courts, defending drunks and widows and solving all sorts of problems. He was probably the major employment agency of his district, devoting considerable effort to placing people on private and public payrolls. He attended Catholic and Jewish funerals and confirmations and weddings constantly and conspicuously, gave to charities, and favored the causes of his people; he provided feasts and excursions to brighten the lives of his constituents.

In all of this Plunkitt followed some clear if unarticulated theory. First, he served his people as they wished to be served, asking in return only that they vote his way—something that, especially to economically and culturally marginal people, was a small price to pay indeed. Second, he avoided judgments as much as he possibly could; he took people on their own terms and did not try to change them. Third, he expended tremendous quantities of time and money to keep his system going; it was a full-time occupation, and it was one that demanded considerable resources as well. Plunkitt did grow rich as a politician, but he dispensed more than he kept. True to his own conception of things, he was the major social service agency in his district, and the major employment agent as well. Although he, and others like him, may have done this inefficiently, at considerable undue cost to the taxpayers generally, the fact was that in these areas the machine politician had little competition at the turn of the century and was thus indispensable.

To Plunkitt it was natural and reasonable that people would be active in politics only if there was something in it for themselves: "How are you goin' to interest our young men in their country if you have no offices to give them when they work for their party?" Likewise, it was equally reasonable that those who received jobs—high or low—from the party, "help along the good cause" by contributing part of their salaries to the party: "A political organization has to have money for its business as well as a church." Thus civil service reform was a "curse," "free silver and the tariff and imperialism and the Panama Canal are triflin' issues when compared to it." This provincialism is a key characteristic of the urban machine, whether in Plunkitt's day or in Daley's. Unlike his contemporaries, who disparaged partisanship and machine politics, Plunkitt had tremendous respect for political parties as a source of the republic's strength; and since the parties revolved around jobs, patronage was crucial and civil service was a great danger.

He disdained "reformers" as much for their methods as for their advocacy of things like civil service reform. They were, as he put it, "only mornin' glories," who did not take politics seriously enough and thus were foredoomed to ultimate failure. Politics, after all, was "as much a regular business as the grocery . . . or drug business" and required the same kind of full-time professional attention. Likewise, Plunkitt was unimpressed by Lincoln Steffens's *Shame of the Cities;* Steffens was too simplistic to please him, failed to see the difference between honest and dishonest graft, between a statesmanlike institution like the New York Democracy and the Philadelphia Republican "gang."

Plunkitt had an implicit sense of what made for stability in the political organization. Ingratitude was one of the great evils, as was disloyalty: the hierarchical structure had to be respected. Likewise there must be reciprocity, even across party lines, so that everyone who worked at politics got "something out of it" and so that provision could be made for the day when one's party might be voted out. The individual politician, for his own part, must stay ever close to the masses; elegant dress or other accoutrements of wealth must be disdained. He must also be a man of great probity—honest graft being an entirely separate area—whose personal morals were beyond reproach; successful politicians, while they defended the drinking habits of their constituents, out not to drink themselves—they need their energy and their wits at all times.

Another of his major concerns was the power of the "hayseeds" (anyone outside of Manhattan). Hayseeds were too often Republicans, and even beyond party considerations they were unfair to New York and conspiratorial toward Tammany. Like many urban politicians before and since, Plunkitt sensed the urban-rural tension of his state, and he had to deal with the problem of a rural-dominated legislature's frequent opposition to both the city and its political machine. Indeed, "the feelin' between this city and the hayseeds that make a livin' by plunderin' it is every bit as bitter as the feelin' between North and South before the war." The solution, he felt, was separation, for the city to "become a state itself. . . .

Just think how lovely things would be here if we had a Tammany Govern-or and Legislature . . . and a Tammany Mayor and Board of Aldermen. . . . How sweet and peaceful everything would go on!" It was a district leader's dream.

Plunkitt did reflect, however, flamboyantly, the concerns and con-ceptions of the professional urban politician. Issues were secondary to organization and were important only to the extent that one's constituents really seemed to care about them. It was, to be sure, an extremely pro-vincial view, but it can also be argued that the machine served the needs of provincial people. It was certainly a view of politics, and of the urban masses, that differed considerably from that of critics of bossism. Plunkitt would argue that the vindication of his position was seen almost constant-ly at the polls; Tammany was "the only lastin' democracy," and the evi-dence thereof was its success in the free marketplace of the voting booth.

Right or wrong, good or bad, Plunkitt's defense of the machine antici-pated later, more scholarly, and less colorful writing on urban politics. The themes of the machine as a social welfare agency; as an uncritical responder to the wants of the masses; as a buffer between the low and weak on the one hand and the powerful and wealthy on the other; as a democratic agency which better than any other reconciled the variety of interests in the modern city—these would be central to later interpreta-tions of the machine's success. Plunkitt's own argument did not convert many away from progressive reform. Indeed, it reinforced the conclusions that many opponents of the machine already had. But it did at least shed considerable light on why the machine did flourish; and the reformers continued on the whole to lose elections because they rarely involved themselves in the social fabric from which the machine ultimately drew its nourishment.

The 1920s saw a lessening of popular writing on bosses and machines. The city was somewhat less new, and less newsworthy. And there were other concerns which seemed to draw more attention. The problem had not disappeared, and at the individual city level it remained a major con-cern and issue in urban politics, as we shall see in Chapter 4. But in general people were reading about other things.

The academic, as opposed to the popular, concern did not flag, how-ever. A whole new approach to the study of politics by modern social scientists was just developing at this time, led especially by the political scientists at the University of Chicago. People like Charles E. Merriam and Harold F. Gosnell were beginning a more systematic and nonnormative study of American urban politics which provided a new theoretical per-spective and a new knowledge that remains important down to our own day. Some of these scholars, like Merriam, were personally concerned with governmental reform; but they managed nonetheless to look deeper and more objectively at just why the machine succeeded. If this did not necessarily facilitate defeating the machine at the polls, it did certainly expand the understanding of how urban politics did work.

Merriam's *Chicago: A More Intimate View of Urban Politics* (1929), and Gosnell's *Negro Politicians: The Rise of Negro Politics in Chicago* (1935) and *Machine Politics: Chicago Model* (1937) were among the important contributions emerging from the "Chicago school." These two writers and their students used Chicago as a laboratory for developing a theoretical and functional understanding of the nature of urban politics. They probed for the success of the machine by looking more directly at who voted for it and why. Thus they were aware of its social context and its social role. Gosnell especially was able to see the weakness of traditional reform in its failure to come to terms with the urban masses. Moreover, he was one of the first writers to understand the fundamental error of the progressives in focussing on economic motives to the exclusion of cultural ones. He was highly aware of the force of ethnicity—national, racial, and religious—and of its force in politics.

Part of the greater perceptiveness of the Chicago school came from advanced methodology. They were among the first social scientists to develop quantitative techniques for measuring voting and other kinds of behaviors, giving them one thing their predecessors had lacked: a clear picture of who voted for whom. Merriam and Gosnell were able, for example, to carefully investigate the phenomenon of nonvoting (in their *Non-Voting: Causes and Methods of Control*, 1924, and in later works) and what it might represent.

Gosnell characterized his study of black politics as an effort "to describe in realistic fashion the struggle of a minority group to advance its status by political methods." To this end he and his students compiled great quantities of statistics, attended many ethnic and political meetings at the lowest level, and interviewed racial and political activists and participators. It was a far cry from James Bryce's or even Lincoln Steffens's going to the "leading citizens" of various communities as their main sources of information.

The contributions of the Chicago school were at least twofold. First, they led to a better understanding of the real operation of the machine and the real reasons for its success, at least for those whose minds were open to alternatives to the progressives' explanation. For the first time it was suggested that the urban masses were not by any means entirely "controlled" by the politicians but, rather, tended on the whole to make rational—if not always ideal—choices among the options open to them. The relationship of one's place in urban society—of one's level of assimilation, skills, and status—to one's perception of the political world and its potential for serving one, was made clear for the first time. Writers like Gosnell and Merriam were by no means apologists for the machine; on the whole they saw it as generally an inefficient and dishonorable form of urban government. But they did suggest reasons why its support was a reasonable choice for people on some levels of the American urban social structure. They also paved a way for our understanding of the cultural basis of American elective politics.

Second, the Chicago school played a central role in the development of modern theory and methodology for the study of political behavior. Both conceptually and in terms of specific techniques they made a contribution to which all social scientists interested in the study of politics are indebted.

This stage of the study of the machine did not immediately supersede more traditional approaches. Indeed, in popular writing, and in school textbooks, the progressive view did not die easily. Interest in the boss and the machine waxed and waned with many extraneous factors. But when it was evinced, it followed no one path. Two other studies of about this same time may be taken as examples.

Harold Zink, a political scientist trained at Harvard, published his *City Bosses in the United States: A Study of Twenty Municipal Bosses,* in 1930. The book included, in addition to chapters on the careers of each of his late nineteenth and early twentieth century bosses individually, seven introductory chapters which formed a kind of impressionistic collective biography. This first part of the book was most original, although it lacked the systematic rigor of the contemporary Chicago school.

Zink looked at a variety of potential common characteristics among the bosses, including such superficial ones as height, weight, appearance, health, and dress—none of which proved an accurate predictor of successful bossism. The "racial stock" of the bosses was mixed, although about a third had risen to power in areas where their own groups were strong. Significantly, he found, all of them had lived for a long time in their cities, twelve of the twenty having been born in them. Thirteen had no education beyond grammar school, and seven had been leaders of gangs.

The bosses studied by Zink did have in common "better than average personal morality," in that they were not drinkers, wife-beaters, etc. They were all hard workers, and they did "tend to be loyal to their friends and true to their promises." These were indeed important attributes of urban political success, as we shall see. On the other hand, Zink concluded, the bosses tended to seek wealth, they "kept the quest for gold fairly well to the fore in their lives"; ten of the twenty were millionaires. Most of them, however, did not accomplish this through direct theft from the public, but indeed were about as honest as most businessmen.

The apparent key to successful rise to bossism, Zink found, lay in the characteristics which Plunkitt had urged. The bosses started in politics young, respected the system, and worked hard within it. They were very much a part of their cities, manifested "generosity to the poor," loyalty to their friends and the organization, good personal morals, and practicality. Beyond these characteristics, however, Zink did not feel that any "theory of the 'typical' boss" could be derived; too many other characteristics he had apparently expected them to share did not seem to be shared.

Zink found that his twenty bosses ended their careers for the most part for "natural causes." Moreover, "reform movements do not seem to play much of a part in breaking city bosses in spite of the fact that such movements have dogged the footsteps of almost all of them." There was not a single case where reformers were "entirely responsible for a knockout."

If Zink's book was part of a new social scientific effort to understand, without *a priori* assumptions, the nature of urban government, J. T. Salter's *Boss Rule: Portraits in City Politics* (1935) fits the description even more. Salter was, as he put it, trying to study politicians as they were, "without advocating what I thought they ought to be." He relied more on theory, seeing the political process as pretty much the same regardless of level, party, or location. His was an early example of what has come to be called a "participant-observer" study; using Philadelphia as a test case, he lived and worked there as he studied the political organization and politicians firsthand.

Salter focussed on party organization and the individual precinct politician as the key factors in the political process. And he rapidly learned that their "service function is the raison d'être" of their existence; that service function may be public and general, as in the case of a president of the United States, or "private and personal," as in the case of a precinct leader, but it remained essentially the same: "The votes are invariably cast because the voter has received, or expects to receive, service or service's worth. This service may be an old-age pension law, a tariff, or merely a friendly smile." Here Salter was articulating an important basic principle to which I shall return shortly.

Since service was the key element, and personal and private services were the specialty of the urban political machine, it was not surprising that the machines had better control in those parts of the city which had the "most unemployment, most conflict with the law, most difficulty in paying rent . . . and these areas are more often than not districts in which a preponderant number of foreign-born or colored people live." For these people, especially, the party served as an "intermediary between the citizen and the state," just because they needed that intermediation most. But the party served the same role for those higher in the social order also, only in different ways and with different parts of the apparatus of the state.

Salter focussed his book on the Philadelphia division (precinct) leader, again making discoveries that seem to be those of a more scholarly and analytical Plunkitt. The machine district leader was very hard working, sincerely interested in people, and made a primary, face-to-face contact with his constitutents. Conversely, the "anti-organization candidate, unlike his opponent, invariably relies on a secondary—not a primary—appeal"; and he sought votes on a nebulous, ideological base, rather than a service one. This is why the latter tended to lose.

The district leaders of the Philadelphia Republican machine had backgrounds as varied as Zink's bosses, but their behavior was quite similar, and almost all of them also were on the public payroll, permitting politics to be a full-time occupation. They did profit from politics, not only in their public salaries, but also from a variety of other sources of varying legitimacy. But they operated in a real merit system, the measure of which was the vote one's division turned out: you produced or you were through. Ideology didn't count; many of the division leaders, for example, had been strongly attracted to Democrat Al Smith in 1928, but their duty was in the other direction.

Service for their constituents, and an ability to deal with them, argued strongly for cultural consistency. What tended to be true for Zink's city bosses was even truer for Salter's division leaders: they shared the race, religion, and national origins of their constituents. Likewise they shared, and reflected, their constituents' values and positions on issues, honesty, and just about everything else.

Salter included nine chapters on individual leaders of various Philadelphia districts. Their careers and labors did reinforce his generalizations and Plunkitt's model. Salter himself realized that although the social welfare aspects of the machine were crucial to its strength, it was not a "scientific" social work; it was spotty, *ad hoc,* and often inefficient. Moreover, it often maintained dependence (an argument later made most forcefully about governmental social welfare as well), kept crooks out of jail, and probably worked against the evolution of really "efficient and honest" government, which in the long run would serve the whole society. This, however, was almost an aside, since Salter did not really define how "efficient and honest" government would deal with the social problems addressed by the machine.

One interesting thing about Salter's study is that he was dealing with a well-entrenched Republican machine which during the course of his study (1933) lost control of the city. It was a strong indication of the interrelatedness of political behavior at the various levels of government; the factors behind the rise of the New Deal had made the American population more Democratic generally; and the rise of the Democrats to power nationally had put important tools into the hands of local Democratic organizations. Salter did not see it entirely that way. Rather, he stressed the impulse for "change" resulting from the depression, the dying-off of some local Republican leaders, and a popular Democratic governor who fought the machine. Moreover, he said, the problems of the depression had made the voters more concerned with the issues and the economy; and even in terms of the machine's traditional social services, those services were in so much greater demand because of the problems of the depression that the machine was simply not able to deliver. Finally, public employees and professional politicians, guessing the likely path of the future, jumped to the Democratic party. In fact, it was too early to tell exactly why Philadelphia Republicanism was collapsing, and one can hardly expect Salter to have the benefit of hindsight for what was only just then developing.

Salter made some effort to reconcile his more academic view of the machine with that of the progressives. While the machine was primarily supported by the poor and dependent, parts of the "capitalist and upper middle class" also supported it, either to maintain the status quo or for privileges it granted them. Partisan reasons were also important in this phenomenon, but Salter did not consider them.

Salter saw the New Deal and Roosevelt as intruding an important new variable into the political equation; more and more people found government real and attractive, a possible alternative to the machine in terms of providing the services they needed. That is, if real government becomes more active and responsive, the machine as unofficial government will become less important. He felt that the concept of people receiving services from the government as a right rather than from the political organization as a favor was liberating and socially beneficial. From the standpoint of 1935, he could not see the direction this would take, but it in fact soon became a key element in the scholarly and popular debate over the fate of the political boss.

Popular and scholarly concern with the boss and the machine began to change at the end of the 1930s. The traditional progressive view of the evils of the boss system did not disappear; in fact it was a central theme of political opponents of machines in numerous cities, and, as we shall see below, continued in the battle against Mayor Daley. But at the same time there arose an increasingly sentimental view: the stereotype of the boss as shrewd, kindly, very, very Irish, and—most importantly, I think—eminently human in an age of increasingly remote and impersonal politics.

The very fact that the number of old fashioned bosses and machines did appear to be declining after the 1930s was important in this sentimentalization. It also raised the question of just why this phenomenon was on the way out, and what the effects of its demise on urban government might be. Scholars, for their part, had the advantage of time and distance, and with the arrival on the scholarly scene of people who did not share the nativist assumptions of their predecessors and who were also increasingly imbued with the new methodology of the social sciences, the unemotional and systematic study of the institution itself could be expanded. Thus interest in the boss and the machine did not flag with the nationalization of American political life.

One of the most striking examples of all this can be seen in what has been probably the most widely disseminated and popular of modern pictures of the boss, Edwin O'Connor's best-selling novel, *The Last Hurrah*, published in 1956 and soon made into a feature film. O'Connor's story, based loosely on the life and career of James M. Curley of Boston, combined high melodrama with some insight. Boss "Frank Skeffington" and his organized machine were colorful, very much oriented to serving the needs of the people as individuals, reflective of the ethnic makeup of the city—although almost tribally Irish overall—and kindly if inefficient. Their political strength came almost entirely from the poor, and largely from the nonyoung.

O'Connor's view of the machine's strength was more akin to Bryce's analysis than to Steffens's. While he certainly disagreed with Bryce on the worthiness and basic value of the masses, he did agree that they were the source of Skeffington's machine. And, unlike the progressives, O'Connor did not see business as in any way supportive of the machine; the entire middle and upper class of Boston, and especially those in commerce and finance (always excepting the contractors, who were Irish anyway) were committed to the machine's destruction.

More than this, O'Connor popularized what is still the most generally held explanation for the decline of the boss and the machine. Developing, with hindsight, what Salter had more or less anticipated, O'Connor argued that the New Deal had killed the old politics and the old politicians; this was why Skeffington, obviously the better of the two mayoral candidates in question, lost the election. The New Deal had oriented the lower-class voter toward Washington, whence, via Social Security, labor legislation, federal employment programs, etc., the kind of support traditionally provided by the machine now came. The key to the machine's success, as O'Connor explained it, had been its social welfare activities, and these were now a national service rather than a local one.

Moreover, a new age and a new generation had arrived. The children and even grandchildren of the immigrants were more secure and more assimilated. They were both less needful of the kinds of services the machines offered, and more interested in the broader kinds of issues to which the machines had never been attuned. The boss was the proverbial dinosaur—well-intentioned, competent (often more than his opponents), intensely and attractively human. But he no longer had a role to play in the new politics of national over local, organizational over individual, issue over service.

O'Connor, as a novelist, was more interested in his story than his thesis, but the latter entered the popular mind along with the former. It was an argument that had merit and was being developed at about the same time by scholars as well. After all, the bosses were disappearing; even Tammany Hall, oldest and greatest of the machines, had lost most of its power by the 1960s. So what has come to be called the "Last Hurrah" thesis continues to be a matter of importance to scholars and to receive widespread support. There are individual cases where it seems to be true. But there are others where it is less applicable; in a 1970 study entitled *The New Deal and the Last Hurrah: Pittsburgh Machine Politics,* Bruce M. Stave argued that New Deal relief and welfare programs helped in the building of a modern Democratic machine in that city. And, as we shall see below, Mayor Daley's machine was hardly rendered senile by the nationalization of welfare.

One of the most important single contributions to our understanding of the political machine comes from Robert K. Merton's *Social Theory and Social Structure* (first published 1949, with a revised and much enlarged edition published in 1957), one of the most important and impressive of modern works in theoretical social science. Merton was primarily concerned with developing theory for social science and with directing us to the basic human behavioral patterns which underlie all forms of social action, including politics. His chapters on reference groups, for example, have been very influential in our understanding of the group basis of politics and in directing our attention to the role ethnicity has played in American political behavior.

From the standpoint of the "functional analysis" to which he was contributing, Merton argued that the machine was successful because it served functions that were "at the time not adequately fulfilled by other existing patterns and structures." His analysis was both *functional* and *structural;* one had also to look at the structural context—wherein the boss and the machine could serve a centralizing purpose not available to other agencies by virtue, for example, of the legal constitutional limitations on formal governmental bodies. Duly constituted national, state, and local governments at the turn of the century lacked the power to deal formally with conflicting ethnic, economic, and other group interests the way the boss could deal with them informally. The boss system was thus *relatively* efficient.

The political machine, like any social organization, had both manifest and latent functions, the latter best illustrated by its ability to reconcile the interests of various subgroups of the society and to provide aid to those needing it in a culturally acceptable manner, or by its role as a vehicle for upward social mobility. To focus only on its manifest functions—its wastefullness, corruption, even illegality—is thus to see only the more superficial aspects of the machine, and not really to understand it. This error was made not only by earlier students of the machine but by the reformers who had battled it since the late nineteenth century. The former had erred and the latter had failed—mainly because they lacked a functional understanding of what the machine and boss were really doing and how they did it.

Merton's analysis has been instructive, among other things, in the light it has shed on inquiries into the relationship between bosses and "reform"; were the bosses and their supporters for or against reform? What were the social, cultural, and economic origins of the supporters of the bosses as opposed to the supporters of reform? Was the opposition to the boss or the machine "reform" in any neutral construction of that term, or just a battle for power between opposed groups of people?

These are questions at the root of much contemporary scholarly debate, about which there is currently no general agreement. Many scholars, similarly influenced, will agree with the thrust of this book, the argument that the urban political machine rested upon a mass lower-class and working-class base which was involved with issues of individual and group survival—in economic, social, and cultural terms. By and large the "great issues of the day," matters of foreign policy or national, even of state economic and political policy, were remote and at best of secondary importance to these voters. Ethnic concerns and jobs were central and tended often to be served far better by the machine than by its alternatives.

Some scholars differ. J. Joseph Huthmacher (*Senator Robert Wagner and the Rise of Urban Liberalism,* 1968, and several other works), and many who have been influenced by him, argue that the urban masses were very interested in and supportive of progressive reform. Their work is interesting but unconvincing. All too often they infer mass support from support of unions, or just union leaders; but the urban masses were not on the whole unionized in the early twentieth century. Or they focus on the support of the masses, and the machines, for individual "progressive" candidates, failing to consider the partisan, social, and cultural context in which those candidates presented themselves to the voters.

As we shall see, a boss like Charles F. Murphy or Richard J. Daley was not so much for or against "reform" as he was concerned with the life of the machine. Indeed, the entire concept of reform is being questioned, since it defies nonnormative definition. In one of the most impressive and influential articles on American history in recent years, "The Politics of Reform in Municipal Government in the Progressive Era" (1964), Samuel P. Hays, in looking at reform, also shed considerable light on its alternative. Hays argued that urban reformers tended to be from the upper-middle and upper-class business and professional elite, a group which endeavored through "reform" to reshape the city into a form congruent with its own economic, social, cultural, and ethical interests and beliefs. Lower-class, and even middle-class, groups "vigorously opposed reform" because it was in their own interest to do so, because "reform" meant a diminution of their own power in the city.

A clear example of this was in the very general effort of the "reformers" to centralize governing agencies. They wanted to decrease the size of city councils, for example, and often to have councilmen elected citywide rather than from individual districts; they preferred commission or city manager governments to the old large council and mayor form. And their attitudes toward other agencies like boards of education were similar. This, they argued, would make government more honest and efficient, even more democratic. But it was precisely the large city council kind of government, with small enough districts that individual ethnic and social groups could have determining power, which had been the key to the strength those groups had in the past. It had also been the key to the rise of the urban machine.

Thus the boss and the lower-class voter had a common rational opposition to many of the basic desires of the urban "reformer." They wanted quite different kinds of governments, to serve quite different interests. And the fact that the upper-middle and upper-class reformers were often also nativist and antilabor, for example, only served to expand the reasons for the masses' preference for the machine rather than "reform."

The questions of the relationship of the masses to alternate kinds of politics and of the precise reasons for the decline of the machine remain open, subject to lively and creative scholarly debate. The public is less concerned with such questions now, since they do not seem really contemporary. With the exception of Mayor Daley's Chicago almost alone, thoughts about bossism seem thoughts about the past—a colorful but no longer relevant aspect of earlier American history.

One wonders, however, if this is true. To the extent that the urban machine has existed primarily because of the presence of a poor and unassimilated urban mass, that group continues to exist in significant numbers in most cities. We have to try to see just which agency is filling the "latent functions" demanded by those groups. It may well be that the machine is not dead, as it appears to be, but vested differently and so not entirely recognizable.

In the next four chapters I shall look in some detail at four machines and five bosses, spanning a century in time. I hope that some—definitely not all—questions thus far raised will find answers in these case studies.

Neither any boss, machine, nor city, is entirely "typical," and for this reason any general theory of either the rise or decline of bossism is bound to find exceptions. Indeed, I shall try in each chapter to introduce the city in which each boss functioned, because it is my conviction that the individual city is an important variable in any political equation. A city's composition—especially ethnically but also in general social terms, in physical character, economic specialization, and so on—provides forces that very definitely affect its political development. Much of the difference in the political histories of Cleveland and Los Angeles, for example, can be explained by the kind of people who came to live there, how they made their livings, how they related to one another, etc. And efforts to theorize on any aspect of urban political behavior without giving due credit to this variable are doomed to fail.

The key to the machine's success has been its ability to provide services that government has been unable or unwilling to provide, and these services have been as importantly cultural as they have been economic. Thus the "Last Hurrah" thesis is probably correct in explaining some of the reasons why machines have declined. They have not declined everywhere, however—not only because there remain marginal people who still need survival services, but also because there are services of group recognition, for example, as well as some of administration, which government has not preempted and which the machines have sometimes used to maintain their lives.

In fact, everyone "sells" his or her vote, in terms of exchanging it for something which one or another candidate, or party, or organization delivers or promises to deliver. That one person sells his vote for a promised government policy on southeast Asia, and another for a direct payment of five dollars or promise of a job, is a function not of their having conflicting conceptions of politics, but rather of their existing in different social situations. It may well be argued that the society would benefit from everyone's being in a sufficiently secure social position to exchange votes on matters of broad societal policy. But thus far in American history there have always been considerable numbers of people for whom such behavior would be a waste of the major bit of currency they possessed. It is those people who were, relatively, best served by the boss and the machine. Both have declined with the years, but not disappeared.

I hope that in looking, as we have, at what scholars and the general public have thought about bosses, and then in looking in some detail at examples of the species, we will develop a clearer understanding of this fascinating and important aspect of American history.

2

WILLIAM MARCY TWEED:
THE FIRST BOSS

It is not surprising that the first modern urban political machine developed in New York City, in many respects the first modern American city. In size, heterogeneity of population, and diversity of economic groups and activities, New York was the first place that was ripe for the functions of machine politics. Rapid mid-nineteenth-century growth strained not only New York's government, but also its physical facilities, its recreational and welfare institutions, indeed almost every aspect of organized life. And the city itself was little prepared to deal with such problems. Its government was old-fashioned, very limited in power, and reliant upon the state legislature. And on the whole its leaders—too interested in the fantastic possibilities of economic expansion—preferred to stay out of government service, confining themselves to an insistence on minimal and economical government.

Legal New York, the political entity in which the Tweed Ring arose, was still quite confined at the end of the Civil War, consisting principally of Manhattan Island. The other boroughs of the city would be added later. But in any but the political sense—socially, economically, culturally —it was already a metropolis. Rapid ferry service as early as the 1830s had made commuting from the suburbs possible; and by the 1870s the city's newspapers, for example, were distributed throughout the area, which suggests that it was a unit, no matter what the legal geographic lines might be. Even legally, police, fire, and other services were metropolitan in nature. One of the Tweed Ring's great successes, in 1870, would be to undo this and make New York City again self-contained.

Nor was all of Manhattan Island full of New Yorkers in Tweed's day. The city's population was very much concentrated in the southern 20 or

25 percent of the island's area. North of Fourteenth Street the population thinned out rapidly; and north of Central Park, the island was still almost rural. Its population of about one million people in 1870 was compressed into very tight space, surrounded by relatively vast hinterlands within the city's borders.

Within that focus of population was pent up the city's personality. Here not only lived the vast majority of the population, but also were focussed its industrial, commercial, and mercantile life. It was a scene of daily and nightly activity—small factory next to commercial house next to tenement building. And it was indeed a walking city for most of its inhabitants. Public transportation consisted of a number of private horsecar companies, jockeying with one another for franchises from government and providing, in the process, unreliable transport for people and goods on poor, largely unpaved streets, through dirt and garbage that were infrequently and imperfectly removed.

Like other rapidly growing cities in the nineteenth century, New York lacked the will, the legal ability, and the money to provide urban services. Thus it was not only dirty and often ugly, but also unhealthy; its death rate of 35/1,000 at the end of the Civil War was one of the highest in the Western world. Illiteracy was commonplace as well. The city was "disconnected" in very many ways—a highly variegated mixture of individuals, interests, and forces living and working in a tightly circumscribed geographic area in noncomplementary, even cross-purposed ways. What it needed perhaps more than anything else was leadership and coherent planning. This was something that the city's limited powers made very difficult; and it was its very opposite that would be the key to successful political organization.

American cities accentuate many of the nation's most distinctive characteristics, and this is nowhere truer than in terms of their striking ethnic heterogeneity. And New York City was, from its colonial origins, a composite of national, racial, religious, and cultural groups. This was even more true in the middle of the nineteenth century. The age of Tweed came before the tremendous influx of southern and eastern European immigrants of the turn of the century, but others, particularly Irish and Germans, were there in great numbers even before the Civil War. In 1860, for example, in a population of just over eight hundred thousand, a bare majority (52 percent) were native Americans; and since almost 2 percent of those natives were blacks, and far more were of the second generation, the white "old stock" was in fact a minority. Irish-born, in 1860, made up 25 percent of the city's population, and German-born 15 percent. With their children, these were important population groups for the city. And with considerable elements of English, Scotch, French, and blacks, plus a few of almost every nationality the world had to offer, they made up the motley divided population around which everything, including politics, revolved.

National heterogeneity was accompanied by religious. On the eve of the Civil War, New York City had 24 Catholic churches and 10 synagogues, in addition to its 218 Protestant churches. These numbers are somewhat deceiving, since the 24 Catholic churches had 100,000 parishioners in "usual attendance," only slightly below the Protestant total of 118,225. The number of Jews listed by city census as "usual attenders" was 3,825.

In 1870, at the height of the Tweed machine's power, the population had changed little from 1860. The foreign born made up 44 percent of the city's population. The two largest immigrant groups remained the Germans and the Irish. The former made up 16 percent of the city's population and 36 percent of the total foreign born, the latter 20 percent of the total population and 48 percent of the foreign born. The next largest group was the English, about 3 percent of the city's population; and after them—none totaling more than 1 percent—came the French, Scots, Canadians, Italians, Poles, Swiss, Swedes, and Russians. Blacks were just a bit more than 1 percent of the city's population.

Thus what is distinctive about Tweed's New York, unlike later boss-ruled cities, is that it was a bit less foreign overall than its successors would be, and that its ethnic population was overwhelmingly dominated by only two groups, the Irish and the Germans. The nature of ethnic politics would thus be different in Tweed's day than, say, in that of Boss Murphy a generation later. In many respects Tweed had it easier, since he did not have to jockey quite so many groups as his successors did. Moreover, the ethnic population was not in ghettos as much as it would be in New York and other cities by the turn of the century. In New York's twenty-two wards, for example, the foreign-born population varied only from a low of 31 percent to a high of 56 percent. And even in election districts (the smallest political unit, with an average population of two or three thousand) the population mixture was generally the same as that of the ward. This not only makes it more difficult for the political researcher, but also limited the ability of the political organization to operate at its lowest organizational level on a purely ethnic basis. In the early twentieth century, when individual ethnic groups made up 70, 80, or even 90 percent of election districts (precincts), a more precise variety of machine politics would emerge. But in Tweed's day, groups were less clearly organized, and the group basis of politics was more diffuse.

Moreover, the nature and relative social position of the immigrants in

Tweed's day was very different from what it would be a generation later. In seeking background variables for the analysis of the pro-Tweed vote, I isolated, in addition to percentage of foreign born, the number of persons per dwelling, the number of persons per family, and the percentage of the population living in "tenant houses and cellars." The relationships between these variables are given in Table 2.1, which is a matrix of correlation

TABLE 2.1
Relationships among Socio-Economic Indicators for
New York City Wards during the Time of Tweed
(Pearson's r)

	Percentage foreign born	Persons/ dwelling	Persons/ family	Percentage in tenant houses and cellars
Percentage foreign born	----	.502	—.081	.389
Persons/ dwelling	.502	----	—.785	.741
Persons/ family	—.081	—.785	----	—.635
Percentage in tenant houses and cellars	.389	.741	—.635	----

Source: Data compiled for the twenty-two wards of New York City from *Tenth Census,* 1870, and U.S. Industrial Commission, *Report,* vol. 15.

coefficients (Pearson's r), showing the strength of association of each variable with every other variable. This data should suggest not only the extent to which these apparently interrelated phenomena are in fact related, but also—in comparison with what we shall see in later chapters—the extent to which the variables of ethnic voting behavior were consistent over time.* One would ordinarily expect a strong relationship among all of these variables, and especially between foreign birth and each of the others. In fact, for New York wards, foreign birth had a significant correlation (and that marginal, at .502) only with persons per dwelling. As one

---

*The coefficient of correlation (Pearson's r) is a popular statistical measure of association, which we shall have frequent occasion to use. Essentially, it measures the relationship between two variables. For example, if we are studying the fifty wards of Sample City and are interested in the relationship between wealth and voting for candidate X, we could design a graph wherein we plotted on one axis the average wealth and on another the voting percentage for X, for each of the fifty wards; this would give us a graph with fifty dots, each representing an individual ward's position

would expect, the foreign born lived in crowded conditions. But the correlation between foreign birth and domicile in tenant house and cellars was not significant (.389), which suggests that this measure of dire poverty was not particularly conspicuous among the immigrants in the city. And there was no relationship between foreign birth and persons per family. Indeed, persons per family had strong negative correlations with persons per dwelling (−.785) and with percentage in tenant houses and cellars (−.635). In the nineteenth century, at any rate, large family size appears not to have been associated with ethnicity or even socioeconomic position, and the number of single males appears to have been large.

There was a strong measure of association (.741) between persons per dwelling and percentage in tenant houses and cellars, suggesting that these were common measures of relative poverty. But it is worth repeating that only the former correlated significantly with foreign birth.

In sum, then, one can infer that the immigrants in New York City were considerably more spread out geographically, socially, and economically than would be the case a generation later. They were, on the whole, poor, but made up only one part of the generally poor population of the city. Because industrialization was only partly completed, the clearer socioeconomic and cultural divisions that would become characteristic of American cities were imperfectly developed in 1870. The immigrant poor of New York were poor, however, and like other people and other newcomers, tended to be disproportionately represented in crime and lesser social affronts. This, augmented by their "strangeness" in nationality and often religion, led to an increasingly nativist reaction from older New Yorkers. And their lack of intellectual and social resources, coupled with lack of material ones, left them more in need of outside assistance than were the other poor of the city. Thus Tweed.

---

on the two variables. The correlation coefficient is a number which summarizes this graph, describing the relationship, positively or negatively, within a possible range from −1.00 to 1.00.

The nearer the coefficient is to 1.00, the more the two variables are related to one another—the more the scores on the two variables rise and fall together. The coefficient shows only relationship, not causation, although the student may or may not want to infer causation from that relationship. Just what level of relationship (e.g., .555, .700, etc.) is "significant" varies with the data and other factors, and is in fact open to argument. For our purposes we will be interested when the level is about .400 or higher, and impressed when it is about .700 or higher. Often we will be interested in comparative relationships—in determining which, among several pairs of variables, seem most closely related.

A negative relationship can be as important as a positive one. For example, a coefficient of .820 between wealth and voting for X tells us that the two variables are highly related: the wealthier the voters were, the more likely it was that they would vote for X. Conversely, a relationship of −.820 is just as strong in the opposite direction; it says that the more wealthy the voters were, the less likely it was that they would vote for X.

The black population, likewise, was highly dispersed throughout the city. Every ward but one had some black residents; no ward had an appreciable number. A couple of individual election districts—one in the Fifth Ward and one in the Eighth—were about 30 percent black, and that is as concentrated as that population group got. They were numerically insignificant to the politics of Tweed's day, and did not play a real role therein.

The study of New York politics inevitably requires some understanding of the unique nature of Tammany Hall, that famous but often misunderstood force in the history of the city's Democratic party. Tweed's control of New York politics was both a function of and a contributor to the fact that at the end of the nineteenth century, and for much of the twentieth, Tammany *was* the New York Democratic party. This had not always been the case, however, nor would it be so a century later.

The Society of St. Tammany, or Columbian Order, had been founded in 1789 as a patriotic and democratic organization, not a political or partisan one. Its future development, however, was early anticipated; Aaron Burr was one of the first to try to turn its organizational strength and its popularity to political purposes, in 1800. As a basically middle-class organization, Tammany was, in the early nineteenth century, rather nativist and anti-Irish. It was dominated by merchants and bankers and for a long time excluded Roman Catholics and foreigners. But during the age of Jackson, two phenomena served to change this policy: first, the expansion of the suffrage made exclusivist policies politically counterproductive; and second, the rise of large-scale immigration had the same effect. No ambitious political organization could with impunity ignore such a large group of potential voters.

Thus Tammany became, by the middle of the nineteenth century, more open to the immigrant and the worker. There was still a theoretical division between the Tammany Society (as a social organization) and the General Committee of Tammany Hall (as a leading faction of the local Democratic party), but the division was largely fictional; the same people led both, and the purposes were political.

Under Fernando Wood in the 1850s, Tammany emerged as by far the most powerful force in the Democratic party, and as a boss-led one as well. And under Tweed, Tammany achieved the careful and successful organization for which it became famous—the ward and assembly district clubs, rigidly controlled decentralization, etc.

The rise of Tammany was in no small way assisted by the traditional nature of New York City government. Well into the nineteenth century, the city was governed by an aristocratic elite—old-stock Dutch and Anglo-Saxon families who controlled its public affairs as well as its commerce.

Only in 1834 did the mayor's office become elective, and only in the late 1840s was democratic government widespread. Moreover, legal power was highly decentralized, with myriad commissions, departments, and agencies each controlling its own little empire and no real centralizing power over them all.

Various "reform" charters were largely unsuccessful. And the Tweed Ring would be able to use the city's governmental decentralization to build its own power while at the same time appearing as the champion of home rule—which the city and the Ring both needed, albeit for different reasons.

The importance of a political party, or even a dominant political faction like Tammany in such a situation was that it could provide a centralizing force in this power vacuum. Thus while the various and more or less autonomous branches of government in New York City were not coordinated by any governmental agency, if Tammany men were to hold all or most of them, Tammany could serve this purpose. To a considerable extent this is what happened. And in this process is explained the rise and success of the Tweed Ring.

The Tweed Ring was called a "ring," in the definition of Samuel Tilden, one of its foremost enemies, because it controlled enough people in both parties to ensure the success of its nefarious schemes. Whether this differs in some real way from a machine, as some have suggested, is moot. I think not, since this is an aim of the machines we shall consider as well. Thus for our purposes, *ring* is simply a customary name for the Tweed machine, which, as I have already suggested, differs from an "organization" only in very mysterious ways. In these terms, the argument of Tweed's most recent biographer that no ring existed seems to me to ignore the realities of Tammany's organization and strength.

William Marcy Tweed, who would eventually become the first undisputed individual boss of Tammany Hall and, through its triumphs, of New York City, was born of a middle-class New York family, of Scottish and Protestant background, in 1823. In his twenties, Tweed joined one of New York's highly competitive volunteer fire companies, a rather common entry to political life. These seventy-five colleagues provided him with some leverage, for a start. And after one unsuccessful election campaign in 1850, Tweed turned around the next year and was elected alderman (thus becoming one of the famous "Forty Thieves").

It was a propitious and well-chosen start. Aldermen had considerable power in their districts—they appointed policemen, granted saloon licenses and streetcar franchises, and so on. It was not only a focal point for anyone who sought graft, but it was also ideal for the building of a strong and loyal ward machine.

Tweed went on to Congress in 1853, but was never really happy outside of local affairs. His ambitions were fairly clear, and residence in Washington and federal patronage had little relationship to what he wanted to do. In 1854 Tweed was defeated by a Know-Nothing candidate, which had the double-edged effect of returning him to New York City and making him more aware of the question of immigration and the role that immigrants were playing and would continue to play in American politics.

Fernando Wood would try to win over both the Irish Catholics and the Know-Nothings, to the pleasure of neither. But Tweed read the situation more clearly, and eventually realized—as other old-stock bosses would—that the immigrants were numerically more important for the inchoate metropolis, and that they must therefore be deferred to.

Unlike some bosses, Tweed did not operate from offstage, but rather was very much involved in running for office himself. This gave him more leverage, a coterie of his own personal supporters, and, through his careful selection of offices, a voice in legislation affecting his city and party.

In 1855 he was elected to the Board of Education. More importantly, in 1857 he was elected to the Board of Supervisors, of which he would continue as a member until it was abolished in 1870. This position was a key to Tweed's developing powers, and, when he no longer needed it, he was a leader in the popular movement to get it abolished. Tweed held other offices as well during this period, including deputy street cleaning commissioner, which gave him control of thousands of jobs for lower-class and immigrant voters; member of the state senate, where he could be at the place where taxing and other decisions relative to the city were really made; and commissioner of public works, which again controlled many jobs and thus was a rich source of power through patronage.

As it happened, Tweed was as concerned with the possibilities of graft as those of political power, but in this he was typical of only some American bosses. It will be more instructive to concentrate on the latter for the moment.

Tweed's career was not unaffected by luck. He came on the Board of Supervisors in 1857, the same year that state legislature made that body bipartisan and more powerful—really a county legislature. Although designed to be a "reform," it became a boon for Democratic politicians, and Tweed was able to use it for purposes of graft and power.

But Tweed's ability was more important than his luck, by far. As one recent student has said of him, "It was his mastery of urban politics, abetted by the political astuteness of other members of the Ring, that consolidated, centralized, and modernized politics in a way never seen before their time." Tweed was single-minded, never deviating from his aim of control, and this was a key to his success. Thus, for example, in the state senate he chose as committee assignments the Committee on

Municipal Affairs and the Committee on Charitable and Religious Societies. The relevance of the former to his aims is obvious; that of the latter will become apparent below.

Similarly, in his rise to control within the Democratic party and Tammany Hall, both of which were faction-ridden and full of suspicious ambition, Tweed insinuated himself in key positions and chose his people well. As early as 1861 he had become chairman of the New York County Democratic Central Committee, and two years later was chairman of the General Committee of Tammany Hall. Shortly after that he became grand sachem—the first man to be both general chairman and grand sachem, and the first one-man boss of the New York Democracy. Like many successful bosses, Tweed was shrewd in his personal alliances and able to maintain them. This was through a rigorous personal honesty, which is often the key to successful political organization. Indeed, one might argue that the more corrupt a political machine, the more it requires scrupulous honesty among its members to function well. So important are verbal agreements within and between factions, and so informal are crucial arrangements, that a boss or would-be boss with a reputation for reneging on his word cannot long survive. Here, Tweed met the test, as he did to some extent in his choice of people. Tweed's men were loyal and worked well with him for a time. But they were too like the boss in being themselves corrupt, which hastened the downfall of the Ring.

Among Tweed's most important allies was Abraham Oakey Hall, "The Elegant Oakey," who served as mayor from 1868 to 1872. Hall was a fop, showman, actor, and sometimes fool. He was well educated and mannered, scholarly (in a superficial way) and, despite his obvious limitations, respectable—and a kind of liaison between the Tweed Ring and the leaders of New York. Hall was interested less in corrupt practices than in popularity and the spotlight; but these desires made him unconcerned with the others' corruption, and he served, for a while, to divert attention from the real activities of the Ring.

Peter Barr Sweeny was quite the opposite of Oakey Hall. He came from a poor Irish Catholic family, his parents being saloon keepers (one of the best possible introductions to the realities of voter-centered politics). He himself ran a saloon for a while, making many of the contacts he would need for entry into political life. He attended college and read law, and eventually became an excellent lobbyist in Albany. Sweeny was the Ring's political realist, a wheeler-dealer and backstage operator of real ability and some respectability. His appointment as city treasurer in 1866 looked fairly good in public eyes and at the same time gave Tweed another agent in a central position.

Richard "Slippery Dick" Connolly was the least respectable of Tweed's lieutenants, but no less useful for that. Irish born, of a lower-middle-class family, he slowly worked his way up in New York politics. He became very powerful in his district and ward, and this gave him the currency that any politician would respect. As Tweed put it, "He was a powerful man in his ward and district. We could not get along without him, and annexed him for the vote he controlled" (quoted by Alexander Callow). Connolly was a Tammany sachem, a "tribal" leader among the Irish, and comp-troller of New York City—again, a central position for both power and graft, particularly the latter.

A boss like Tweed would inevitably accumulate some wealth, but Tweed had ambitions that were in no way moderate. In the end, he seems to have valued wealth even more than political power, which removed that one crucial restraint—ambition—that has kept so many politicians out of corruption, and prison. His tastes and ambitions were upper class, not those of the urban masses, and somewhere along the line he lost touch. It is estimated that he became New York City's "third largest holder of real estate" (an estimate his most recent biographer questions). And his daughter Mary Amelia's 1871 marriage was an extravaganza of oriental opulence. Her gifts, valued at about $700,000, demonstrated not only the extent to which various people were anxious to ingratiate themselves with her powerful father, but also the scale on which the Tweeds were living at the time.

But the year of his daughter's marriage was also the beginning of Tweed's decline. He was arrested shortly before the election. And, al-though Tweed himself was nonetheless reelected to the Senate, in the long campaign of revelation and revilement against him, his associates, and Tammany candidates generally, were overwhelmingly defeated.

Thus the man and his history, which are central to the drama of the Tweed Ring and the rise of the modern machine. We must now look at the machine itself, and the elections in which it rose to control and then lost everything.

Table 2.2 gives some basic sociocultural data and voting for selected Tammany candidates over the period 1868-1871. The broad picture of the Tweed Ring's rise, success, and fall is quite clear. It is equally clear that New York was a very Democratic city, whether one is talking about the Tweed era, or its predecessors and successors. Also striking is the rela-tive lack of variation from ward to ward. This reflects the general spread of ethnic and socioeconomic forces throughout the city, as described above.

There is a difference in loyalty to the Democracy between more and less foreign wards, as one would expect. The wards with the fewest foreign born (e.g., the Ninth, Twelfth, Fifteenth, and Sixteenth) are among the weaker supporters of the Tweed Ring; and the Fifteenth Ward is the only ward to show somewhat consistent opposition to the Ring during its heyday. But on the whole this difference, like the differences in proportion foreign born per ward, is very slight, and the city's consistency is a good deal more impressive than its variations.

TABLE 2.2
Sociocultural and Voting Data for New York Wards
during the Time of Tweed

Ward	Percentage foreign born	Persons per dwelling	Persons per family	Percentage tenant house and cellar	President, 1868	Governor, 1868	Register, 1868	Supervisor, 1868	Mayor, December 1868	Corporation counsel, December 1868	Secretary of state, 1869	Comptroller, 1869	Governor, 1870	Mayor, 1870	Register, 1871	Supreme court, 1871
1	55	21.0	5.0	50	91	91	96	90	94	94	85	75	73	64	80	75
2	50	1.8	9.7	00	72	62	70	61	79	79	65	60	66	51	49	37
3	53	8.7	6.1	35	77	75	74	36	83	83	74	71	75	69	49	37
4	56	24.6	4.8	82	86	80	94	69	91	91	86	80	89	78	82	8
5	46	13.3	4.8	50	73	75	75	59	85	85	75	71	64	55	33	28
6	55	21.5	4.7	86	92	93	90	70	96	96	91	89	92	82	87	8
7	46	18.8	5.0	51	83	82	91	44	89	89	82	78	86	77	82	87
8	42	13.6	4.7	43	71	74	72	58	80	80	75	74	76	77	51	49
9	31	12.2	5.1	34	51	56	55	41	53	57	53	51	52	51	23	22
10	55	21.9	4.5	64	82	73	72	50	73	73	55	64	74	66	24	21
11	46	20.8	4.4	99	78	80	76	56	85	85	67	68	80	72	42	47
12	34	8.2	6.0	00	60	65	53	36	70	67	64	61	72	69	48	49
13	42	19.9	4.7	48	71	76	70	45	78	78	69	66	79	69	63	57
14	49	18.0	4.6	73	87	86	84	56	90	90	84	80	80	56	60	61
15	39	11.7	5.9	19	48	51	48	42	61	61	47	47	53	51	22	18
16	39	12.7	5.4	74	57	60	56	44	63	63	54	52	56	42	29	29
17	52	24.1	4.5	91	69	74	68	42	79	79	55	66	75	63	26	19
18	46	15.2	5.3	63	64	68	75	32	77	77	67	63	68	59	28	27
19	44	12.9	6.2	50	64	66	60	37	74	74	63	60	68	52	34	34
20	43	14.9	4.8	49	61	64	68	45	78	78	64	65	70	51	34	35
21	41	13.3	6.0	75	64	66	65	64	78	78	79	70	63	51	17	14
22	42	11.7	5.2	75	65	68	60	32	72	71	63	61	68	51	32	33
City Total	45	14.7	5.1	55	69	71	71	52	78	78	69	67	71	61	40	35

Source: Socioeconomic data from Tenth Census, 1870, and from U.S. Industrial Commission, *Report*, Vol. 15. Voting data from *New York Times*. The vote given is the percentage Democratic of the two-party vote, where the second party is the Republican, except: (1) in 1870, when the opponent of Tammany incumbent mayor Hall was Thomas A. Ledwith, running as a "Young Democracy" (anti-Tammany fusion) candidate; and (2) in the race for supervisor in 1868, split three ways between Tweed (Tammany), Oliver (Republican), and Chanler (Democratic Union): here the vote given is Tweed's share of the three-party vote.

For this reason one feels the need for somewhat more precise statistical measures, given in Table 2.3, a matrix of correlation coefficients of the relationships between these same sociocultural and voting measures, wherein each individual variable is related to every other one. Here we find further evidence of the relationship between foreign voters and the success of the Tweed Ring, in the string of significant, and sometimes quite striking, coefficients between this background variable and voting for the Democratic candidates. And here, too, one sees the beginning of a decline in

TABLE 2.3 Pearson's *r* Correlations for Variables in Table 2.2*

	Percentage foreign born	Persons per dwelling	Persons per family	Percentage tenant house and cellar	President, 1868	Governor, 1868	Register, 1868	Supervisor, 1868	Mayor, December 1868	Corporation counsel, December 1868	Secretary of state, 1869	Comptroller, 1869	Governor, 1870	Mayor, 1870	Register, 1871	Supreme court, 1871
Percentage foreign born	—	.502	-.081	.389	.831	.703	.771	.497	.766	.772	.509	.672	.645	.454	.485	-.036
Persons per dwelling	.502	—	-.785	.741	.558	.644	.588	.338	.475	.497	.321	.532	.601	.518	.372	-.001
Persons per family	-.081	-.785	—	-.635	-.243	-.435	-.279	-.037	-.189	-.205	-.157	-.331	-.342	-.363	-.116	-.042
Percentage tenant house and cellar	.389	.741	-.635	—	.389	.485	.393	.184	.376	.396	.265	.384	.402	.184	.061	-.229
President, 1868	.831	.558	-.243	.389	—	.942	.921	.629	.901	.908	.788	.900	.834	.661	.764	.308
Governor, 1868	.703	.644	-.435	.485	.942	—	.892	.584	.905	.910	.817	.934	.845	.694	.766	.368
Register, 1868	.771	.588	-.279	.393	.921	.892	—	.642	.909	.932	.840	.907	.780	.629	.794	.313
Supervisor, 1868	.497	.338	-.037	.184	.629	.584	.642	—	.617	.639	.626	.658	.313	.273	.501	.115
Mayor, December 1868	.766	.475	-.189	.376	.901	.905	.909	.617	—	.995	.879	.939	.825	.615	.745	.305
Corporation counsel, December 1868	.772	.497	-.205	.396	.908	.910	.932	.639	.995	—	.884	.943	.813	.608	.746	.291
Secretary of state, 1869	.509	.321	-.157	.265	.788	.817	.840	.626	.879	.884	—	.934	.712	.568	.780	.286
Comptroller, 1869	.672	.532	-.331	.384	.900	.934	.907	.658	.939	.943	.934	—	.823	.683	.780	.288
Governor, 1870	.645	.601	-.342	.402	.834	.845	.780	.313	.825	.813	.712	.823	—	.852	.786	.249
Mayor, 1870	.454	.518	-.363	.184	.661	.694	.629	.273	.615	.608	.568	.683	.852	—	.710	.199
Register, 1871	.485	.372	-.116	.061	.764	.766	.794	.501	.745	.746	.780	.780	.786	.710	—	.461
Supreme court, 1871	-.036	-.001	-.042	-.229	.308	.368	.313	.115	.305	.291	.286	.288	.249	.199	.461	—

*Pearson product-moment coefficient (*r*) calculated for twenty-two New York wards, for each variable against each other variable, for the values expressed in Table 2.2.

Tweed support by 1870, although the foreign born were more consistently loyal overall than the natives. This is one reason why the Tweed Ring was involved in election frauds—to register, for example, as many real or imagined Irishmen as it could. Although the Irish made up a bit over 20 percent of the voters, their "illegitimate voting strength," according to one student of the Ring, was much greater than that.

It is interesting, and puzzling, that Tweed himself fared less well among the foreign born than did his candidates (coefficient of .497 in his 1868 race for supervisor). Why this was so is unclear, and it is the only Tweed campaign for which we have citywide data. It was a three-way race, with an anti-Tammany Democrat as well as a Republican opposing him, which may explain much of the difference. Perhaps also Tweed's reputation as "the boss" cost him some votes that stayed with his supporters and subordinates, who were less blatantly a part of the machine.

It is worth noting that in 1871, when the Tweed Ring suffered an irreversible defeat, it nonetheless maintained a good deal of foreign support. The very different ward votes for register and supreme court, and the very different correlation coefficients between foreign birth and voting on these two offices, result from the fact that the Democratic candidate for register, Shandley, was a Tammany man, whereas anti-Tammany Democrat Thomas Ledwith had won the nomination for supreme court. Thus even when the Ring had lost its power to assure the election of its own candidates, it continued able and willing to limit the possibilities for Democrats who tried to buck its control of the party.

On the economic side, the category persons per dwelling has generally significant correlations with voting Democratic in the Tweed years, but there are frequent exceptions. More striking is the lack of significant correlation between percentage dwelling in tenant houses and cellars and Democratic voting. It suggests that the Tweed Ring, contrary to general assumptions, did not mobilize the poor as poor, or appeal to the poor as poor, despite its extensive "social welfare program" (described below). There is some reason to believe this measure is not as precise as one might desire, and I hesitate to generalize much from it. But at least one can say that the Tweed Ring appears to have been less universally successful with New York's poor than most students have assumed.

The Tweed Ring, like any political organization, operated in various ways and took its power through equally various tactics. The vote was always the ultimate goal, but the ways of attracting votes and of using them to the organization's ends were many indeed. The Ring never had complete control of New York's vote; it did not necessarily command complete loyalty of even a majority of the voters. Thus it was, as all political organizations since that time, constantly active to refine the machine, to guarantee as fully as it could that a majority would be there for the next intraparty battle, and the next election. Always, there were the questions of Tammany's controlling the party and of the party's winning the election; sometimes one was the more difficult, sometimes the other.

The Tweed Ring, again like every political organization, was very much obligated to partisanship—that backlog of voters who identified with Tammany's party and were thus relied upon as the basis of its strength. To get as many reliables as possible is the goal of any political movement. And here one sees the interrelationship of national, state, and local politics —reliable Democrats were those who stuck with the party at all levels and in all situations. And this required cooperation among various levels of party organization. The state and national Democratic organizations might not have liked Tweed, but if he was in control of the city's Democracy they needed him; and, in the long run, he needed them as well. This is one of the forces which finally fell apart for Tweed and helped contribute to his downfall. But so long as he controlled the New York City Democracy, and as long as a large number of voters—like the Irish—continued to identify themselves as Democrats, he would not be easily undercut.

For related reasons, the Ring was highly reliant upon ward and election district leaders. Decentralization of government and power is a key to the rise and success of the machine, and it also demonstrates the importance of the local political leader. Disaffection of important ward leaders could greatly enhance the power of anti-Tammany factions within the party and threaten Tammany's control; if this happened, there could be disaster.

Thus every machine skates on thin ice, and the boss is hardly omnipotent; rather, he is constantly manipulating and compromising with local leaders in order to stay where he is. The device Tweed most relied upon to hold the loyalty of these various elements was graft—gigantic payoffs to one and all. This worked for a while, but was not openended. The extent of this largesse is a sign of Tweed's realization that his power would last only as long as he maintained the support of local leaders.

This is not to say that the Tweed Ring ignored patronage, that most hoary of devices for the maintenance of a machine. On the contrary, the Ring took great advantage of the opportunity afforded by governmental decentralization and its own control of several levels of government. But even in patronage matters, decentralization had its effects. The Board of Aldermen, for example, whose nature had changed frequently over time, had in the late 1860s both legislative and executive powers, and each alderman had many appointments and jobs at his disposal.

Key elements in Tweed's own personal power were the elective and appointive jobs he kept for himself, giving him a considerable amount of personal patronage. Tweed personally, and Tammany as an institution, appointed great numbers of inspectors of this and assistant commissioners of that, creating thousands of jobs for the poor and for recent immigrants. This not only guaranteed a certain number of voters, but, even more, an equal number of party workers and contributors to the party—for campaign funds or slush funds, as the party leaders desired. Likewise the Tweed Ring was enthusiastic about building—streets, docks, buildings, etc.—which provided additional thousands of jobs and party loyalists, and possibilities for graft as well.

The operation and use of the police force is a good example of the effects of decentralization and patronage. The New York police had been professional only since the 1840s. Members were appointed on nomination of the aldermen; appointment was looked upon as a patronage device, and the jobs were ideal for the new immigrants. The district police captain was a virtual dictator in his district, and police from the captain on down realized the essentially political nature of their appointments. This did not make for a very efficient or honest police force, but it did contribute to the strength of Tammany.

The police were used directly in politics, also. For example, in their role of enforcing law and preserving order in elections the police were very handy. The *New York Times* charged in 1870 that they had been used to prohibit Republicans from voting in their own primary, and had also permitted Tammany men to stuff the ballot boxes. Since Tammany was the source of their having and holding jobs, the sensitivity of the police to Tammany's needs on election day was not surprising.

The Ring did not rely on shrewdness alone. It would, when the need seemed apparent, rely on skulduggery, violence, and brute force. The Ring did recruit bums, winos, and others to act as repeaters; it did pad registration lists with false names—tens of thousands of them, according to contemporary critics. It was apparently linked with crime in the city, as an important source of revenue. Payoffs from brothels, after-hours bars, etc., have long been a staple of machine finance, and they seem to have existed in Tweed's day as well as later.

When all else failed, Tweed was not unwilling to bully his way through. Thus when the Ring lacked the votes in party caucus to nominate the judges it wanted, it sometimes just went ahead—Tweed being chairman of the meeting—and ignored the vote.

Another source of strength and funds for Tammany came in the practice, common to many cities in the nineteenth and early twentieth centuries, of paying certain public officials a percentage of the money their offices took in. This applied to offices like that of sheriff or county clerk, both of which produced huge sums for their incumbents, and through them, for the party. This practice naturally provided a strong motivation for the officeholder to generate funds, to the neglect of other duties associated with his office.

In all of these ways, then, Tammany cemented its economic and political strength, creating a reciprocal and highly resilient link between itself and a large part of the city's poor.

This link, and the ways in which the Tweed Ring built the loyalty of the urban mass, require somewhat more careful examination. We have already noted some differences between New York City in 1870 and the "classic" boss-run city of the twentieth century: New York had fewer large ethnic groups; poverty was general rather than group-specific; and the population was fairly evenly mixed throughout the city. From this it is reasonable to infer that the practice of boss politics, and the role of ethnicity in the Ring's politics, would be a bit different from what we shall see in later chapters. However, because the Irish and Germans were large and definable groups, and there were definable religious groups also, it will be instructive to see the extent to which the Ring gave special attention to their needs.

Part of the Ring's work was done for it by its opponents. Those middle-class groups generally referred to as the "reformers"—groups whose interests included greater honesty in government—were often decidedly anti-immigrant, and sometimes antipoor as well. As Alexander Callow has noted, many of these people were immigrants to the city from upstate New York and New England; they came of old-stock Protestant background and had a sense of order and propriety that almost forced the immigrant and the machine together. Their viewpoint was reflected in the *New York Times*, which was outspoken in support of middle-class reform and was anti-Irish and anti-Catholic as well.

A recent student of the Tweed Ring has stated that "Tammany ruthlessly exploited the immigrant. The fundamental interests of Tammany were not those of the immigrant but the cold, calculated pursuance of the narrow self-interests of Tammany Hall." This is undoubtedly true, but it is not really the point. The question is whether these quite discrete elements developed a symbiotic relationship, and whether we can understand the rise and success of the Ring on the basis of its relationships with the ethnic lower class. Motive is always difficult to discover, and generally not very important. A poor Irish immigrant, for example, is not too concerned with the motives of political leaders and organizations—only with which among them are most responsive to his own personal and group needs.

And we have already seen that Tammany did well under Tweed with the immigrant vote. This is not surprising, simply in terms of patronage, as discussed above. Moreover, the Tweed Ring had an extensive public welfare program of its own. This operated at several levels, including the distribution by Tammany leaders of direct aid. At the time of the 1870 election, for example, Tweed gave each alderman $1,000 to buy coal for the poor and in his own ward spent $50,000 for the same purpose. But beyond that, there was a well-orchestrated program of public aid to private institutions, especially churches; this was, as one recent scholar put it, "systematic and sustained" giving—self-interested to be sure, but nonetheless effective, especially in times of limited and highly qualified philanthropy. And the Ring not only solicited immigrants through patronage and favors, but did respond to some of their real desires. It was not against organized labor, but encouraged unions to organize and did not oppose strikes. And it supported such ethnic aims as Irish opposition to Great Britain. Tammany had a Naturalization Committee—to serve its own ends, of course—but nonetheless an agency that facilitated the naturalization of thousands of immigrants. Gustavus Myers estimated that in the six weeks prior to the 1868 election, between 25,000 and 30,000 new citizens were naturalized, of whom "85 percent" went on to vote for Tammany. There was a great deal of bribery, perjury, and phoniness in all this, including the registration of thousands of nonexistent voters. For example, one naturalization office was in a saloon on Centre St.; it printed over 40,000 certificates that were to be presented to the clerk of any court. The tickets were numbered and read "Please naturalize the bearer"; they were signed by "M. D. Gale, Chairman, Naturalization Committee Tammany Hall." All fees were to be charged directly to the Hall.

This was largely corrupt and self-serving; but the fact nonetheless remains that it did facilitate the naturalization or even "renaturalization" of many immigrants, gave them some money, and—by enfranchising them, even if under several names—some political power as well.

Tweed's charitable activities developed on a very large scale because of his strength in both city and state government. It is estimated that the city treasury, between 1869 and 1871, gave about $1.4 million to the Roman Catholic church, $57,000 to the Protestant Episcopal Church, $25,000 to Jewish organizations, and lesser amounts to various Protestant denominations for schools as well as charities. That the largest amount was given to Catholic churches simply reflected the religious loyalties of most of the immigrants and the poor in New York City.

Tweed's committee assignments in Albany (including Charitable and Religious, Financial, and Municipal Affairs) facilitated his endeavor to get state participation in his welfare programs. State aid to parochial schools was an old and divisive issue in New York politics, and Tweed pushed it hard. A state Board of Public Charities had existed, but was removed in the constitutional convention of 1867-69, primarily because of religious division. This was the kind of thing that Tammany disdained. Tweed labored mightily to get new state aid for parochial schools, something that produced much criticism from agencies like the Union League Club, from the *New York Times,* and from upstate politicians, who opposed the political and economic principles involved, the power of the Catholic church, and the power of Tammany. Failing to get direct aid, Tweed tried to get a bill passed which would permit the city and county of New York to pay part of the annual expenses of parochial schools; this, too, failed, but it was obvious to Catholic leaders that Tammany was trying.

Tweed finally succeeded by sliding state aid for parochial schools into a complex annual bill for financing New York City government. This produced increasing criticism of what the *New York Christian Advocate* called the "Irish Democratic Party" in 1869 and 1870. That Protestant journal warned of a "papal conspiracy," and its opposition was reflected by journals like the *New York Times* and even the state Republicans at their annual convention.

Apart from schools, there was a New York state tradition to grant money to private hospitals, orphanages, and other charities on an individual basis through an annual charity bill. This had always been a great pork barrel measure, and was made to order for Tweed when he arrived on the scene. During the three years that he sat on the Senate Committee on Charitable and Religious Societies more money was appropriated ($2.25 million) than in the preceding seventeen years combined. Of this money, New York City got almost $2 million, and of that about $1.4 million went to Roman Catholic charities and schools.

It is not surprising, then, that Irish support of Tammany and Tweed was as strong and consistent as has been seen. This alliance preceded Tweed, but he did a good deal to maintain it and even increase it. The 1870 campaign came in the midst of the furor over state aid to parochial schools, and much of the publicity centered on the campaign for governor. Tweed's man, John T. Hoffman, led the ticket in New York City, with 71 percent of the vote. And in the poorest wards and those with the greatest number of Irish, like the Fourth and Sixth, his vote was about 90 percent. The correlation between foreign birth and percentage of Democrats was higher for Hoffman (.645) than any other candidate in the election. And thus, in the anti-Tweed crusade of 1871, there were special appeals to the Irish-Americans of New York that recognized their overwhelming Democratic allegiance but nonetheless solicited their support against Tweed.

The Germans were more mixed in their political loyalties. They were as much Protestant as Catholic, for one thing; and there were greater social and economic variations within this group than among the Irish. Indeed, the control that the Irish had asserted over the Democratic party through Tammany alienated even German Democrats, to the point that they were relatively open to the idea of reform through the overthrow of the Ring. Nonetheless the wards with the greatest numbers of Germans and the poorest wards, like the Tenth and Seventeenth, demonstrated the effectiveness of Tammany politics and welfare, and, in the election of 1870, for example, they voted 75 percent for Hoffman and Tammany. The very fact that Tammany was running a German-American for governor was important. The Democratic reformers of 1871 would finally recognize the reality of Tammany's appeal and slate a German and two Irishmen on their own ticket.

Blacks showed no real affection for Tammany. Group leaders were overwhelmingly committed to Frederick Douglass's famous dictum, "The Republican Party is the ship; all else is open sea." To the extent that they voted (property qualifications remained for blacks until 1870), one can assume that black voters stuck with the Republicans. But the Ring did not entirely ignore blacks. Rather, it sent in "repeaters" to vote black registrations, so that when the black voter arrived at the polls he found that he had already "voted." Just as Tammany had reflected its supporters' views in refusing to oppose slavery, so, too, in 1870, it reflected their fear and dislike of the black man, making no effort to enlist blacks' loyalty.

In its greatest success, the election of 1869, the Ring, in the words of one student, "linked Albany to City Hall." Its success in this election gave the Ring great power in state government and the ability to kill legislative or other state action that might have changed the nature of city government in such a way as to minimize the Ring's control.

No political organization is omnipotent, however, and the Ring was confronted, in 1870, with the inevitability of a revision in the city's charter. The question, really, was how seriously this revision might undermine the Ring's control. And it is great testimony to the astuteness of Tweed that he moved on the offensive, played a leading role in the proposed "reform," and ended up with the "Tweed Charter," which gave something to upstate Republicans, something to the middle-class reformers of New York City, and at the same time reinforced the Ring's own power against its Democratic rivals and over the city as a whole.

The politics behind this success was quite brilliant—and reinforced by perhaps a million dollars in well-placed bribes. The results were worth the effort and the price. The power of the mayor of New York City was considerably increased; the office of comptroller (a very sensitive one, in view of that official's ability to spot fraud and corruption) was changed from elective to appointive (by the mayor); and a new Board of Audit was created to audit all municipal expenditures. The personnel of this new agency were the mayor (Hall), the comptroller (Connolly), the president of the Board of Parks (Sweeny), and the commissioner of Public Works (Tweed). And thus the major "reform" of urban government of the time was turned by Tweed into perhaps his greatest personal success. Never before had the party in power had so much control over patronage, nor had there been more jobs available for it to fill. It was a classic case of the machine using "reform" for its own ends, and rather like the many cases where "reformers" used machine tactics for theirs.

From this point, until the beginning of the great exposé of the Ring's frauds in the summer of 1871, the Tweed organization was at its height. In the 1870 state and local elections it continued its string of successes, not only over the Republicans but over its Democratic competitors as well. The city elections for mayor, sheriff, and clerk were between Tammany candidates and Young Democracy (anti-Tammany Democrats) competitors; and here Tammany showed the extent to which its support was more than just partisan. With majorities of from 61 to 68 percent, Tammany candidates overwhelmed their intraparty rivals almost as completely as they defeated the Republican candidate for governor.

The Tweed Ring was in fact short-lived for a political machine. This is sometimes lost sight of because of the Ring's great power and notoriety. But the heyday of its power was only from about 1868 to 1871—short indeed. Moreover, the fall of Tweed also brought about a temporary decline of Tammany Hall. Tammany, however, had obviously institution-alized strengths, which permitted it to reassert itself as the dominant faction in the New York Democracy in rather short order; but it would be a Tammany under entirely different leadership. The Ring did not return.

The main reason for the fall of the Ring was that its leaders were far more concerned with the perquisites of power than with power itself. This led them into kinds and degrees of corruption that almost guaranteed that they would be undone. George Washington Plunkitt's famous distinction between honest and dishonest graft perhaps defines the true borders of politically acceptable corruption in late nineteenth and early twentieth century urban politics. The Tweed Ring recognized no such distinctions, and ran so afoul of any reasonable standard of graft—if one can speak in such terms—that they not only fully aroused the middle class, but did so to an extent and with a brazenness that removed their immunity from the legal system and in the long run undercut some of their popular base as well.

This chapter is concerned with the Tweed Ring as a political phenomenon, and particularly with its relationship with the lower-class immigrants. As such, we are not particularly interested in the corruption of the Tweed Ring. But a brief look at this phenomenon is not entirely out of order, since it says something further about the way in which the Ring operated. Moreover, the extent of the Ring's attention to its corrupt aims inevitably deterred it from otherwise productive politicking, and as such is a measure of the extent to which it detoured from a single-minded attention to building a successful political machine.

The Ring's corruption was both political and economic. These monies came from corrupt practices in city and state government and in private business. Sometimes it was what George Washington Plunkitt would call honest graft: Tweed or another Tammany leader would, for example, take advantage of the prior knowledge his political position gave him of land the city planned to buy, and buy it on the open market in anticipation. Then, however, the honest graft would often become dishonest, when the same man would take additional advantage of his position by getting the city to buy that land at a much higher than free market price. Tweed, for example, seeing how much money printers could make on city contracts, bought in 1864 controlling interest in the New York Printing Company. Using the power of his position, he saw that all the city's business went to that company, and at very high prices. Moreover, he forced companies which wanted city business to give their printing jobs to his company as well.

Similarly, Tweed got himself admitted to the bar, not out of any particular interest in the law, but because the combination of his political position and his being a certified lawyer made possible tremendous fees. He was perhaps the first of the great "influence peddlers," a breed more famous in the twentieth century. The large number of jobs that Tweed had in his control, in his position as deputy street commissioner, for example, was used not simply for political purposes but also for money gathering. Job aspirants were frequently expected to show their gratitude in tangible ways.

What the leader did on the grandest scale, his major and minor functionaries copied as well as they could. His chief aide, "Slippery Dick" Connolly, as comptroller, was in a position to make a fortune—and did. He was also on top of much that was going on, which put him in a sensitive position.

Politically, the Ring also broke the law. Most notable were the naturalization frauds mentioned above. Though the main purpose of these was to rapidly and greatly increase the number of loyal Tammany voters, the leaders of the Ring were not above making some money from it, too, when they could. And lesser lights were more than willing, often, to accept bribes in return for facilitating the fraudulent registrations.

Overall, students of the Ring's corruption have estimated the extent of its graft at anywhere from fifty to two hundred million dollars. Even the lower figure was a true fortune in 1870. Most of it went to the men at the top, but enough drifted down to hold the machine together and to suggest that corruption was widespread. But very little of this money was turned to political purposes. It was "pure" graft, the result of the avarice of a few men who put pecuniary gain even ahead of power.

It is generally held that the overthrow of the Tweed Ring came as a direct result of this corruption. The *New York Times* and cartoonist Thomas Nast in *Harper's Weekly* began their campaign of exposure, criticism, and humiliation against Tweed and his organization in July 1871. And as already noted, the extent of this corruption was sufficient to arouse to political concern and action a middle class which was decidedly apolitical in that era. More and more, New York's merchants and business-men galvanized one another to "do something about Tweed."

This middle-class organization and propaganda was not only politically powerful; it had economic cutting edges as well. Mandelbaum suggests that the anti-Ring publicity had the effect of making it impossible for the city to float more bonds. The European buyers were frightened off, as were domestic ones. Moreover, the bankers refused to extend further credit to the city. Thus even if Leo Hershkowitz is correct that the corruption was less than alleged, and the opposition of Nast and the *Times* went well beyond the bounds of due cause, the effect was the same as if all the allegations were true. A high-flying machine like that of Tweed constantly needed cash flow and tended inevitably toward increasing deficit financing; thus this kind of middle-class pressure was real indeed, and was hard to overcome, especially if it was politically influential at the polls as well.

In November 1871 Connolly resigned as comptroller and a few days later was arrested. His bail was set at one million dollars (a rather hefty sum for nonviolent crimes, it would seem today; but Connolly no longer had powerful friends in high places), and since he couldn't meet it, he went to jail. Tweed himself had been first arrested at the end of October, and this helps explain the great Tammany defeat at the polls on November 7. We have seen how broad was this defeat, but also that the most heavily Irish and German and poorest wards were least anti-Tammany; they were not part of the middle class, and the battle against Tweed was, after all, largely a battle of classes. Tweed himself was reelected, but he was one of the few elected survivors, and a Tammany chief without braves could not last very long.

By December of 1871 Tweed had been indicted on a felony count; he was released on bail, but did resign his last office. During 1872 the pressure continued unrelentingly, so that the chances for a Ring rebound were virtually nil. Finally, in 1873, Tweed was tried, found guilty, and sent to prison for twelve years. He got out after one year, but was rearrested on civil charges and held in lieu of bail of three million dollars! Even this he avoided for a time, escaping to Cuba and Spain. But he died in jail, in 1878.

The rapid growth and increasing demographic heterogeneity of New York City, combined with woefully inadequate city government and insensitive state government, created the situation that made the Tweed Ring possible. With a rapidly increasing urban lower class, consisting largely of immigrants and their children, and a ruling middle class which not only had no sensitivity to the problems of these newcomers but was too intent on the economic challenges of the time even to care very much about control of their political environment, all it took was some shrewdness, organization, and hard work.

Thus the genesis of the Tweed Ring is no mystery. Likewise its maintenance in power came from its providing to these lower-class groups at least more assistance and urban service than they had been used to previously. This gave the Ring the votes, and that, in a democratic government, was all it needed.

The Ring did not long survive, however, since its provision of these services was not as consistent as it might have been. Had it been otherwise, all the *New York Times* editorials and all the Thomas Nast cartoons in the world would not have undone the Ring. Individuals might have been destroyed, on the basis of illegal activity, but the Ring itself, the machine, would have survived. Never in the history of democratic electorates has the pen toppled a political organization.

The Ring's base was not broad or deep enough; its hold on the voters was insufficient. And this was primarily because, in the final analysis, the leaders of the Ring, and Tweed himself, were incomplete politicians—they were after financial gain more than they were after power. This led them to concentrate on the wrong things and to spend too little time doing what they should have done if political survival had been their goal.

With the whole middle class and commercial force of the city arrayed against them, their own crimes to make them vulnerable, and a popular base that was less secure than they imagined, the leaders of the Ring were able to maintain their machine for only a few years. Tammany was more than Tweed, and Tammany not only survived, but, after a brief decline, rose to new heights.

But Tweed, in some ways, had shown the way. He had proven that the urban lower class, and particularly the immigrant sector thereof, formed a usable base for political control. From this start, shrewder and even more dedicated people would build more permanently and constructively.

3

CHARLES FRANCIS MURPHY: THE ENDURING BOSS

Charles Francis Murphy, like William Marcy Tweed, was the boss of Tammany Hall; through that position, again like Tweed, he was the boss of the New York Democracy and thus in considerable control of the governments of New York City and the state of New York. Moreover, the similarities between the two men extend beyond the positions they held in common. Tammany Hall and the New York Democracy continued as political movements resting on a base of the lower-class and working-class elements of the city. The *modus operandi* of Tammany Hall continued much the same as before. And its structure persisted also; Tammany continued to function through a system of structured decentralization, wherein each political worker down to the precinct level operated independently and on his own terms so long as he delivered the vote. But the forces of central authority, with the boss at their pinnacle, were constantly vigilant to see that the vote was indeed delivered; few leaders of district, precinct, or any other level were able to contest the powers of the central authority.

But these similarities between Tweed and his situation, and Murphy and his, cannot mask the considerable differences between the men and between the cities they attempted to rule. Indeed, the changed nature of New York City alone was reason for the considerable differences between Tweed's and Murphy's Tammany Halls, and the different ideas and ambitions of the two men added another important dimension.

New York City in 1900 was a very different place physically from what it had been in 1870. In 1897, the Bronx (soon Bronx County), Queens (Queens County), Brooklyn (Kings County), and Richmond (Richmond County—Staten Island) were added to Manhattan (New York County) to create the five boroughs of the new city of Greater New York. A Manhattan of about 31 square miles in Tweed's day was now a large metropolis of about 365 square miles, jumping rivers and other apparently natural dividers to form a new unity.

Along with this increase in acreage were other physical developments that served to turn it into a real whole. The Brooklyn Bridge, begun in Tweed's day, was finished in 1883. It was complemented, in Murphy's day, by the Williamsburg, Manhattan, and Queensboro bridges, and the beginning of construction of "tubes" under the water as well. Transportation in Manhattan to about 1890 was in the hands of four private companies holding perpetual franchises from state government, which together had about 32 miles of track. More rapid development was taking place at the same time in the other cities, all of them, like Manhattan, using steam-powered locomotives to pull their trains. But the 1890s saw the expansion of the elevated railroads, and 1900 the plans for the first subway. With conversion to electric power in 1902, the basis for a reasonably clean and efficient transportation system for this disjointed city had begun. Under Murphy, both municipal and private construction contributed to the development of a reasonably complete interborough rapid transit (IRT) system.

Better transportation made possible a more specialized city, where residential and industrial/commercial districts could be separate from one another. The "walking city" was no longer essential. This specialization was not so thorough in New York as in other cities, partly because it was less industrial than, for example, Chicago, and also because some of its most important industries—textiles especially—were decentralized and tenement-based for a long while. But nonetheless a more distinct neighborhood development and characterization did take place.

The city modernized in other ways. The Tweed era had seen, whatever the waste, the first development of more active government and government-centered urban services. Tammany and non-Tammany governments after Tweed continued this, so that by the turn of the century, things like city-run street cleaning and refuse collection were general. Despite the crowding of the tenement areas, New York was a healthier place in Murphy's day than it had been in Tweed's. The death rate, for example, which had been 35/1,000 in Tweed's day, was 21/1,000 in 1900 and 13/1,000 in 1920.

But in many respects the most important changes in New York were neither physical nor economic. They were demographic, and they stemmed from the tremendous increase in population, and the variety thereof.

The newly integrated New York City had a population of almost 3.5 million in 1900, which increased to 4.75 million in 1910 and over 5.5

million in 1920. Manhattan had a bit less than half of this population, and Brooklyn a bit more than a third. The Bronx was next largest, then Queens, and finally Richmond, by far the smallest of the boroughs. Thus, at the outset, a prospective "boss" of New York politics in the twentieth century would have far more people to deal with than had Boss Tweed; this alone required changes in the operation of politics.

But numbers were only one part of the changed population of New York City. Starting with the 1880s, immigration had begun to increase more and more. Between 1860 and 1900 alone over 750,000 immigrants came into New York City, accounting for about a third of its population growth during that time. (Considering that so much of the rest came from annexation, the immigrant aspect of this is yet more impressive.) Even up to 1890, immigrants made up over half of Manhattan's population growth. After 1900 the volume of immigration grew ever larger; as New York continued to be the major port of entry for new immigrants, it also continued the largest permanent settling point for them. From Ellis Island, established by the federal government in the 1890s, awesome numbers of people moved into New York City proper in the years up to World War One. By 1920, the foreign born and their children made up 76 percent of the city's population (78 percent in Manhattan and 81 percent in the Bronx).

Moreover, the source of this immigration was greatly changed from the time of Tweed, introducing new cultural and political factors. The essentially old stock, Irish, and German city of 1870 became, by the First World War, a major center of settlement for southern and eastern European nationalities as well. Italians and eastern European Jews began their immigration in the 1880s and never stopped. Close to a million foreign-born Jews lived in New York City in 1920, as well as almost 400,000 Italians, plus still-large Irish and German communities. Jews, native and foreign, made up perhaps as much as a third of the city's population in 1920, making it a leading Jewish center for the world.

Blacks, too, came to New York, as did other Americans looking for the opportunities provided by the modern metropolis. Black immigration from the South was steady, but only became large-scale with the employment opportunities of the First World War, to make a total population of 152,467 in 1920. This was only 3 percent of the city's population, so that, in Murphy's day as in Tweed's blacks were still essentially unimportant in the city's politics.

Along with the rapid increase in number and size of immigrant groups came increasing residential concentration, or ghettoization. We have seen that in Tweed's day, differences in ethnic composition from one district to another were not very large. In Murphy's time, however, the picture of the ethnically ghettoized metropolis that we have come to associate with twentieth-century America was much clearer. For reasons both of choice and necessity, new immigrants did tend to live among themselves, often in extremely high concentrations. In 1920, for example, there were four assembly districts (basic political units, often with populations over 100,000) that were more than two-thirds Jewish (in one of them, on the East Side, Jews made up 85 percent of the population of about 95,000 people).

While other groups were neither so large nor so concentrated as the Jews on the assembly district level, there were nonetheless districts like the Third, which was 51 percent Irish; the Eighteenth, and which was 39 percent Italian; and the Twenty-first, which was 48 percent black. If we had data available for the smaller election districts (precincts), these concentrations would be both higher and more numerous.

In addition to, and partly because of, their residential and sometimes occupational concentration, as well as their lack of institutionalized power, New York's ethnic groups were much better organized in Murphy's day than in Tweed's. And they had the political power that comes from concentration and organization. With ethnicity as the most powerful variable behind group actions, the party or politician that wanted their support would have to meet the needs of the group. It would be much harder in the twentieth century to get around ethnic aspirations and demands; and it would be difficult to please all groups with the same actions. What was called for was an elastic and decentralized politics catering to the largely subsistence needs of poor and unacculturated people. And it is testimony to Tammany and the men who ran it that they were able, much of the time, to do this, and thus to stay in power. Their success was not constant, however, which was the most effective kind of reminder that the voters were fickle and not easily gulled.

The death of the Tweed Ring was a setback but by no means a catastrophe to Tammany Hall. Because of its innate strengths, the Hall proved resilient indeed, and as early as 1874 a Tammany mayor once again graced city hall. Gustavus Myers, an early and hostile historian of the Hall, explained its continuation as due to the fact that "a large part of the thoughtless mass of the Democratic voters were still willing to follow its leadership." But he had no evidence that such voters were indeed "thoughtless." Rather, one can argue, these voters were committed either to Tammany or to the Democratic party; and given the fact that no viable long-term opposition arose against Tammany within the party, the answer continued to be "regular" voting. Tammany's social services, its relative concern for the urban masses, and its rigorously hierarchical organization continued to function; for these reasons, rather than because of thought-lessness, it continued to attract a large part of the New York electorate.

An example of this, from the other side—that is, the standpoint of the reformers—can be seen in the mayoral career of Abram S. Hewitt. Hewitt was a millionaire, as independent in his politics as he was financially, who was first elected with Tammany support in 1886, defeating Henry George and Theodore Roosevelt. Both his independence and his ill humor gradually alienated the Tammany leaders, and his insensitivity to the sources of Tammany strength was the last straw. When delegates from several Irish societies came to him in 1888 to ask that he review the annual St. Patrick's Day parade—something that every mayor of New York had done for thirty-seven years—Hewitt lectured them:

Let us understand each other. I am Mayor of the city and you want me to leave my official duties to review your parade. . . . You started off by a reference to the Irish Democratic vote. . . . We all know that the Irish vote is strong enough to elect any candidate in this city for which it is cast. But for the purpose of getting that vote I shall not consent to review any parade, be it Irish or Dutch or Scotch or German or English.

The delegates told the mayor that "We do not ask this as Irishmen, but as Irish-Americans," but he was adamant. This was, to Hewitt and perhaps others, high-minded and even very American, but it was bad politics and offended a large part of the Democratic electorate. Tammany refused to support him for reelection that year, and he was defeated.

But Tammany was by no means universally successful in these years. It frequently lost the mayoralty and was rarely able to control enough offices to give it unified control at city, county, and state level. This would change only after the turn of the century, when Charles F. Murphy took control, but even in Murphy's day Tammany never had the control of New York City that other machines would develop in other parts of the country.

Tweed's successor in Tammany Hall leadership was "Honest John" Kelly. Kelly had been born in Hester Street in 1822. He came from a poor Irish family and rose to some influence through his reputation as a good fighter and his activity as a volunteer fireman. He served as alderman, had two terms in Congress, and then three terms as sheriff, which made him a wealthy and reasonably powerful man. His career was not without charges of corruption, but on the whole, as leader of Tammany, his reign was scandal-free. Unlike Tweed, Kelly was not a blowhard; rather, he operated quietly, and with as little bombast as possible. In several of these characteristics, he would serve as a model for Charlie Murphy; and he was Tammany's first Irish Catholic leader.

Kelly was also foresighted in bringing "reformers" into Tammany leadership and campaigns. Samuel Tilden, Horatio Seymour, and August Belmont were all Tammany sachems during his time. And he even nominated for mayor in 1872 one of the Committee of Seventy which had been instrumental in the overthrow of Tweed. The economic crisis of 1873-74 helped him return Tammany to the mayoralty in 1874. From that point on, his success was frequent but not constant for the next ten years. He failed, however, to expand Tammany's power to the state level, and this impaired the machine from functioning as completely and efficiently as it had in Tweed's day.

It was under Kelly that rival Democratic organizations made their greatest effort to replace Tammany Hall as the real heart of the New York Democracy. Both the Irving Hall Democracy and the County Democracy operated for some years; but it became soon obvious that, at least within the Democratic party, it was virtually impossible to remove Tammany Hall for any extended period. Thus the unique importance of "fusion" in New York politics.

The mid-1880s witnessed increasing allegations of corruption against Kelly's machine. This was almost unavoidable, since it was the start of the period of tremendously lucrative street railway franchises, wherein the opportunities for graft were enormous.

When Kelly died in 1886, several factions vied for control from within Tammany. Eventually Richard Croker won out and until about 1901 was the preeminent leader of the New York Democracy. Croker had been born in Ireland, of a blacksmith father. He himself was trained as a machinist but grew more famous as a fist fighter; he even fought in some prizefights, which made him widely known. He became leader of the "Fourth Avenue Tunnel Gang" and a Tammany activist at a young age. He was an alderman under Tweed but then sided with the County Democracy against him. He had also served as coroner, a position for which his main qualifications had been party regularity.

At one point, Croker was indicted for murder in a shooting—a political quarrel—but was eventually acquitted by a jury. His career was marked by accusations of corruption and violence, and he was probably under more long-term scrutiny from state, county, and private groups than any other Tammany leader.

From perhaps the humblest origins of any nineteenth-century leader, Croker rose to greater wealth and perhaps even greater power than Tweed himself. He had a real taste for opulence, again like Tweed, and again dangerously for a mass political leader. Croker became a horseman, having his own stud farm and racing stable, along with a $200,000 house. He traveled extensively, especially to Ireland, where he spent a great deal of time.

By the 1890s Croker was under pressure comparable to that Tweed had been under. Several state investigations—particularly those of Lexow and Mazet—and a good deal of city pressure from "reformers" like the Reverend Charles Parkhurst revealed much honest graft and much dishonest graft, such as payoffs from gambling and vice. The *New York Times*—hardly sympathetic to Tammany Hall—estimated that gambling payoffs in the year 1900 amounted to $3 million. Croker's own reasonably frank and revealing testimony before the Mazet Committee reinforced middle-class opposition to Tammany Hall, even though he set up his own Committee of Five which "proved" that Tammany had no connection with vice.

But there were reasons for Croker's long leadership of Tammany Hall. He never forgot where the votes came from. He was parochial or practical —depending upon the prejudice with which one viewed him. He was not averse to some real political issues, as in the 1899 mayoral campaign, when Tammany boasted in speeches of the role played by the Democratic party in Albany. Arguing about "What Democracy Has Done for Labor," the Tammany list included the creation of a Bureau of Labor Statistics, the prohibition of cigar making in tenements, maximum hours legislation for women and children, the Saturday half-holiday, and so on—a list of twenty-nine "pro-labor" laws passed by the Democratic state legislature. These were real issues and help explain the mass working-class support that the Democrats received. And on national issues, Croker and Tammany reflected the practical politician's cynicism: thus on free silver, a major issue of the day, Croker argued, "What's the use of discussing what's the best kind of money? I'm in favor of all kinds of money—the more the better." And his view of the imperialism question was equally acceptable to the masses of New York voters: "My idea of Anti-Imperialism is opposition to the fashion of shooting everybody who doesn't speak English." A *Harper's Weekly* writer commented that "If every man who cannot speak English were to be shot tonight it is doubtful if there would be ten members of Tammany Hall left alive tomorrow." Similarly, the Reverend Mr. Parkhurst commented, after a tour of the dives and flophouses of New York, "Yet from just such sad places at election time comes a host of men to cast their ballots. I feel like revolting against my generation, when I think that from just such lodging houses are built up political careers."

These critics of Tammany politics were not only accurate, they were derogatory, and evinced a parochialism that was no more enlightened than, if different from, that of the Hall itself. The basics of Tammany operations were, at the least, closer to the masses. In the Second Assembly District, for example, Croker's man Patrick Divver was competing with Tom Foley for the district leadership. Their contest had a strong ethnic tinge: each man attended weddings, funerals, and other Jewish and Italian affairs (the district was 96 percent foreign stock, with Jews composing 58 percent and Italians 24 percent of its population). They competed in the lavishness of their giving, for the rewards in power and/or money were potentially very great. Foley stationed men at the marriage bureau at city hall so that he could be the first to congratulate the parents of the prospective brides and grooms; and he endeavored to discover the nature of Divver's gifts so that he could exceed them in an ostentatious way. And Foley won.

Even the best-intentioned reformers, on the other hand, could hardly help offending New York's ethnic groups, or appearing culturally arrogant. Theodore Roosevelt, who would become one of the most generally attractive politicians of the early twentieth century, had real problems as police commissioner of New York City in the 1890s, since he truly wanted to alleviate the squalor and exploitation of the immigrants, but was forced by his position to enforce Sunday closing laws, antigambling laws, and the like—all of which conflicted with the immigrant's way of life and was offensive to him.

Croker, meanwhile, managed to overcome the great pressure upon him in the late nineties, forcing his own personal choice for the mayoralty, R. C. Van Wyck, upon the party, and to success in 1897. But, while he did not give up his claim on the helm of Tammany Hall, he did begin spending more and more time abroad from then on.

In 1899, Tammany once again swept the city, even to the point of defeating Assemblyman Robert Mazet, Republican chairman of the state investigating committee, in the Nineteenth Assembly District (interestingly, this generally Republican district was only 64 percent foreign stock —low for New York City, and 33 percent old stock—the highest in Manhattan). But the effect of the investigations was seen in general Republican victories throughout the state and in Republican control of the state legislature—which meant that Tammany's power was far from secure.

In 1901, Tammany and Croker suffered a crushing defeat in the success of Seth Low and a whole Fusion ticket in taking over city government. Low, a former president of Columbia University, had lost the mayoral contest to Tammany in 1899. But he won in 1901 due to tremendous middle-class unity against Tammany and Croker—and also to a more intelligent campaign. As in 1871 against Tweed, it seemed that the commercial and other leaders of the city had really decided to defeat "Crokerism" and that the time was ripe for another general housecleaning. Certainly the rather devastating results of the Mazet Committee, linking Tammany and Croker personally to graft and corruption, were very timely. But also important was the fact that Low and his running mates—especially district attorney candidate William Travers Jerome—carried their arguments to many groups that the reformers had largely ignored before.

There was, for example, a great deal of German-American activity in favor of Fusion. The Germans had always been somewhat marginal in the Democratic party, since Tammany was so rigorously controlled by the Irish. And this was heavily played in 1901, as were appeals to the Germans' middle-class sensitivities. Low even spoke to newer immigrant groups, like the Bohemians—to whom, as to the Germans, he implied that he would not try too vigorously to enforce Sunday closing. The Jews and Italians were also considered, the stress being on "Crokerism" and its moral turpitude and its ignoring the real needs of the populace. This strategy resulted in some support even from the garment unions.

On the other side, there was the more traditional anti-Tammany support, especially as seen in the city's Protestant churches. On the Monday before the election, the *New York Times* devoted most of a page to summaries of the previous day's sermons on politics. With a single voice, the Protestant ministers condemned Tammany and all it stood for. The preacher at St. Andrew's Methodist Episcopal Church, for example, complained not only about traditional Tammany immorality but stressed also the "illegally registered" aliens who didn't even know English and would be voting the Tammany ticket. He also worried about the "floater vote—that great mass of ignorant and unprincipled people" which was also committed to Tammany. Another Protestant minister noted in his sermon that the largest Tammany vote would come from the East Side of Manhattan, where the worst "urban abuses" were common.

This theme was reiterated from sermon to sermon, not only among Protestant ministers, but also by at least one rabbi (of an upper-middle-class, assimilated, Reform congregation) and by Felix Adler, the head of the Ethical Culture Society. The only sermon for Shepard (the Tammany candidate) reported by the *Times* was that by the priest of the St. Leo's Roman Catholic Church on Eighth Street, which criticized the Protestant ministers for calumniating him. The cultural divisions of New York City politics were very clear.

The election of Seth Low and the Fusion ticket really ended Croker's role in New York politics, although he remained theoretically active for a few more years. He did name his own successor in 1901, and a particularly bizarre one at that. Lewis Nixon was an Annapolis graduate and businessman, one of a number of "respectables" whose political interests had led them to activity in Tammany Hall. But Nixon's avocational interests in politics had ill prepared him for the realities of Tammany leadership, and the demands for patronage and dispensation of power overwhelmed him. After only four months he quit, declaring that "I could not retain the

leadership of Tammany Hall and at the same time retain my self-respect."
So much for amateurs.

For another six months a triumvirate ruled Tammany Hall, but this
was contrary to tradition and inefficient as well. Thus one of the three,
by his ability and with strategic support, rose above the others, and
Charles Francis Murphy became the new boss of Tammany Hall.

Charles Francis Murphy was born in 1858 in a tenement in the Gas
House district of Manhattan; he continued to live in the general area for
the rest of his life. He was the second of nine children of a working-class
family and attended public schools until the age of fourteen, when he
went to work—none of which was unusual for the time. Like other political leaders, Murphy first attracted attention and popularity by his physical
prowess. He was a baseball player and leader of a crew that won a famous
boat race. In 1875 he got a job as a horsecar driver, a position which permitted him to greatly expand his circle of acquaintances. From the roots
of his baseball team he organized the Sylvan Social Club, which gave him
a reliable group of friends upon which to launch both his political career
and his business activities in saloon keeping.

Murphy actually followed his brothers into Tammany affairs, and later
he would be no hindrance to their careers; one was on the Board of Aldermen, another on the police force, and a third also held several offices.
At one point, the local assemblyman, who had been dumped by Tammany, asked the popular young Murphy to run his independent campaign;
Murphy did so, and successfully, but that was the only time he ever operated outside the organization.

By the 1890s Murphy owned four prosperous saloons, which provided
him a ready-made constituency in the Gas House district. He rose in
Tammany affairs and became leader of the Eighteenth Assembly District
organization at age 34; one of his saloons became the headquarters of the
Anawanda Club, the Tammany district association.

Murphy was an ideal Tammany leader. He worked hard at his job and
delivered his votes. For example, records were kept on each voter, and if
he hadn't voted by three o'clock on election day, a party functionary
arrived at his home or work to remind him. In addition to thoroughness,
Murphy stressed accessibility: he was always available. Every night a certain lamppost on Second Avenue was Murphy's station; he did not fail to
show up. Likewise he was generous, as a political leader had to be; but
unlike many, he gave much anonymously. Nonetheless, he developed a
reputation for charity and generosity.

Under Mayor Van Wyck, Murphy was appointed one of the four dock
commissioners—his only public position ever. For the rest of his life he

enjoyed being addressed as "Commissioner." It was a lucrative position, both directly and in terms of graft. And Murphy did take money, one way or another. He eventually owned a small estate on Long Island with a nine-hole golf course, and when he died left an estate of about two million dollars—a large sum indeed for a saloon owner of the day. But Murphy seems to have been a true example of the "honest" grafter; he did take advantage of his position, but he appears to have had no connection with rackets of any kind.

Charlie Murphy was, in fact, rather old fashioned and a bit of a prude; his saloons, for example, never admitted women, although it was common to do so at the time. And one suspects that part of his refusal to profit from gambling, prostitution, and other kinds of dishonest graft, was his real moral aversion to such practices. He was also, quite unlike Tweed, famous for his taciturnity. Rarely did he speak out in public. One famous story tells of a Fourth of July celebration where Murphy did not join in the singing of patriotic songs. When a reporter asked a Tammany official why the boss was not singing, he was told, "Perhaps he didn't want to commit himself."

When Murphy came into control of Tammany Hall in 1902, he had some advantages he could count on. He had, after all, a going, successful organization—under a cloud, perhaps, and temporarily out of power, but nonetheless with real resources. Moreover, as General Theodore A. Bingham had written in an anti-Tammany article in *McClure's*, the Tammany leader was powerful because of his relative permanence. Mayors or police commissioners, for example, were fleeting figures on the public scene, but the grand sachem was more or less permanent; it was therefore natural, or at least logical, for the policeman or the businessman to look to him, rather than to more duly constituted figures. And if the Democrats were temporarily in decline in the nation and state, this was surely temporary, and one of Tammany's most potent political weapons continued to be the fact that it was the Democracy for New York City.

Murphy continued his practice of being accessible, although in somewhat altered form. Now, as leader, he divided his public presence into three spheres. First was Tammany Hall itself, where he appeared each morning to conduct organization business and to receive party workers and the interested public. Then, every noon, he lunched at Delmonico's restaurant, where party higher-ups and important nonpoliticians could meet with him. And finally, he maintained close ties in his home neighborhood—to whose more affluent reaches he had moved without ever leaving the Eighteenth District.

It was a one-man leadership: about that there was no doubt. Murphy was ever vigilant about the protection of his position and control. He early abolished the Tammany Finance Committee and set up a puppet office of treasurer, in fact keeping the purse strings entirely in his own hands. He never forgot that the hierarchy spread from his own single position. But he maintained this authority not via dictatorship but via cooperation. He respected the positions of his district leaders and would never, for example, recommend a man for a public job if the man's district leader did not approve. Likewise he followed that key aspect of extra-legal political leadership that we saw in Tweed before him: he was famous for being a man of his word.

Murphy was entirely aware of the way in which Tammany Hall actually operated. He did not try to follow every detail of every district's activities. The bureaucracy was well established, the key forces were in his own hands, and when things moved smoothly he was quite content to let much decision making reside at the district level. But when things went badly, when elections were lost, the structure permitted the removal of the weak cogs in the wheel while the leader continued.

He had many problems as well. Not least of these came from the consolidation of Greater New York. To be sure there were real advantages in having a unified organization that included the Bronx, Brooklyn, Queens, and Richmond as well as Manhattan. But there were also a lot more miles, and people, and leaders to be dealt with. The other boroughs had their own ongoing Democratic organizations at the time of consolidation, and these did not take kindly to incorporation—and thus disappearance—into Tammany Hall. Brooklyn boss Patrick H. McCarren, for example, fought him for six years, saying "The Tiger shall not cross the bridge." But Murphy went around him, building up his own rival Brooklyn organization; and by 1909 the Tammany Tiger had Brooklyn. Not only did political rivals trouble him here, but now the Hall was liable to blame for malfeasance on the part of any Democrats in the city. John Purroy Mitchel, long a bane to the Hall and later a Fusion mayor, gained his first fame in Murphy's early days with accusations against the several borough presidents relative to contracts for street work.

Even in Manhattan itself Murphy had to struggle to establish his dominance. Most of the local Democracy accepted his accession to power; one who did not, and who fought him for some time, was William S. Devery. Devery, who was hardly a piker, struggled to maintain his base in the Ninth District with such affairs as an outing for ten thousand women and children on nine boats and barges in 1902. This was followed by barbecues with beer for the men, as well as tremendous largesse—and some fraud. He stayed leader of the Ninth for a while, but never really managed to threaten Murphy's control of the Hall, although he was ever present in the wings as a powerful opponent.

Withal, Murphy did manage to hold onto the reins of Tammany down to his death in 1924, by means and with effects that will be seen below. Some of the few things he would boast about toward the end of his career were modest but important developments like the removal of the police force from politics and the development and introduction, through Tammany Hall, of some first-rate men for American politics. Whether he was in some way as distinctly "good" a boss as Tweed was a "bad" one is a personal judgment. But he did endure, in a democratic politics, for over twenty years.

In his muckraking history of Tammany Hall, Gustavus Myers felt that he had gone a long way toward exposing "Tammany corruption and inefficiency." It is notable that Myers would couple the expected first factor with the more debatable second one. Indeed, one might argue that Tammany's long life and frequent success challenge the notion of "inefficiency"; the inefficient rarely flourish. A good answer was provided by Murphy himself, in a statement toward the end of his career cited by his recent biographer: "When Tammany can elect its candidate so often in a city of 6,000,000, in a city of intelligence, in a city dotted all over by the church spire and the school house, it seems silly to use the time-worn campaign cry that there is nothing good but everything corrupt in Tammany." That is a point worth considering, and thus a closer look at the operation of Tammany Hall under Charles Francis Murphy is called for.

We are chiefly concerned with the Hall's ability to build long-term support among the urban ethnic masses, and we have already noted that those groups were considerably more varied and numerous in Murphy's day than they had been in Tweed's. On the whole Tammany was successful, in conjunction with the Democratic party, in attracting considerable immigrant support. This was not, however, as consistent as the Hall would have liked, as we shall see when we get to the election returns themselves. Murphy, like many urban Irish politicians, followed an ethnically sensitive politics because he had concluded, rationally, that it was necessary for victory; but it was always something that had to be done. Only consummately ethnic-oriented people, like Anton Cermak, had a basic belief in the virtue as well as necessity of ethnic recognition and carried the practice to its greatest development.

The best example of the above is seen in nominations for public office. While Tammany tended to respect the ethnicity of an assembly district in terms of its party workers, most Tammany leaders and candidates for public office continued to be either Irish or old stock. Murphy's recent biographer sees his choices of candidates as being based on their "vision and ability," but this seems to me to evade the question at best. If, indeed, Murphy's Tammany Hall wanted only highly qualified candidates for public office, it was hardly required to confine these choices to so narrow an ethnic spectrum as it did. Rather, regardless of whether or not the desire for quality was real, Murphy and his advisers were reluctant to support those whose loyalty was not as reliable as possible; and for this they tended to turn to those like themselves and to be leery of the newcomers. This is one reason, I think, that the Democrats did not fare better than they in fact did under Murphy; ethnic party identification was weaker than it might have been because recognition of each group by the party was weaker than it might have been.

On the other hand, Tammany did demonstrate continuing concern for the poor as poor, and some ethnic sensitivity, in its treatment of the urban masses. The traditional social services continued—aid to widows and other deprived individuals, food baskets, coal, entertainment, and above all jobs—lots of jobs in city, county, state, and private employment. (Murphy's biographer, Nancy Weiss, differentiates this aid from that of earlier bosses by saying it emanated from "a sincere philanthropic spirit"; in fact, it was precisely the same as earlier and later Tammany activity.)

Almost every weekend, at College Point or another pleasant location— generally on the water to facilitate transportation—Tammany district associations held clambakes and other outings. The local district leader would distribute tickets, and steamboats took the people to the site of the festivities. In addition to free food, and beer for the men, there would generally be gambling, baseball, entertainments, and so on. Often local saloonkeepers, business people, or even gamblers would foot the bill, to cement their relations with the local party organization, and then the district association could even make some money on the affair. Frequently, the day's festivities ended with a torchlight procession through the district to Tammany headquarters and a finale of fireworks. For people who worked fifty, sixty, or more hours a week, for five or ten dollars, and lived in crowded, unpleasant tenement apartments, this was no small thing.

And the Tammany functionary, be he lofty assembly district leader, election district captain, or even lower on the hierarchical ladder than that, worked hard with his constituents. As George Washington Plunkitt had noted, the professional politician put in as long a day as any of his constituents, and the key to work was service. The point is not whether this service was selfishly or unselfishly motivated, but simply that it was done; and moreover that in many cases, had Tammany not provided these services, there was no other agency to fill the role. Thus the actual material aid of jobs, gifts, and charity, plus the cultural or social service of recognizing group legitimacy and particularism, were what endeared Tammany Hall and the Democratic party to immigrant voters.

"Big Tim" Sullivan, a Tammany leader famous for his Christmas dinners for about five thousand people, was a good example. As state senator, Sullivan paid relatively little attention to legislative business and introduced very few bills. But of the legislation that he did introduce, one bill was for making Columbus Day a legal holiday, and another—the famous Sullivan Law—was to make the carrying of firearms without a license a crime. Both appealed to the voters (the latter was intended to diminish gangster influence) and are examples of practical Tammany legislation.

Another Tammany man, Tim Campbell, gained some fame for his practical approach to running for Congress. He had one speech, which dealt with one national issue, the McKinley tariff bill, which he opposed. The bill was "for protection with nothing free. Do you want everything free or do you want to pay for everything?" Campbell continued:

Having disposed of the national issue I will now devote myself to the local issue, which is the Dago Rinaldo [his opponent]. He is from Italy, I am from Ireland. Are you in favor of Italy or Ireland?

Having thus disposed of the local issue, and thanking you for your attention, I will now retire.

Campbell did not have the makings of a national statesman, but for an Irish immigrant district he expressed a sense of the world that his constituents understood. And his approach to extra-local issues suggests that the immigrant and the poor, concerned with their economic and cultural survival in a new and often hostile environment, really could not afford the luxury of worrying about tariffs, or the Philippines, or even about graft—problems that seemed to have no real relationship to their own lives.

Tammany's relationship with the immigrants was, to some extent, facilitated by the actions of its opponents. The middle-class groups, the "reformers" who were the crux of the fusion forces against Tammny, generally included very few representatives of recent immigrant groups. Moreover, these people had little sympathy for the problems of the lower class, or, at least, little understanding of what those problems really were. When these people came into power, they enforced the law, which was perhaps proper; but the law included Sunday closing and the removal of unlicensed pushcarts from the streets, to cite only two examples. Thus the cultural practices and economic survival of many immigrants were threatened. Jewish pushcart peddlers, for example—a large and economically very marginal group—learned that they could ignore the annual fifteen-dollar license fee and also be protected from other dangers if their associations pledged and delivered their votes to the local Tammany leader. It was a bargain; why not?

Another example of the reformers' obtuseness can be seen in reformer-backed Police Commissioner Theodore Bingham's famous article in the

North American Review in 1908, charging that Jews, making up about 25 percent of the city's population, contributed about 50 percent of its criminals. Not only was it a politically questionable charge to make if true, it was not true. He included in his statistics on crime things like pushcart peddlers without licenses, and violators of Sunday closing laws (an especially obnoxious law to observant Jews); and he did not mention that, in terms of felonies, Jews had committed only 16 percent of the total in the previous year.

Finally, while Tammany did not really try very hard to get representatives of new immigrant groups into elective office, its opponents went so far in the other direction as to make the Hall look good by comparison. Of the forty-six members of the Board of Education appointed by Seth Low, fully one-third were in the Social Register; and the figure was almost as high—31 percent—under Fusionist John Purroy Mitchel a dozen years later. By contrast, under the Democrats in between (that is, 1903-13) only 15 percent of the appointed members of the board were in the Social Register. And not only were newer immigrant Jews and Italians, and for that matter even the children of earlier German and Irish immigrants, not very likely to be found in that almanac of respectability, one might also argue that the people so honored were a good deal less likely to understand or sympathize with the educational aspirations of newer immigrants than were people who at least lived and worked near them. Had the Board of Education been elected rather than appointed, one can assume that its character would have been somewhat different.

One of the problems of machine politics is its cost. Person-to-person relationships and extensive social services do not come cheaply, nor did they at the turn of the century. Whether one is speaking of a bucket of coal to a voter, a bribe to a judge to let off a juvenile offender, or the various other services described by boss Plunkitt, a great deal of revenue was required. Much of this came from those who received the largesse at Tammany's disposal. Those who held public office, government jobs, or contracts were expected to repay the hand that fed them with a share of their salaries. As Murphy himself acknowledged, "When I can do it without violating the law, it is perfectly right to give out contracts to organization men. If I can, I will." Graft played a role also; the honest or even dishonest graft that people like Plunkitt received was not simply for their own personal enrichment. Indeed, one might well conclude, from reading Plunkitt or from watching Murphy, that far more of their gains, however gotten, were plowed right back into their enterprise—just as in other successful businesses. But one can also note that it was a system that made graft almost essential. And thus the Murphy years were hardly immaculate in this regard.

Murphy's biographer argues that he truly opposed dishonest graft and would have nothing to do with vice of any kind. She cites his removal of Eighth District leader Martin Engel because of involvement with gambling and prostitution, as an example of this. And it does seem true that Murphy did not want Tammany associated with vice. But Police Commissioner Bingham was probably closer to the mark, in a 1911 book, when he agreed that it was not so much that Tammany "officially recognizes these fellows [pimps] . . . but if they pay their dues regularly and perform their part willingly at election time, Tammany does not ask questions, and when a faithful henchman runs afoul of the police, Tammany will 'take care' of him." Whatever his own moral scruples, Murphy was not likely to remain leader long if he did not seek votes and support where they could be found.

Moreover, Tammany's decentralization permitted a wide variety of activities over which Murphy had no effective control. If a district leader delivered his district, he was doing his job. Murphy could not practically establish a code of proper conduct. Martin Engel, before his falling out with Murphy, was running a kosher chicken racket in his overwhelmingly Jewish district; this was something that an Irish Catholic leader would not be very likely to anticipate, or even perhaps understand. And "Big Tim" Sullivan is alleged to have philosophized over the idea of running for Congress: "Say, what is the graft over there?" He asked how long it took to get to Washington, and then continued:

Say, those guys that flag the Washington graft get famous and get to be the main squeeze at the White House if their gang is in, don't they? They are the whole cheese in national conventions. That ain't a bad lay. I will think it over. Maybe I will go down there and look the game over. It ain't a pikers game, and maybe I may take a stack and sit in.

Sullivan went to Congress. His role as a national statesman has yet to be chronicled, but when he died in 1913, more or less insane, 25,000 people attended his funeral, many of them congressmen, most of them just people. All of this is an integral part of the history of Tammany Hall in the time of Murphy.

It should be noted, while considering the problem of graft in Tammany Hall, that it all seemed somewhat less significant to many people—and not only new immigrants—than it might have been because of the nature of the times. This was a period of tremendous and rapid economic growth, with little regulation thereof by any public agency. Allegations of bribery, graft, and corruption were very general, and not only against political entities. Early in Murphy's leadership, for example, the state legislature was investigating insurance companies, which had been accused of huge bribes to both political parties. And the average small businessman was quite accustomed to paying off various people and agencies almost all the time. Thus it might well have appeared to many people that the reformers were making a big deal out of accusing Tammany of doing something that was endemic at the time, a "natural" human activity.

Murphy did a somewhat better job than most Tammany leaders in achieving the elusive aim of broad control—spanning city, county, and state government. This was so small accomplishment, and in return it gave Tammany greater control over the political life of the city than it had previously enjoyed. The control of the Brooklyn Democratic organization was an important first step in this process, because it made possible the control of the state Democratic convention (most of Murphy's era was still in the period before the primary, which gave the party organization greater control). He made deals with potential Democratic rivals like William Randolph Hearst and seems to have been able to find some bases for occasional deals with Republican leaders as well.

This broad base of control was not easy to maintain. First of all, the Democrats had to win enough elections to make it possible. And then there was the question of getting enough of these elected Democrats to defer to his leadership, a problem that was never completely solved. The most famous such case was that of William Sulzer, whose election to the governorship had Murphy's support in 1912, and whose 1913 impeachment and removal from office had Murphy's even more enthusiastic support. The battle against Sulzer left a bad taste in many Democratic mouths and resulted in some pressure for Murphy's removal; but it came to nothing.

A related question is that of Tammany's response to the so-called reform impetus of the Progressive Era. J. Joseph Huthmacher and Nancy Joan Weiss argue that Tammany under Murphy underwent a major change: it became more ideological, less parochial, more concerned with local, state, and national issues, and in fact moved to the left. Weiss sees what she calls a "market basket liberalism" in Murphy's Tammany Hall, and a sense of real social and political responsibility in Murphy's effort to improve the quality of candidates presented to the public.

I have already argued that *reform* is not a very useful word, and while not denying that Murphy took politics seriously and professionally and tried to make it as good and honest as he could, nonetheless I think that a less normative perspective is more useful. He tried to find candidates who were both "respectable" and competent, because he took his job seriously. Thus, one of his first acts as boss was to nominate the eminently respectable George B. McClellan (son of the Civil War general) for mayor. And he did indeed actively encourage the political careers of young men like Alfred E. Smith and Robert F. Wagner. This made sense; why run a candidate likely to be incompetent or dishonest if an honest and competent one can be found who will also be loyal to the organization? More than one aim could often be accomplished at the same time. Murphy urged Wagner to run for the state senate in 1908, and in Wagner's victory he broke the hold on the Sixteenth Senate District of "Silent Maurice" Featherstone, a Tammany leader whose loyalty he questioned. This benefited Murphy, Wagner, and, one might argue, the public—all at the same time. And in 1911, when Franklin Delano Roosevelt and others were leading a revolt in the legislature against him, Murphy chose Smith and Wagner as Tammany's candidates to head the House and Senate, respectively. He won, they won, Tammany won, and the legislature was put under what was generally conceded to be first-rate leadership.

One of Murphy's cleverest moves came also in the 1903 local elections, when he successfully ran McClellan for mayor. On the Fusion ticket with Seth Low when Fusion swept the city in 1901 had been Edward M. Grout for controller and Charles V. Fornes for president of the Board of Aldermen. Murphy was able to get both men to see the advantages of Democratic backing and thus to accept the Tammany endorsement and appear as the Democratic candidates for reelection. Thus he continued two "reformers" in office, undercut his opposition, and helped assure a Democratic victory. Many in the party had opposed this failure to nominate party regulars, but Tammany's sweep of the election was Murphy's strongest defense.

Certainly Murphy did not oppose help for workers or the poor generally. Tammany never had. (Weiss is wrong in thinking that this was something new.) If anything, state support for the working class would result in private employers or the state itself financing some of the services which Tammany had traditionally supplied out of its own coffers; that was not harmful. And Murphy was even willing to learn from his subordinates. When Wagner introduced the famous "Five-cent Fare" bill (for the subway) in 1907, it was not a Tammany measure. But it was extremely popular with the masses, and Murphy was willing to go along—even actively supporting it. Murphy could be adamant in insisting on party regularity from his people; it was made clear to both Smith and Wagner that they were to support the impeachment of Sulzer, for example. But many things, like women's suffrage, direct election of senators, regulation of business, and so on, he either lent his support to or simply ignored. If it did not affect Tammany's position or its narrowly construed interests, it was fine.

Thus the relationship between Tammany and "reform" is best understood if one does away with the term *reform* and with a normative approach. It was a political movement primarily geared to the lower- and working-class urban masses, and was not very likely to oppose their social, economic, or cultural desires. It did not do so. As Murphy modernized and rendered more efficient Tammany's operation, he came to realize that a broad area of power required more than a great list of "Big Tim" Sullivans. Competent, hard-working, even reasonably independent young men were quite acceptable, so long as they remembered those areas in which the organization brooked no exceptions.

Because the urban masses of New York City had interests and needs very different from those of the upper middle class, their expectations from politics were very different. Middle-class progressive reformers generally had little interest in labor unions, Irish independence, or Sunday beer, and they tended to oppose free immigration and cultural pluralism. The ethnic masses of New York, in return, had very little concern with imperialism, trust-busting (except in the most general, antibusiness way), or the conservation of natural resources, and they were violently opposed to Protestant and old-stock-derived cultural reform. So the point really is not whether or not the working class also participated in progressive reform. And the fact that the Italians perhaps responded positively to arguments for workmen's compensation does not make them "progressives." Different groups had different needs, operated in different spheres and via different means. And the primary concerns of what is called the Progressive Era, if they had any unity at all, had a unity to which the urban masses had no sense of relationship.

Let us now look more directly at Tammany's successes and failures in the age of Murphy, focussing on the scene of the action—elections. Table 3.1 presents data on ethnicity, some socioeconomic indicators, and voting, for the thirty-five assembly districts of Manhattan and the Bronx for selected elections between 1897 and 1913. The inclusion of only Manhattan and the Bronx is dictated both by methodological problems and by convenience; since our central concern here is the relationship between ethnicity and support for Tammany, the data are more than sufficient. Since district lines were greatly revised after 1913, Table 3.2 provides similar data for Manhattan districts in 1920 and for the 1918 elections, permitting a more careful look at two of Murphy's most famous protégés, Alfred E. Smith and Robert F. Wagner.

It should be remarked at the outset that the tables do not cover all elections, but rather a selection thereof. Those included were chosen for their usefulness in understanding Tammany's development at this time, showing major defeats, victories, and contests that were significant in other ways. In 1897, for example, the first mayoralty of Greater New York was held, and this was the first time the mayoralty was to be a four-year term. (This was the result of action by the state legislature, which erroneously anticipated an anti-Tammany victory; when Tammany won anyway, the legislature changed the mayor's term back to two years,

TABLE 3.1
Sociocultural and Voting (Percentage Democratic) Data for New York Assembly Districts during the Time of Murphy

Assembly District	Percentage, foreign stock	Percentage of those age 6-20 in school	Families per dwelling	Percentage homes in district rented	Mayor, 1897	Mayor, 1901	Controller, 1901	District attorney, 1901	Mayor, 1903	President, Board of Aldermen, 1903	Mayor, 1909	Controller, 1909	President, Board of Aldermen, 1909	Governor, 1910	Supreme court, 1910	Mayor, 1913	Controller, 1913	President, Board of Aldermen, 1913
1	90	57	5.50	65	65	63	61	61	77	77	61	61	62	73	68	60	64	63
2	96	57	9.25	94	72	70	70	69	77	76	65	66	66	78	74	62	63	63
3	93	55	7.77	93	53	56	54	53	70	70	71	71	72	83	82	69	71	70
4	98	61	12.01	95	57	58	48	56	60	61	55	57	58	75	72	57	59	56
5	76	57	5.29	87	38	40	37	37	46	47	57	58	58	74	67	65	70	69
6	99	57	12.03	96	60	66	65	66	76	76	36	40	40	47	44	25	70	25
7	73	56	4.56	94	53	54	53	52	65	65	52	53	53	69	64	55	60	59
8	99	57	10.98	97	45	51	49	51	64	65	49	54	52	65	62	45	46	47
9	72	55	6.29	94	51	43	42	42	59	60	49	52	51	70	62	60	66	66
10	97	53	11.20	96	51	49	48	49	60	61	42	43	43	59	53	34	37	36
11	77	60	7.10	93	56	52	52	51	66	66	52	53	53	70	62	58	65	64
12	88	57	8.44	97	60	58	58	59	63	64	64	64	64	77	73	68	72	72
13	63	61	8.09	96	60	55	54	56	70	69	54	54	55	66	58	61	67	66
14	85	56	6.64	96	52	52	51	51	68	69	51	51	52	68	63	56	61	61
15	63	56	3.53	94	53	55	54	53	66	66	31	34	33	60	42	34	33	30
16	86	57	5.57	96	58	59	58	58	62	61	52	52	52	70	63	53	59	57
17	66	61	5.92	94	58	54	53	52	65	66	32	34	33	57	37	31	33	30
18	89	61	7.27	92	60	65	64	62	75	75	49	51	51	67	59	48	54	52
19	64	58	9.37	85	34	34	32	33	43	43	33	34	34	57	46	34	36	33
20	89	62	8.04	92	60	62	53	52	65	64	55	55	55	75	66	49	56	54
21	58	60	5.66	90	31	33	31	30	42	42	32	33	32	47	40	31	36	33
22	86	61	7.54	90	60	61	59	59	69	69	43	44	44	66	55	43	51	49
23	64	63	7.79	89	41	40	38	37	48	48	34	34	34	54	44	31	35	34
24	91	64	10.63	89	57	58	56	56	68	68	49	49	51	71	64	55	61	61
25	65	51	2.96	83	32	32	29	30	40	39	35	37	36	52	41	35	37	33
26	93	62	9.65	94	53	48	46	48	60	61	33	33	34	51	43	34	37	35
27	63	50	2.21	69	32	32	31	32	39	38	32	34	33	59	42	37	37	35
28	93	61	8.90	92	57	59	57	57	69	69	47	48	48	66	60	46	49	49
29	69	56	2.81	71	30	31	29	30	38	36	33	35	35	61	44	33	34	31
30	78	61	6.41	94	52	54	52	51	66	66	41	41	42	61	53	44	49	49
31	79	56	5.25	88	31	34	32	33	42	43	28	28	27	49	40	24	22	25
32	76	66	2.87	96	52	57	56	56	66	67	40	42	42	61	52	34	39	40
33	81	61	5.40	92	49	52	51	51	64	63	40	42	43	62	53	35	45	45
34	79	64	3.48	90	45	51	49	49	63	64	41	44	44	60	51	37	43	44
35	75	66	2.36	75	46	46	46	44	57	57	41	43	43	59	51	38	43	44
New York City	79	81	3.34	85	48	47	46	47	56	56	43	44	44	61	—	40	46	44
Manhattan	82	58	6.54	92	49	48	47	47	58	59	43	45	44	63	54	44	47	46
Bronx	78	64	3.27	77	*	*	*	*	*	*	*	*	*	*	*	35	41	42

Source: Data on foreign stock (immigrants and children of immigrants), percentage attending school, and families per dwelling from the Thirteenth Census, 1910. Data on percentage of homes rented from the Twelfth Census, 1900. The vote is given as the percentage Democratic of the two-party vote, the second party being Republican, with the following exceptions: for 1897, vote given is percentage Democratic of four-party vote; for 1901 the second party is Fusion rather than Republican; for 1903 the second party is Fusion rather than Republican; for 1909, mayor, the vote given is percentage Democratic of the three-party vote; for the other two offices it is percentage Democratic of the two-party vote, with Fusion being the other party; and for 1913, the second party is Fusion rather than Republican. Voting data from the *New York Times.* Manhattan consisted of Assembly Districts One through Twenty-nine and part of Thirty; the Bronx consisted of the rest of Thirty and Thirty-one through Thirty-five. The asterisk (*) indicates that these votes were reported as part of combined Manhattan and Bronx; their vote was reported separately only after 1910.

which again backfired when Seth Low defeated Tammany in 1901!) As at other times in New York's history, it was a multipartisan affair, which redounded to the advantage of Croker's man, Robert A. Van Wyck. Seth Low was the hope of fusion (called Citizen's Union that year), but Republican boss Platt would not accept him, and so there was a Republican

TABLE 3.2
Sociocultural and Voting (Percentage Democratic) Data for Manhattan, 1918

Assembly District	Percentage foreign stock	Percentage of those age 16–17 in school	Families per dwelling	Governor, 1918	Supreme court, 1918
1	87	24	9.00	85	84
2	97	22	9.73	78	74
3	72	19	5.29	80	79
4	97	28	9.30	81	82
5	68	18	7.92	81	80
6	96	27	10.39	58	57
7	60	46	5.31	55	48
8	96	30	9.11	72	64
9	64	44	6.40	55	47
10	60	34	3.45	53	49
11	65	46	9.90	59	52
12	82	23	5.94	82	80
13	61	34	8.85	60	56
14	87	19	7.07	80	78
15	68	53	3.30	53	48
16	84	22	7.30	81	82
17	94	30	8.56	63	49
18	91	21	8.78	75	62
19	48	34	4.91	52	49
20	83	28	5.81	72	71
21	34	38	8.52	46	43
22	68	35	11.43	63	58
23	65	38	13.22	56	51
New York City	76	27	3.49	69	———
Manhattan	77	28	6.95	72	62

Source: Data on foreign stock (immigrants and children of immigrants), percentage in school, and families per dwelling from the Fourteenth Census, 1920. Vote for governor is Democratic percentage of the two-party vote. Vote for supreme court, where there were three vacancies to be filled and three nominees per party, is derived by adding the vote for Wagner and that for the most successful Republican candidate, then taking Wagner's percentage of that total. Voting data taken from the *New York Times*.

candidate as well. Additionally, Henry George was running again, under the label of the Jeffersonian Democrats. George died in the midst of the campaign, to be replaced by his son, Henry, Jr. Even without the four-way split Van Wyck would probably have won, since he carried 48 percent of the total city vote and had a comfortable plurality. Thus Tammany had control of the newly unified city. Van Wyck did well among the most heavily foreign districts.

Having learned their lesson, at least for a while, the anti-Tammany forces really united in 1901, again behind Seth Low; the addition of William Travers Jerome to the Fusion ticket, for district attorney, was another popular move. In addition to the traditional complaints of Tammany corruption, the Fusion forces also raised the issue of social problems in the immigrant East Side, and such related ills as the forced prostitution of young girls. The combination of scandal and old animosities brought a tremendous cross section of the middle class—from Protestant ministers to Mark Twain—out against Tammany, and this time it was successful. The whole Fusion ticket swept to victory, with very similar levels of support across the board. The Democrats increased their vote from 1897 only in a few districts, particularly the most heavily Jewish and the poorest; but it was a small amount of erosion of support almost everywhere that gave Low his 52 to 48 percent victory over Edward M. Shepard. This campaign marked the end of Croker's career as the boss of Tammany Hall.

The year 1903, on the other hand, was the inaugural of Charles F. Murphy, and it was a remarkable beginning. Murphy's choice of George B. McClellan to run against Low was a shrewd one. McClellan, in addition to being the son of the famous general, had served in Congress, had a reputation as a respectable gentleman, and was at the same time a Tammany loyalist. Shrewder yet was Murphy's coup in getting Low's controller and president of the Board of Aldermen, Edward M. Grout and Charles B. Fornes, to accept the Democratic nomination. Grout and Fornes expected also to be renominated by Fusion, but were not; but their choice was in the end the proper one.

Low had run a reasonably good administration and had strong support from clergymen and other middle-class interests. But his legally proper enforcement of the blue laws and an increase in the liquor excise tax had alienated many ethnics; and some businessmen found him inflexible and harder to work with than Tammany. As Plunkitt would have it, the reformers did not work hard enough at politics.

Thus Tammany swept all the local offices in 1903, and by very comfortable margins for the time. One can see in Table 3.1 that its vote reached or exceeded 70 percent in some of the most foreign districts (District One, for example, was about 55 percent Italian; District Two was 58 percent Jewish and 24 percent Italian; and District Six was almost 90 percent Jewish.)

In 1905, for which we do not have data on the table, Murphy renominated McClellan, who won again. But that campaign was interesting for the entry of William Randolph Hearst. Hearst, the powerful newspaper publisher, had previously served as a Democratic congressman but now wanted to operate on a wider stage. Failing to receive the Democratic nomination for mayor, he formed the Municipal Ownership League, which was less interested in municipal ownership than it was in unseating Tammany Hall. McClellan and Murphy were saved by the fact that the Republicans did not join with Hearst, and thus it was a three-way race. McClellan carried 39 percent of the vote, Hearst 38 percent, and the Republican 23 percent; it is not unlikely that Tammany stole the election through fraud. Murphy and Hearst never really had a good word to say about one another, but they must have made some kind of deal, because in 1906 Murphy supported Hearst's nomination for governor (he lost to Republican Charles Evans Hughes).

Even McClellan grew more independent in his second term, a good example of the fact that, while the machine can put people in office, it cannot necessarily control them after they get there.

The pressure on Tammany continued, and in fact increased with the increasing number of years that the Hall had controlled city affairs. Thus the 1909 elections threatened to return the forces of fusion to power. Once again, Murphy demonstrated why he was the leader of the New York Democracy. He chose as his candidate for mayor William J. Gaynor, a judge from Brooklyn with a reputation for independence and integrity. It was a controversial choice, since there was a fairly large chance that Gaynor would not be very controllable in office; but winning elections was always the first priority, and Murphy knew this. The Fusion candidate in 1909 was one Otto Bannard, and William Randolph Hearst again ran for the office, this time under the banner of Civic Alliance.

Gaynor ran into some trouble with traditional sources of Democratic support because he was a lapsed Catholic. He had been born into an immigrant Irish Catholic family and had even, at age 16, entered a lay teaching order for a few years. But he fell away from the church, and he eventually divorced his first wife and remarried. He tried to downplay his background, but because he was unusually outspoken and quite caustic, a certain anti-ecclesiasticism often came through. It was charged by a Bronx priest that a local archbishop had tried to halt Gaynor's nomination, but Murphy vehemently denied this. The same priest, the Reverend William J. Dougherty, also preached at preelection Sunday mass that his parishioners should use their own judgment; personally, he would vote the Democratic ticket, but "cut off the head of that ticket." How many other New York clergymen preached similarly one cannot tell. Three of the four most heavily Irish districts (Eleven, Thirteen, and Fourteen) voted about fifteen percentage points less Democratic in 1909 than they had in 1903, and all four were less Democratic than they would be in 1913. On the other hand, the spread in these districts in 1909 between voting for mayor and for the other offices was very slight, and thus we do not have a clear answer—unless the nomination hurt the entire slate.

Gaynor did carry the city, with 43 percent to 28 percent each for Bannard and Hearst. Gaynor's strength was in traditionally strong Democratic areas, among the foreign and the poor. Hearst's strength varied considerably from borough to borough and district to district, and is worth looking at more closely. He won in two Manhattan districts (Six and Twenty-six), both overwhelmingly immigrant and overwhelmingly Jewish, as well as poor. And he ran a strong second in four other Jewish districts (Two, Four, Eight, and Ten) and one with a relatively high German element (Twenty-two). But he also did well in several Bronx districts that were not particularly immigrant, Jewish, or poor. What particular attraction Hearst had with immigrant Jews at this time probably came from his paper's extensive coverage of and strong opposition to czarist pogroms, as well as his "radical" stance on some urban issues.

While Gaynor won the mayoralty in 1909, Tammany did not really do well, as Fusion swept the remainder of the races, particularly the borough presidencies and the important posts of controller and president of the Board of Aldermen. John Purroy Mitchel won the latter office and continued a career that would frustrate Murphy frequently. Nonetheless Tammany bounced back the very next year as Murphy chalked up one of his most impressive victories, the Democrats taking control of the executive and legislative branches of the state government for the first time in nineteen years.

The year 1910 was Democratic nationally, and the New York Democrats profited therefrom. But it took more than just that to win both the state House and Senate as well as the governorship and all county offices as well. An example of this is the case of Edward B. Whitney, a state supreme court justice, who was not renominated by Murphy. The Republicans put him on their ticket, and two other parties (including Hearst's, this year called the Independence League) also nominated him. Whitney got a lot of favorable publicity, and he did run better than Henry L. Stimson, the Republican candidate for governor against John A. Dix; but Whitney nonetheless lost, learning a lesson, one supposes, in the power of party. Hearst, running for lieutenant governor, did very poorly, getting less than 10 percent in every Manhattan district.

Murphy and Tammany Hall would continue to hold the governorship of New York for eight of the fourteen years that Murphy still had to live. But they would not always be easy years, as 1912 proved. In that year, both the Progressive and Republican parties entered the gubernatorial race, and Murphy, in what he later characterized as "the greatest mistake of my life," nominated William M. Sulzer, a nine-term congressman and Tammany loyalist, if something of an independent.

Sulzer and Murphy soon had a falling-out over patronage and appointments as well as certain Progressive Era issues that Sulzer pushed and Murphy opposed (a state investigation of corruption and a direct primary law, for example). Murphy decided to have Sulzer impeached, putting all his force on state Democrats to see that it was done. In what started out purely as a power play, the investigation did ultimately turn up some evidence of real impeachable malfeasance—relative to campaign financing—and the governor was impeached and removed from office in 1913.

The whole affair left bitterness in the party and intensified Tammany's general reputation for ruthlessness and corruption. And in the midst of it, Murphy suffered a defeat in the city which was a real setback.

Gaynor had been a good mayor. He had started out as a rather traditional nineteenth-century reformer, believing in good people and minimal government and taxes. But as time went by he grew increasingly realistic and assertive. Moreover, despite a certain insensitivity and outspokenness, he also developed a good working relationship with immigrant groups. He defended Jewish pushcart peddlers, for example; cooperated with the *kehillah,* or communal organization, which had been organized in reaction to Bingham's charges of Jewish criminality; and refused to grant a license to a missionary who wanted to convert the Jews. He appointed Jews and Germans to office and defended both Saturday and recreational sabbaths.

On the other hand, in the midst of a police scandal emanating from the 1912 murder of a minor underworld figure and police inaction thereupon, he tried to excuse the force by noting that, "We have in this city the largest foreign population of any city, and a large number of them are degenerates and criminals." Some of the same Jewish organizations and leaders who had lauded him for his stand against the missionaries reacted strongly against him now.

Gaynor was a difficult man and, despite a good deal of popular support and respect, many were not distraught when Murphy, fearing his independence, decided not to nominate him for reelection in 1913. Fusion, shortly thereafter, nominated John Purroy Mitchel; and Gaynor, who was not well, finally decided to run on an independent ticket but died before his campaign really got under way.

The Sulzer impeachment, getting headlines during the course of the 1913 mayoral campaign, did not help Tammany. Nor, for that matter, did the passage of time. And Fusion triumphed all across the board. Table 3.1 suggests that the largest Democratic fall-off came in Jewish districts (e.g., Four, Six, Eight, Twenty-six), but there was a general Democratic decline as well; Mitchell won 56 percent of the vote in Manhattan and a whopping 60 percent in New York City as a whole.

The Democrats did bounce back in 1917, through a combination of luck and compromising strategy. Judge John F. Hylan was Hearst's man for the office, and Murphy decided to compromise and support him, despite the fact that Al Smith, who was then sheriff, also wanted to run (Murphy persuaded him to run for president of the Board of Aldermen instead, which certainly strengthened the ticket). Additionally, Mitchel found that reformers were not necessarily popular, losing in the primary to William Bennett; he then decided to run as an independent, thus splitting the anti-Tammany vote into two parts. Moreover, he ran a weird, and perhaps nativistic campaign, focussing on international issues and accusing Hylan and Morris Hillquit (the Socialist candidate) of being pro-German. Hylan won, and was reelected in 1921, giving the Democrats eight straight years of local control.

Finally, the results for 1918 are included in Table 3.2 because of several interesting factors. We can see here the political success of two of Murphy's most famous products, Alfred E. Smith and Robert F. Wagner—who are often cited as personifications of the idea that machine politics and good government are not mutually contradictory. Moreover, their victories in a generally Republican year should illustrate the real hard-core Democratic support. And finally, this was the first statewide election in which women voted—although, as it turned out, this had no appreciable effect on the parties or the issues.

It is perhaps hard to believe that Smith barely won the governorship in the state returns, since he carried New York City with 69 percent and Manhattan with 72 percent. Wagner, running for one of the three places on the supreme court, was ten points behind Smith, but still decisively victorious. Their strengths were very similar, and they had overwhelming support from traditional Democratic voters and tended even to win in districts which were more native and middle-class (e.g., Thirteen, Fifteen, and Twenty-two).

It is interesting to note that the districts where Wagner ran noticeably behind Smith (e.g., Eight, Seventeen, and Eighteen) were Jewish districts, where the Socialist supreme court candidate, Morris Hillquit, was very popular. Smith's popularity was such, however, that the Socialists did less well against him.

In order to analyze more systematically the relationships between background variables like ethnicity and the results of these elections, and between the various elections themselves, it is necessary to prepare correlation matrices as we did in studying Tweed. Table 3.3 presents such a matrix for our data on the thirty-five assembly districts of Manhattan and the Bronx for 1897-1913; Table 3.4 does the same for the twenty-three assembly districts of Manhattan for 1918.

First, in looking at the four background variables, we can say that the information available is not always the information one would most like to have. The percentage attending school turns out not to be a useful indicator

TABLE 3.3
Pearson's r Correlations for Variables in Table 3.1

	Percentage foreign stock	Percentage of those age 6-20 in school	Families per dwelling	Percentage homes in district rented	Mayor, 1897	Mayor, 1901	Mayor, 1903	President, Board of Aldermen, 1903	Mayor, 1909	President, Board of Aldermen, 1909	Governor, 1910	Supreme court, 1910	Mayor, 1913
Percentage foreign stock	----	.044	.662	.462	.575	.646	.596	.608	.507	.536	.398	.533	.313
Percentage of those 6-20 in school	.044	----	.082	.166	.278	.326	.308	.316	−.040	−.023	−.031	−.024	−.098
Families per dwelling	.661	.082	----	.535	.446	.430	.394	.408	.307	.318	.181	.347	.203
Percentage of homes rented	.462	.166	.535	----	.664	.659	.692	.717	.417	.422	.270	.449	.417
Mayor, 1897	.575	.278	.446	.664	----	.954	.929	.923	.609	.625	.556	.638	.615
Mayor, 1901	.647	.326	.430	.659	.954	----	.951	.944	.581	.607	.522	.608	.453
Mayor, 1903	.596	.308	.394	.692	.929	.951	----	.997	.551	.583	.468	.570	.421
President, Board of Aldermen, 1903	.608	.316	.408	.717	.923	.944	.997	----	.547	.579	.459	.573	.418
Mayor, 1909	.507	−.034	.307	.417	.609	.581	.551	.547	----	.993	.921	.953	.935
President, Board of Aldermen, 1909	.536	−.023	.318	.422	.625	.607	.583	.579	.995	----	.917	.952	.924
Governor, 1910	.398	−.031	.181	.270	.556	.522	.468	.459	.921	.917	----	.939	.914
Supreme court, 1910	.533	.024	.347	.449	.638	.608	.570	.573	.953	.952	.939	----	.896
Mayor, 1913	.313	−.098	.203	.324	.507	.423	.421	.418	.935	.924	.914	.896	----

Note: Pearson product-moment coefficient (r) calculated for the thirty-five assembly districts of Manhattan and the Bronx, for each of fourteen variables against each other variable. To make the table more legible, four of the variables in Table 3.1 were not included, since their correlations with the other variables were virtually identical with the race(s) for that year which were retained. Data is otherwise identical to that in Table 3.1.

TABLE 3.4
Pearson's r Correlations for Variables in Table 3.2

	Percentage foreign stock	Percentage of those age 16-17 in school	Families per dwelling	Governor, 1918	Supreme court, 1918
Percentage foreign stock	----	−.550	.259	.687	.588
Percentage of those 16-17 in school	−.550	----	−.131	−.813	−.799
Families per dwelling	.259	−.131	----	.094	.056
Governor, 1918	.687	−.813	.094	----	.966
Supreme court, 1918	.588	−.799	.056	.966	----

Note: Pearson product-moment coefficient (r) calculated for the twenty-three assembly districts of Manhattan, for each of the five variables against each other variable. Data identical to that in Table 3.2.

of socioeconomic status; at least it has no significant correlation with any other variable. Families per dwelling does have significant correlation with the other two background variables, but not with Democratic voting in any of the studied elections. Apparently, these three variables all have positive relationships to low economic status; but poverty covered such a broad cultural spectrum in the early twentieth century—as we have also seen in Tweed's day—that the fact that voting was a largely cultural response means that a measure solely associated with poverty is not a very good predictor.

The percentage of the population that was first or second generation, and the percentage of homes that were rented, while they relate to one another in a positive but just less than significant degree, do have significant correlations with Democratic voting. Reading down the first column or across the first row, we can see that Tammany did indeed profit from its activities among the immigrants.

Looking more precisely, one can pinpoint inconsistencies, as in the 1909 mayoralty, where the strength of the relationship drops somewhat. This is probably explained by Hearst's strong campaign in that year, eating into the traditionally Democratic Jewish immigrant vote. And 1910 is a problem: while Democrat Dix carried the city for governor with an impressive 61 percent, the relationship between his vote and foreign stock—or percentage homes rented—is quite low. We can suggest two possible explanations for this: Dix did so well in the election, even among traditionally non-Democratic voters, that the variation from district to district upon which the calculations are based did not follow its usual pattern. Moreover, the governorship, being a statewide rather than local race, has a somewhat different constituency; people vote at that level who do not vote for local candidates, and vice versa; and party workers at the lowest level are less concerned about a statewide race than a local one. As witness to this one can look at the supreme court race of the same year, which was for a district embracing only Manhattan and the Bronx; here the correlation with foreign stock was much stronger; and, all down the line, its correlations with Democratic voting in other elections were also stronger than those of the voting for governor.

The second obvious area of inconsistency is the election of 1913, where the correlations with foreign stock and with those renting homes are notably lower and are not significant. This cannot be explained by population movement over time, since our demographic data come from the 1910 census. Rather it seems to be related to Tammany's losses of the whole election. Fusion in 1913 was broader than ever, including not only the Republicans and traditionally anti-Tammany Democrats, but also the National Progressive party, and—for mayor and sheriff—Hearst as well.

Correlation coefficients need not change much from a successful to an unsuccessful campaign, if the sources of Tammany support remain constant; but in 1913 this was not the case. There was a real falloff of ethnic support. On the other hand, voting Democratic for mayor in 1913 does have strong associations with Democratic voting in the various elections closest in time to it, which suggests that this falloff was by no means catastrophic, as was shown by Tammany's return to power the next time around.

Indeed, as with Tweed, one can see here strong indications of the strength of party, and of the partisan basis for Tammany success as the representative of the Democratic party. All of the mayoral elections, for example, correlate significantly with one another; the strength of these associations does diminish with time, but even between 1897 and 1913 it is a significant .507. The same holds for the other offices studied, although for those the passage of time had a somewhat greater effect.

Turning to the election of 1918, and Table 3.4, we can see that families per dwelling was again not very useful as a variable. But the more precise measure of those still in school among all those aged from 16 to 17 was more useful than the measure in the previous table which included those aged from 6 to 20. The strong negative correlations between this measure and voting for Smith or Wagner, or between it and percentage of foreign stock, suggest that here we do have a viable measure of higher socioeconomic status. Obviously Tammany's choice of Smith and Wagner not only contributed two of the period's leading politicians but also was wise in terms of attracting very great support from the poor and the immigrant. The relationship between foreign stock and voting for Smith is higher than any other such relationship for the whole period 1897-1918 (and we shall see later that this immigrant response to Smith was no less in other cities and in national elections).

In sum, Tammany was on the whole not only able to attract the allegiance of the mass of lower-class and immigrant New Yorkers, but was able to hold that allegiance with some constancy over a long period of time. Even in 1913, when it lost, Tammany carried many immigrant districts by large majorities. The fact that Tammany represented the Democratic party was crucial; but it is also true that for many New Yorkers Tammany defined, or was, the Democratic party. And if being Democratic helped Tammany, having Tammany also helped the Democratic party.

There were important differences between William Marcy Tweed and Charles Francis Murphy, and the Tammany Halls which each man led. In the final analysis, however, Murphy was a real professional politician, whose interests were in the obtaining and retention of political power (and also, some would insist, in the productive utilization of that power), whereas Tweed was an opportunist whose arena just happened to be politics. Doing what he felt he had to do to keep his organization in power, Murphy seems to have been able to please a large enough proportion of the voters—compared with his various opponents—to have won more elections than he lost over more than twenty years.

Motivation is difficult if not impossible to determine, and I do not know precisely what Murphy's motives were; nor, in understanding the development of modern urban politics, do I think it terribly important to find out. Why Murphy decided to work toward the alleviation of some of the most resented aspects of the lives of New York's immigrant poor, and why he determined that bright, ambitious, and reasonably independent candidates were often worth supporting, are moot points. But he did these things, and they not only perpetuated his machine, but also affected the nature of the government that was provided the citizens of New York in his day. It was not bad government, compared with what was available in other places at the same time, but it was also not nearly as good as it might have been—in terms of efficiency, economy, or solutions to profound social and economic problems.

But Murphy's Tammany Hall served the needs of more people better—as they saw it—than any alternatives offered them in New York City in the first quarter of the twentieth century. There is a reason, after all, why Tweed's machine, and Seth Low's also, lasted only a few years, whereas Murphy's lasted a generation.

4

BIG BILL THOMPSON AND TONY CERMAK: THE RIVAL BOSSES

As the conditions which led to boss-run political organizations were not confined to New York, neither was the institution itself. Indeed, the urban political machine has been found in cities of all sizes and in all regions, so long as there has been a mass base upon which it could be built. Since new immigrants formed the most distinctive of these mass bases, it is natural that boss-led machines followed the path of immigrants as they spread from Ellis Island and other points of entry across the nation.

Other cities rivalled New York in number and variety of ethnic groups, and it is therefore well to leave the Atlantic coast to view the development of the machine in other parts. In many ways, Chicago is an ideal example, both for its similarities and differences as compared with New York. It was, like the larger city, a metropolis of great size in the twentieth century; it also had a huge immigrant population, and many of the same physical, governmental, and social problems. But Chicago was younger, more industrial, a true two-party city, and had a greater variety of relatively large ethnic groups than New York had. And for the period after the First World War it provides perhaps the ideal laboratory for the study of the urban political machine.

Chicago started as a sleepy little village in the 1830s, when New York was already a major metropolis; but the Second City grew rapidly at mid-century and, by the time of Tweed, had about 300,000 people—well over half of them of foreign stock and, as in New York, mainly Irish and German. But even at this early date one can see demographic differences in Chicago: it was also a center of Scandinavian population, something New York never was.

Chicago benefited, in the long run, from its great fire of 1871, which left a third of its people homeless and destroyed a large part of the central city. Its aftermath was the removal of much antiquated building, and the chance to rebuild a central city with the knowledge of the 1870s. While this did not necessarily make the Chicago of the twentieth century more beautiful, safer, or cleaner than New York, it did obviate some of the problems that other cities confronted in a time of rapid growth. And Chicago was growing rapidly: in 1890 its population exceeded a million; another million was added in the next twenty years; and another million by twenty years after that.

From its inception Chicago had been a transportation center, and it became the focal point of a national railroad network. This, plus its position at the foot of the Great Lakes, and its link with the Mississippi River by the great drainage and navigation canal completed in 1900, explain the city's emergence as the second-greatest American city in terms of trade, as well as its leading role in the marketing of grain and livestock. It did not emulate New York as a center of international trade and finance, but far exceeded it as a center of industry. Because of its central position and its key location at the junction of rail and water commerce, Chicago by the end of the nineteenth century was not only the nation's chief slaughterhouse but also the site of steel mills and myriad other manufacturing processes. Thus it was a city with a considerable industrial proletariat, and its industrial structure helps explain its chief demographic difference from New York—a very large number of eastern European immigrants, who manned its great factories.

The heyday of Chicago's ethnic politics was in the 1920s, by which time most of its ethnic groups were present in large numbers and had been in the country long enough to have become citizens and thus be able to vote. Before the First World War, ethnic voters were largely German, Swedish, and Irish; in the years 1900-14 most of the immigrants were Jews, Czechs, Poles, and Italians. Thus ethnic politics before the war was rather different from ethnic politics afterwards. Table 4.1 gives a picture of the nature of Chicago's population as of the census of 1930 and suggests the variety of groups that the successful boss would have to deal with. Among other things, this is the first time that blacks made up a considerable part of a northern city's population, and their role in its politics in the 1920s was an important one.

Moreover, Chicago's working class was dispersed in the kind of residential pattern commonly associated with the modern metropolis—a series of ethnic ghettos, as Figure 4.1 shows. Here, then, was the basis for an ethnically specific and decentralized political organization such as was never available to Tweed or, completely, to Murphy.

In this chapter we shall look at two more or less contemporaneous bosses, each operating in the same milieu but in quite different ways and through different political parties, and we shall examine their direct confrontation, wherein the voters made clear which of the bosses' approaches was more acceptable. I am also able here, due to the kind of data available, to be more methodologically precise in pinpointing the vote of individual groups and measuring the kinds of relationships which emerged in the voting of the urban masses during this period.

TABLE 4.1
Characteristics of Chicago Population, 1930

Group	Foreign born	Second generation [1]	Group percentage of city population
Czechs	48,814	73,725	3.6
Danes	12,502	16,193	0.8
Germans	111,366	266,609	11.2
Hungarians	15,337	15,090	0.9
Italians	73,960	107,901	5.4
Lithuanians	31,430	32,488	1.9
Norwegians	21,740	30,968	1.6
Poles	149,622	251,694	11.9
Russians	78,462	91,274	5.0
Swedes	65,735	75,178	4.2
Yugoslavs	16,183	16,108	1.0
Jews[2]	325,000	——————	9.6
Old stock[3]	943,301	——————	27.9
Blacks[4]	233,903	——————	6.9
White ethnics[5]	842,057	1,332,373	64.3

Source: *Fifteenth Census of the U.S.,* 1930, and *Census of Religious Bodies,* 1926.
1. Includes native born of foreign or mixed parentage.
2. All Jews, regardless of country of origin.
3. Native born white of native born white parentage.
4. All blacks, regardless of place of birth.
5. All white immigrants or children of one or more immigrant parents.

One important difference between Chicago and New York was Chicago's two-party tradition. It had been at the center of the mid-nineteenth-century development of the Republican party, and this relationship continued as the city became a metropolis. As immigrants poured into the city between the 1880s and the First World War, its political behavior was mixed: the Republicans were more successful in national elections and the Democrats in local ones. Cook County, which consisted of Chicago, and its suburbs, was the least stable county in Illinois electorally, reflecting the constant jockeying for power of the two parties and the role of faction within each of them. Indeed, party factionalism was much more

FIGURE 4.1
Ethnic Areas of Chicago

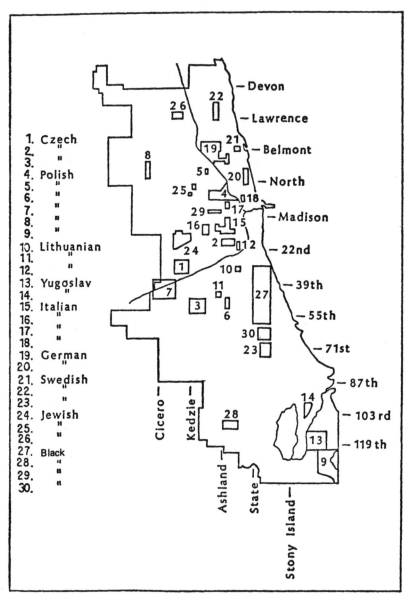

significant in Chicago politics than in New York; rarely did a man or a faction have long-term control of either party, and even more rarely could such a faction or man relax and assume that challengers would not soon be forthcoming.

New immigrants, other things being equal, tend to favor the party in power, since it is the one best constituted to minister to their needs. But other things were not always equal, and ethno-religious conflict, for example, played a role which qualified this generalization. As elsewhere, for example, the Irish had a controlling influence in the Democratic party, prompting non-Catholic immigrants, and even some Catholic ones like the Italians, to seek a home among the Republicans.

Of twenty-five selected elections between 1890 and 1916, for example, the Democrats won ten, the Republicans nine, and the two parties shared the victory in three; the other three were won by third parties. At the presidential level, however, the Democrats carried the city only in 1892; the Republicans carried it every other time except 1912, when Progressive Theodore Roosevelt had a plurality. State voting tended to follow the national vote, although the two parties were somewhat more evenly divided in this area than at the presidential level. Locally, of eleven mayoralties (it was a two-year office until 1907, when it became four-year), the Democrats won seven times and the Republicans four; however, five of the Democratic victories were by one man, and another was by his father (Carter H. Harrison and his son), and so the party element in this predominance is perhaps smaller than it appears.

Third parties did have their effect in the "progressive" years. In the same year—1912—that Theodore Roosevelt carried a plurality of the presidential vote (38 percent), Socialist Eugene Debs also did well, with 13 percent. And the Socialist candidate for state's attorney that same year came within three percentage points of winning the office, in a four-way split. The Progressives continued to show strength in 1914, but after that time the party disintegrated.

But third-party voting in Chicago, whether Progressive or Socialist, seems to have come primarily from the Republican ranks, and thus the relative success of the Democrats in these years appears to be more from Republican failure than Democratic success. And the overwhelming national success of the Republicans in the 1920s—in Illinois as almost everywhere else—would provide an additional source of strength for the local Republicans that the Democrats would not find easy to overcome.

Chicago's established minority groups pretty well reflected the city's political orientation in these early years. Germans and Swedes, for example, voted consistently Republican in national and state elections; locally, they often favored Carter H. Harrison II but were by no means identified with the Democrats as a party. Blacks were almost always very strongly Republican. Newer immigrants, like the Jews, Italians, Poles, and Czechs, were on the whole more Democratic—but only very small portions of these groups were voting in the years before the First World War.

Thus as the country entered the Great War, Chicago lacked a firm partisan tradition like that of New York. Working class political loyalties were only just developing, as the new immigrants—both from abroad and from rural America—began to flex their political muscles. Party organization was more often specific to a given region of the city rather than the whole—and thus faction impeded real partisan city control. And party factions, large or small, had traditionally been much less able to assert control outside the city than Tammany was in New York.

A would-be "boss" of Chicago, then, had a lot of work cut out for him. Not only would he have to carve a majority coalition out of the distinctive—and often mutually antagonistic—ethnic groups of the city; he would also have to override a tradition of party faction and decentralization which was ingrained in the city's modern history.

Quite a few men tried this: none had really succeeded before 1920. No Chicago political leader had ever had the extent of control over the city's life (to say nothing of that of the state) that Charlie Murphy had in New York. But bosses there were, and two in the 1920s had—at various times—a good deal of power indeed. One did develop an effective machine that lasts to the present day; and the other, whose work was much less permanent, was one of the most colorful and controversial urban politicians of his day.

William Hale Thompson began his life in a very different manner from most big city bosses, and in some ways this difference was always with him and played a role in his ultimate failure. He was born in 1867 in Boston, on Beacon Street, to a wealthy, old-stock American family. His father had been a merchant sailor, then a successful Boston businessman, and was a naval officer in the Civil War. His mother came from a wealthy pioneer Chicago family, which provided the impetus for the family's move to Chicago in 1868, where his father became a millionaire in real estate.

Thompson was a less intellectual child than his parents would have liked, and thus did not go east for his schooling. Indeed, he did not really like school, but preferred adventure and a more physical life. At age fifteen he persuaded his family to let him go west for a summer to pursue his dream of life as a cowboy. And for the next half-dozen years he spent nine months of the year in the West and the other three in Chicago attending business college. Thus he pursued a rather different early career from his social peers, who were in eastern colleges at the time; and this con-tributed to his popularity and to a certain aura of romance among his con-temporaries. Even more striking, of course, is the difference between his early years and the more typical background for urban politics of a Charles F. Muprhy.

When his father bought a Nebraska ranch, Thompson took over its operation for six years; he ran it well, and at a profit. But in 1891, when his father died, he returned to Chicago and acceded to his mother's wishes that he remain there.

Then Thompson embarked upon a much more typical career for a political leader. He became an extremely able and popular athlete, excell-ing in baseball, wąter polo, yachting, and other sports, but especially foot-ball. In all of this, plus his organizing activities in amateur athletics, he became very well known—a minor hero in Chicago and a figure of some national prominence in amateur athletics.

Thompson showed no early interest in politics, and his start was a casual one. Since business never interested him greatly, he was ultimately responsive to friends' suggestions that he run for the city council in 1900 (at that time there were two aldermen for each of the city's thirty-five wards). He won in the Second Ward as a regular Republican, even obtain-ing support from the Municipal Voters League, which assumed that his respectable background would make him at least more responsible than his Democratic opponent.

Thompson's background had not prepared him for politics. He was early outmaneuvered by the notorious Democratic aldermen of the neigh-boring First Ward, "Bathhouse John" Coughlin and Michael "Hinky Dink" Kenna. Part of his ward was lost in the process. But Thompson had allied himself with one of the leading Republicans of the day, William Lorimer, the "Blond Boss," and this led to his election to the powerful County Board two years later.

He did early garner a reputation for what we have already seen as a crucial trait for a political leader—loyalty to friends. He even carried this to the extent of testifying in court to his own exuberant visits to houses of prostitution, in order to clear a friend of separate maintenance charges. And he remained loyal to Lorimer when the boss lost a major battle in state Republican factional maneuvering and later when he was ejected from the United States Senate.

By 1905 it seemed that Thompson's career had come to a premature demise and that he didn't really care very much one way or another. He did remain active in Republican politics but did not campaign for office again until 1912, when he ran in the Republican primary for the county Board of Review, on the Lorimer slate. He led the slate, but nonetheless lost in the primary; Lorimer was a bad star to be hitched to at that time.

Nonetheless, Thompson remained popular. His loyalty to his friends seemed admirable. And he had a way with the masses. Fred Lundin, who would be one of his major advisers in the early part of his mayoral career, was sufficiently impressed—and objective—in 1912 that he said, "Y'know, I think we've got a man to go places with. He may not be too much on brains, but he gets through to the people. I think maybe we can do something with Bill Thompson."

It was Lundin, a Swedish immigrant from a poor family (he was known familiarly as the "Poor Swede" and had risen to some wealth, popularity, and leadership in the Swedish community in occupations as various as bootblack and hawker of his homemade, nonalcoholic Juniper Ade) who created a new, highly efficient Republican organization. Having been a precinct captain himself, Lundin realized the importance of organization down to this most fundamental level, and he built accordingly. Lorimer and other local Republicans joined him, with all their efforts focussed on Thompson's election as mayor in 1915. And Thompson's own enthusiasm grew; this was the kind of stage on which he could really see himself.

Unlike earlier bosses, Thompson functioned under the primary system, and in his case this was beneficial. He never was able to unite all the Republican factions in the city; indeed, his actions often exacerbated faction. His base was always among the people, and so the primary served him well. This was certainly true in 1915, when Lundin's organization by no means controlled the Republican county central committee. Thompson defeated his opponent in the primary, with most of the "progressive" and "reform" groups in the city opposing him. (Lundin was no more respectable in the eyes of many Republicans than Lorimer had been.)

He also benefited from the fact that the Democrats were as factionalized as the Republicans. His opponent, Robert M. Sweitzer, had won the Democratic contest over former mayor Harrison, with unhappy feelings on both sides.

Thompson's 1915 mayoral contest set the pattern for his long career. He demonstrated political sagacity and political obtuseness, a nice sense of ethnic realities and a certain fundamental nativism—all intermixed in a complex whole. Thus a strong effort was directed at the older immigrant groups, the Germans and Swedes especially. But there was also religious acrimony, with the Republicans allegedly mailing thousands of letters to voters pointing out Sweitzer's Catholic loyalties. There was talk of the "religious issue," and there were conflicting accusations of who had begun it.

Equally distinctive was the beginning of Thompson's alliance with blacks. He is perhaps the first urban politician to have seen the potential strength of the black vote, and to have positively and openly courted it. Even when he had been alderman, Thompson had been active in this area; he had introduced a bill for the city's first public playground, right in the heart of the Black Belt. In his 1915 campaign, he enlisted the aid of black leaders like Bishop Archibald Carey, and made alliances with rising black politicians like Oscar De Priest. Sweitzer accused him of duplicity in his black politics, but Thompson steamed ahead, spoke often in the Black Belt, and received over 70 percent of its vote.

He also won about 70 percent of the Swedish vote, 65 percent of the German, and majorities among the Bohemians and Jews as well. Among newer immigrants he did less well, but on the whole he demonstrated a strong attraction to lower- and working-class voters. He was off to a good start in citywide politics. But a mayoralty does not a machine make; Thompson had quite a way to go before he could properly be called a "boss."

There is a considerable difference between being a popular candidate who can be repeatedly reelected and being a boss or leader of a political organization covering an entire city. It might be argued that Thompson was never really a boss, since his base was always rather narrow and, more important, he never had a confident hold on the entire Chicago Republican party. However, he did build a successful organization—first with Lundin and others, later largely under his own control—which controlled city government for twelve years and exerted considerable influence at the state level as well. Unlike some machines, Thompson's centered around himself as officeholder, and his three terms as mayor were the crux of his strength. Thus, while he tried to build a strong organization to implement control between elections, his strength nonetheless revolved around his own election campaigns and ability to stay in office.

In 1919, for example, Thompson ran for reelection against the same Democratic opponent he had faced four years before. His victory, with 52 percent of the city's vote, was smaller than in 1915, and there was a question about his further strength since he did not carry any new immigrant groups. But he did win. Moreover, he received about 78 percent of the black vote, over 60 percent of the Swedish and Jewish, and 58 percent of the old stock. He lost the German and Italian vote by only two percentage points, and had 45 percent or better among the Poles and Yugoslavs as well.

His alliance with the blacks proved central in 1919. He had continued working with the leaders—black and white—of this growing population group, and campaigned frequently in the Black Belt. While he was criticized for this by some white groups, the fact was that the vote was crucial to him, and his efforts were very effective; in one speech, Thompson told a black audience, "Enemies have tried to divide us—they are trying to divide us now, but we have always stood together and we always will. I've given you a square deal and you've given a square deal to me." Black leaders reciprocated this feeling, and the city's leading black newspaper exulted after the eleection. "It was a victory not only for Mayor Thompson, but for the *Chicago Defender* as well."

Indeed, during his first term Thompson had achieved a certain national notoriety, not unrelated to his success at the polls. In a period of wartime hysteria and anti-Germanism, he had emerged as a defender of German-Americans and of others who were not ethnically oriented toward the Allied cause. When the Joffre mission from France toured the country during the war, Thompson refused to invite it to Chicago, pointing out that Chicago was "the sixth largest German city in the world, the second largest Bohemian, the second largest Norwegian, and the second largest Polish." Therefore, he said, some of the city's peoples might resent such a visit. And thus, despite the fact that his opponent in 1919 was a German-American, and despite—once again—charges of anti-Catholicism against him, Thompson received passive support from the German-language press and 49 percent of the German-American vote.

He also carried strong majorities among the Jews, Swedes, and old stock in 1919, and, when he was quoted—along with Lundin—as saying that "the party that eliminated the hyphen would eliminate itself from politics," he began to draw national publicity as a leading ethnic politician. In fact, however, he failed with more groups than he won in 1919, particularly the Catholics, and it can be argued that Thompson was relying on the manipulation of interethnic rivalries rather than on a broad appeal to immigrants per se. This was a useful device only in the short term. There is even reason to believe, as we shall see below, that Thompson's real strength was in terms of class rather than ethnicity, which made it a less secure base than one might expect.

Two other factors had emerged by 1919 which promised to limit Thompson's long-term success, one of them important to middle-class groups and the other to a very large part of the city's population. The former was an increasing concern with crime and political corruption in Chicago, along with increasing evidence that the two were interrelated, and that Thompson was a central figure in such interrelationships. Middle-class leaders of Scandinavian and Jewish groups, for example, began to criticize him on this score during the 1919 campaign, despite their general Republicanism, which left them ambivalent about whom to endorse. This problem would worsen during the next decade, when, for example, the Norwegian-American Dovre Club, after reluctantly endorsing him in 1919, became a consistent opponent of his career.

More important was Thompson's vacillating position on the issue of Prohibition, which was central to the interests of most Chicago citizens. Between 1919 and 1930 Chicago held four opinion referenda on the question of Prohibition, wherein its citizens voted from 72 to 83 percent anti-Prohibition. In 1919, for example, the vote was 83 percent against, varying from highs of over 90 percent among Czechs, Germans, Italians, and Lithuanians, to a low of 64 percent among the Protestant Swedes. And for all his later reputation as a proponent of a "wide-open town," Thompson had not been consistent on this issue. In 1915, for example, he had enforced the Sunday closing laws; and the correlation coefficient between opposing Prohibition and supporting Thompson in 1919, for Chicago ethnic voters, was $-.800$; this suggests that they sensed his unreliability on this issue at that time and also indicates the weakness of his hold on much of the immigrant vote.

After winning his second term in 1919, Thompson was obviously a power in Chicago politics and in the local Republican party. He and Lundin had built a strong organization, based on the Black Belt and various other wards in the city. The election of Len Small as governor in 1921 put a Thompson ally in the statehouse and expanded his power accordingly. He had the power to frustrate Republican opponents not only in Chicago but also, for the time, in the state. And he was often referred to as a "boss."

A boss Thompson may have been, but not on the order of a Charlie Murphy. The Republican party in Chicago was as factionalized as ever, with each faction controlling a distinct part of the city and each having its own alliances with downstate Republican leaders. And beyond this, neither Thompson nor any other Republican leader of the period was able to fully override the Democrats. Chicago remained a two-party city during his tenure, and the Democrats tended to control the very powerful Cook County government.

Moreover, since Thompson was a boss whose key strength—again, unlike a Charles F. Murphy—came from his own office-holding, we have seen that his support in this regard was by no means overwhelming. He had been twice elected mayor, but narrowly; and his popular base was hardly overwhelming. As an old-stock, upper-class politician, in a party which nationally was beginning to lose its image of utility for working-class voters, and with a reputation which was beginning to offend the city's middle class, one might say with hindsight that his prospects were not all that great. The very fact that he had to rely on the black vote was itself politically tenuous—blacks were too highly disliked by the fastest growing part of Chicago's voting population.

For all of these reasons Thompson finally decided not to run for a third term in 1923. Rival Republican leaders like Robert E. Crowe and

Edward Brundage were temporarily united against him. His administration seemed suddenly tinged with major scandals: Fred Lundin had just been indicted in a three million dollar fraud, and Governor Small's state administration was also under fire. Thus Thompson did not run, ar! the Republican candidate, Arthur Lueder (Brundage faction), lost to Democrat William E. Dever, a "respectable" judge.

Thompson's role in this election was not untypical of that often played by unsuccessful factional leaders in Chicago. Rather than rallying to the support of Lueder, in the hope of getting united Republican support behind himself at some later date, he appears to have used his political strength to see that Lueder was defeated. His actions here were surreptitious but real, and especially so among black voters. His foremost black political ally, Oscar De Priest, bolted the party to support Dever; and so, too, did Louis Anderson, the black alderman who shared Second Ward political leadership with De Priest. And the staunchly Republican *Chicago Defender* refused to endorse anyone, bemoaning the factionalism dividing the Republican party.

With this one group, at least, Thompson could feel confident of his leadership. Dever received 53 percent of the black vote and 69 percent in the Second Ward Black Belt. But at the same time, Republican factionalism became yet greater, and Thompson's intraparty support would henceforth be weaker. And his close alliance with blacks continued to mark him in a way that alienated other voting groups and could be used against him.

Nonetheless, Big Bill did snap back to dominate Republican politics again, and to be reelected to the mayoralty in 1927. And his ties with the black community were again central in his campaign and his victory. The Democrats, under the leadership of George Brennan, unwisely chose the path of prejudice. They used cartoons, slogans, and calliopes in the streets to impress upon white voters the closeness between Thompson and the blacks. For example, when, early in the campaign, Thompson apparently embraced a black child, Brennan distributed cartoons picturing this, with the caption "Do you want Negroes or White Men to Run Chicago? Bye, Bye, Blackbirds." This theme of blacks taking over the city was repeated often.

Thompson was nothing if not aggressive, and he reacted to Democratic bigotry accordingly. Calling his critics "lily white gentlemen" and "traducers and liars," he also argued that "the black finger that is good enough to pull a trigger in defense of the American flag is good enough to mark a ballot." His support in the black community was virtually unanimous.

Thompson endeavored to rebuild his organization and ensure his election with more devices than his Black Belt politics, however. His "America

First" campaign and baiting of the king of England earned him national publicity at this time. His threat to kick King George "in the snoot" evolved in part from his politics of the First World War, when he had "defended" Chicago citizens of German and Irish ancestry, but it flourished now as he grappled for reelection. And it was influenced also by school problems in Chicago, which were partly real and partly a convenient issue for Big Bill.

Thus Thompson made international politics—of a vague and imprecise sort—a focal point of a mayoral campaign. "America First" was apparently his own idea, and when asked by a friend what it had to do with the campaign, he responded: "That's just it, it hasn't anything to do with it, and that is why it will make a good issue. If anyone opposes us, we will say he is not for America First; he's for America second, or third, or he is perhaps not a good American at all. Everybody is for America First, and if anyone is against us, we will say that he is disloyal." In a way, he was ahead of his time.

All of this made Thompson seem the consummate ethnic politician, according to the pundits of the time. And this seemed reinforced by the third major focus of his campaign—the "wide-open town." Mayor Dever had endeavored to administer the law in Chicago, including the Prohibition law. And Thompson, despite his own enforcement of Sunday closing earlier, grabbed upon this as a most useful issue. Again, it was not so much his stand on the issue (Dever was a committed Wet) but the flamboyance with which he established his position that got him the headlines and publicity he was looking for. When he pledged to open up two "joints" for every one Dever closed, and when he said "I will break any cop I catch on the trail of a lonesome pint into a man's house or car; I will put them on the street and they must catch hold-up men," he drew great press coverage and the image of Wetness that he was seeking.

He was successful, in that he won the election and reasserted his strong position in the local and state Republican apparatus. But he did not in any way override Republican factionalism, he lost a good deal of traditional middle-class Republican support (the clergy and "civic leaders" were almost unanimous in their opposition to him), and he got only a very bare majority (50.4 percent) of the new immigrant vote, failing to carry such groups as the Poles, Lithuanians, and Czechs.

And the limits of his victory became apparent only one year later, in the 1928 Republican primary, when Thompson's machine suffered tremendous defeat. The reasons for this were continuing Republican factionalism, exacerbated middle-class opposition to Thompson, and, especially, increasing charges of malfeasance.

In the fall of 1927 Thompson had carried "America First" into the school system as part of his campaign against the independent superintendent of schools and his continuing effort to expand his own popularity. He harshly criticized the lack of support for America's revolutionary heroes, native and immigrant, and the too-generous treatment accorded England and the English. From this he extended his efforts to the library system in a purge of "un-American" books and the threat of book burning. It was one of Thompson's querulous crusades, done partly for publicity, partly to take the focus off his legal and other problems, partly in the hope of getting political mileage out of it from immigrant groups. Probably its most important effect was in increasing middle-class alienation from him and his career.

The same effect attached to the increasing allegations of corruption in his administration, and ties to the gangsters. Al Capone did have Thompson's picture on his wall, and by 1927 he probably did have an alliance of some sort with the mayor—to the extent that he may have contributed as much as $100,000 to Thompson's campaign.

There were other allegations of corruption as well. And Thompson's on-again/off-again ally, Governor Small, had similar problems. Thus, despite Thompson's reelection in 1927, his Republican enemies were convinced that 1928 was their year.

The 1928 primary became famous as the "Pineapple Primary" because of its violence, and the bombings of the homes of two Republican leaders of the now-united anti-Thompson group. This continued violence only strengthened the growing anti-Thompson feeling and helps to explain his crushing defeat. Table 4.2 gives the Chicago and individual ethnic group vote for Thompson in 1919, the 1927 primary, the 1927 election, and for Thompson's organization in the 1928 primary.

What is most striking in this table is that Thompson and his organization did best in the Republican primaries among the groups that were least Republican. That is, for groups like the Czechs and Poles, who were largely Democratic, those who did vote Republican seem to have been Thompsonites. On the other hand, the more Republican groups—upon whom his strength was ultimately reliant—seem in the primaries to exhibit less attraction to Thompson as their party's leader. And this is most clearly demonstrated in the 1928 primary, coming only months after Thompson's 1927 mayoral victory. Particularly the more middle-class groups, like the Germans, Swedes, Jews, and old stock, had swung strongly against Thompson by 1928. And since this class was increasingly the major source of local Republican support, it did not make Thompson's future all that rosy.

Indeed, the remainder of Thompson's third term was disastrous. Many of his alliances crumbled, and his efforts to expand his control to the state, and even national levels were largely unsuccessful. In 1930, for example, he tried to defeat the Republican candidate for the United States Senate, Ruth Hanna McCormick, of the *Chicago Tribune* family, which had been long opposed to him. Mrs. McCormick did lose, but not because of Thompson's efforts, and many of his black allies broke with him over the issue.

TABLE 4.2
Chicago Vote for Thompson, 1919–1927
(Percentages) *

Group	1919 Mayoralty	1927 Primary	1927 Mayoralty	1928 Primary
Czechs	27	86	41	57
Poles	45	74	46	51
Lithuanians	24	64	43	50
Yugoslavs	48	70	64	42
Italians	49	74	58	74
Germans	49	63	63	35
Swedes	65	60	62	28
Jews	60	69	61	37
Blacks	78	90	93	68
Old stock	58	51	45	22

*Percentage of the two-party vote for Thompson in 1919 and 1927; percentage of the vote of the two major Republican candidates for Thompson in 1927 primary; for 1928, mean percentage of the Republican primary vote for Len Small for governor and Robert Crowe for state's attorney—the Thompson candidates for those positions.

He was also subject to lengthy lawsuits and spent much of his time away from the city. His power seemed rapidly waning, and only a victory in the 1931 mayoralty was likely to reestablish the mayor as a real power in Chicago and Illinois politics.

But between Big Bill and a fourth term in 1931 stood a candidate very unlike any he had faced before, one who was himself a boss, and a boss with more organized and centralized power over his own party than Thompson had ever achieved. And in this campaign the hidden but real weaknesses in Thompson's political base became patent, as the face of Chicago politics was reformulated in a way that has not changed to the present day.

If ever an American politician deserved the title of "the complete ethnic politician" it was Anton Cermak, who rose to party control in the late 1920s and established the political machine that has controlled the city for over forty years. It was not that Cermak's Irish predecessors (Roger Sullivan earlier in the century, and then George Brennan until his death in 1928) were not conscious of the ethnic character of Chicago's mass political base. They demonstrated considerable sensitivity in balancing tickets and so on. But they were Irish particularists, to a good degree, and were generally more concerned with maintaining their own parochial control over the party than they were with victory. Moreover, they positively opposed the inclusion of some groups—like the blacks—into the Democratic coalition, and were ambivalent about others, like the Czechs and other Slavs, who had become increasingly Democratic more or less in spite of the party's leadership.

One thing that had prevailed in the Democratic party under its traditional Irish leadership, however, was relative party unity. After the internal infighting, and the primary battles, the party had tended to coalesce at election time. This had not guaranteed victory, locally or otherwise, as we have seen; but it did provide a tradition that putative future leaders could bank upon. And when George Brennan died in 1928, to be replaced by the first non-Irish leader in the party's modern history, that leader was able to use this tradition to perfect the Democratic machine that continued under the leadership of Richard J. Daley into the 1970s.

Anton Joseph Cermak was born in Bohemia, and at the age of one immigrated with his parents, first to the Bohemian center of Chicago, and then to the mining town of Braidwood, Illinois, again to a section with a large Bohemian population. It was a poor town, working-class and immigrant, and physically primitive; the family preferred Chicago but never seemed able to make a living there. Thus young Tony grew in Braidwood in a typical working-class and ethnic environment, steeped in hard work and some privation, but not poverty. His family was unqualifiedly ethnic, and Bohemian language and culture were the medium of his upbringing. Like others of his background and class, his education was intermittent and very limited. If this period of his life was distinguished by anything auguring his future career, it was in his ability to get along with, even to dominate, his Irish fellows, despite established separation and conflict between these two groups. Ethnic diversity and the possibility of cooperation were very real to him.

In his early teens, Tony Cermak began working in the mines, again a quite standard procedure—putting in long, hard, and dangerous hours, as did the rest of the unorganized workers in the area. Even in these early years, however, Cermak evinced leadership qualities, becoming negotiator for a group of mule drivers who sought a raise; this was sufficient to get him labeled as an agitator and fired; so at the age of sixteen he hopped a boxcar bound for Chicago, where he hoped his prospects would be brighter.

Thus Cermak's early experiences were quite different from those of Big Bill Thompson; but not so far removed from those of Charlie Murphy. Like Murphy, he became—in Chicago—a horsecar driver, and he became involved with a gang centered in a neighborhood saloon. As a strong fighter and a capable drinker, as well as an ambitious and competent leader, young Tony became his gang's leader. Unlike Tweed, Murphy, and Thompson, Cermak seems to have participated in athletics very little apart from fighting. But as the leader of a group of young men, Cermak did come to the attention of local party leaders; he had, after all, something very important to sell them.

In the mid-1890s Cermak went into business for himself hauling wood; it was a profitable business, and he began to prosper in a moderate fashion. He also found related ways to serve the various people he met in his business—such as lighting fires for Jewish customers on their sabbath. Cermak never wasted effort: his alliance with Jewish leaders would eventually be of great political importance. He married, built a house, and became a young man of some rising importance. He had moved to Lawndale, a better neighborhood than Pilsen, but still Czech; it was under the political control of A. J. Sabath, the Czech Jew who may well have served as a model for Cermak's successful ethnic politics.

Cermak worked his way up the party ladder in much the same way as he had the business ladder; moving from loyal flunky to precinct captain, he continued to deliver his votes and serve the organization faithfully. And in 1902 his labors were rewarded with nomination for and election to the office of state representative. In this, as in his business career, he was a representative of the Czechs—that was the base of his support and the thrust of his endeavors, partisan and official. He was loyal to the local Democratic organization, but not strongly identified with either of the major city Democratic factions (the Roger Sullivan or the Carter H. Harrison) at that time.

His career in Springfield was a successful one, and he rose to the party's leadership group there. He continued also to be active in Chicago, most particularly in Czech and interethnic affairs. In 1906, at the behest of the German-language *Abendpost,* and reflecting the rising immigrant fear of the prohibition movement, a meeting was held which led to the formation of the United Societies for Local Self-Government. This was an interethnic pressure group—one of the first instances of real cooperation among the leaders of Chicago's frequently conflicting ethnic groups—and one that grew rapidly as the threat of prohibition became increasingly real (by 1919 it would comprise about 1,087 separate ethnic organizations,

representing over a quarter of a million people). And Anton Cermak became its secretary and leading political spokesman, providing himself
with a forum and a base of interethnic support possessed by no other
political leader in Chicago. Even as he emerged on the local political scene,
he was the leader, for a large part of the population, on the issue that was
paramount to them in their conception of politics.

In 1912 Cermak ran in his first citywide race, for bailiff of the municipal court, and won. It was a good position, keeping him in the middle of
party activities, and he used it while he expanded his interethnic party
contacts. In 1918, he ran for sheriff and, while he carried the city, lost
overall due to the suburban county returns. His practice of not giving up
one office until elected to another left him still politically employed. It is
noteworthy that while losing, Cermak nonetheless showed considerable
strength among the groups that would count. Despite having a German-
American opponent, he had the endorsement of the *Abendpost*—an extraordinary phenomenon; and he received about 47 percent of the German
vote. He also received majorities among all the other major ethnic groups
except the blacks and Swedes; and led the ticket among his own Czechs
with 86 percent. In his first major run for office, he had done pretty well;
and his yeoman efforts as a leader of the antiprohibition forces were
being recognized and rewarded.

Moreover, he had risen in the party; however reluctantly, the Irish
leaders had to recognize this ambitious new man who was a good deal
closer to the immigrant masses than they were. This recognition was made
clear in 1922, when he was nominated for and elected to both membership and the presidency of the Cook County Board of Commissioners—a
position of great power and a traditional major stepping-stone in Chicago
politics. He was reelected in 1926 and again in 1930, becoming known
locally, and even nationally, as a major Democratic leader and as "the
mayor of Cook County."

He had continued his leadership of the Wet forces of the city during the
Prohibition decade. Each time he ran for office he set up another referendum on Prohibition—maintaining the public identity of himself with this
issue. He stepped, also, into other ethnically important issues, like opposition to the new restrictive immigration legislation and to the Ku Klux
Klan. For example, when, in 1927, a joint committee of Poles, Czechs, and
Slovaks was formed to oppose immigration restriction, its president turned
out to be Anton Cermak.

And Cermak began to build his own suborganization in the Democratic
party, outflanking the Irish, who never really wanted him. Starting with
the Jews (it was Cook County Board president Cermak who had created a
kosher section in the county poorhouse) he allied with Moe Rosenberg

and Jacob Arvey of the Twenty-fourth Ward ghetto. And for his own Irish ties he sought out Pat Nash (half of the famous Kelly-Nash organization of the 1930s), who was alienated from the Brennan organization; significantly, Nash was also one of the few Democratic Irish politicians to have ties with the black community. Cermak also used his position as president of the County Board, with its vast patronage, to appoint members of every major ethnic group to office. And he lent his weight to some "reform" organizations, giving himself connections with the city's upper-class leaders as well.

Thus while officially and formally a part of the Brennan organization, Cermak also built to ensure that he, rather than Brennan's chosen successor (Michael Igoe), would succeed to the leadership when Brennan left.

In 1928 Cermak reluctantly let himself to be pressured into running for the United States Senate, to bolster the ticket; he did not, however, resign his county office to do so. While he lost in the statewide returns, he carried the city, doing better among almost all groups than did presidential candidate Al Smith. Between them, Smith and Cermak had a profound effect on Chicago voting patterns, which played a considerable role in the beginning of Chicago's Democratic hegemony.

When Brennan died during the 1928 campaign, the local party leadership did not immediately fall to any one man. But Cermak was able to use his ethnic and partisan alliances and his power as County Board president to gradually assume power. Like Tweed, but unlike Murphy, he used his own power as a candidate to reinforce himself. And with his strong re-election victory in 1930, he had clearly emerged as the new boss of the Chicago Democratic party—one which was, at that time, more powerful than it had been in a generation. It is noteworthy that the 1930 campaign, which marked Cermak's ultimate takeover of the party, saw a Democratic slate of Cermak, Kaindl, Brady, Allegretti, and Smietanka. This is indicative of the manner in which Cermak had built his machine. It also led to Mayor Thompson's famous epigram, "From Szymczak to Zintak to Cermak and the Irish are all out." The Irish were not really all out, and they did not leave the party; but it was true that the top party leadership had slipped from their hands.

What remained for Cermak's Democratic party to achieve was the mayoralty, and Cermak took it upon himself to depose Big Bill once and for all. The 1931 campaign was not the first time these two men had clashed. In 1915, when Thompson had enforced Sunday closing, Cermak led the United Societies' opposition and its great Wet Parade, where forty thousand marchers protested the mayor's action. From that point forward the two men were antagonists.

But the 1931 campaign became not one of issues, really—rather, it revolved around different conceptions of party and, ultimately, different belief systems as well. Although Cermak's entire career had been cast in ethnic terms and his view of the Democratic party was of a vehicle for the success of discrete cultural groups, Thompson had never really seen his own career or party in these terms, despite his occasional rhetoric to the contrary. And this became very clear during this 1931 campaign when, in his hardest political battle yet, the nativism that was very much a part of Thompson's character surfaced and played a central role.

Cermak's popularity, and the Democratic party's new strength—made so clear in 1930 elections—plus Thompson's troubles with the law, had put the latter in a difficult position. Much of the traditional middle-class support of Republicanism in the city seemed lost to him, as one middle-class organization after another openly opposed his reelection. He had squeaked through the primary, but that did not appear to be enough. So Thompson attacked his opponent on ethnic grounds, repeatedly insisting that no man should be mayor of Chicago who was not a native American and jibing "Tony, Tony, where's your pushcart at? Can you imagine a world's fair mayor with a name like that?" Both Thompson's jibe and Cermak's famous reply ("He don't like my name. . . . It's true I didn't come over on the *Mayflower,* but I came over as soon as I could") indicate their very different conceptions of what would appeal to Chicago voters.

Moreover, while Thompson's nomination had come amidst great acrimony and party division, which carried over into the campaign, Cermak reaped the advantage of his own tradition of party regularity—he was easily nominated, and his party was united. Those few Democrats who thought of bucking the organization were rewarded for not doing so; and minor candidates found that the Board of Election Commissioners (under County Board president Cermak) had ruled their petitions illegal.

But the real strength of Cermak and his party came not from malfeasance; rather it was a direct result of the hard work at supporting ethnic issues and aims, and building an ethnic coalition, that Cermak had been putting in for twenty years. And to this was added strong middle-class Republican alienation from Thompson's scandal-tinged administration.

Thompson's nativism clearly backfired. The newspaper of the Polish National Alliance told its readers that "This campaign is not only against Anton Cermak, but also all of those who are not North Americans." Another Polish paper agreed, telling its readers that voting for Cermak was "in defense of the honor of Poland." Thompson's anti-immigrant remarks were constantly satirized, as in "pushcart" cartoons, accompanied by emotional anti-Thompson editorials. Other Slavic newspapers and organizations argued similarly.

Cermak's leadership of ethnic representation and ethnic issues also served him well. The German-American Liberty League, for example, called him "our trustworthy old leader" in the battle against Prohibition, and endorsed him strongly, as did the daily *Abendpost:* Thompson's administration, it said, was marked only by "scandals, an orgy of corruption, squandering and incapability," while Cermak had always been a good friend of the Germans. And the *Jewish Courier* stressed the numbers of jobs Cermak had given to Jews, while other Jewish leaders criticized Thompson's introduction of bigotry into the campaign.

Other ethnic group leaders and newspapers were similar, supporting Cermak both because of Thompson's nativism, and because of Cermak's own careful cultivation of them during his political career. Cermak even got some Italian leadership support, although the Italian-language press remained loyal to Thompson and Republicanism. The Italian gangsters likewise remained supportive of the mayor.

Even among blacks, Cermak had tried to create some sympathy to his party and his own leadership. He was the first Democratic leader to make black appointments to various civic agencies, and really to try to move black politicians toward the Democratic party. It was still too early for this to have had much effect, however, and most black leaders stuck with their old ally, Big Bill. The *Chicago Defender* endorsed neither candidate, however, and gave as much attention to Cermak's campaign as Thompson's.

One important additional area of support coming to Cermak, and through him the local Democrats, consisted of middle- and upper-middle-class groups which had previously been determinedly Republican. Much, but not all, of this support was specifically anti-Thompson and did not stay with the Democrats; but some of it did. Thompson's continuing ties with Chicago's criminals, and his bitter fight over control of the city's schools in 1927-28, had alienated much of the city's leadership. Thus groups like the Municipal Voters League, and leaders like Emily Dean of the Illinois Republican Women's Clubs, came out for Cermak once Thompson had defeated his "reform" opponent in the Republican primary. Cermak also received support from the consistently Republican Scandinavian-American press and organizations. And almost every civic group in the city—representing the city's old-stock Republican elite—came out in support of the Bohemian-born candidate for mayor.

And the vote followed the campaign, as Table 4.3 indicates. Cermak received majorities among every major ethnic group except the Italians and the blacks—and even did better among those two groups than had his predecessor, Dever, in 1927. Groups like the Germans and Swedes voted Democratic for mayor for the first time. He also carried our sample of solidly middle-class old-stock voters by higher majorities than had Dever four years before.

From the newer immigrant groups, among whom he had based his entire political career, Cermak received unprecendented mayoral majorities; and he completely reversed the Jewish vote, from 61 percent Republican in 1927 to 61 percent Democratic in his favor. The size of his vote

TABLE 4.3
Vote for Thompson in 1927 and for Thompson and Cermak
in 1931, for Chicago and Selected Ethnic Groups
(Percentage of the two-party vote won by named candidate)

Group	1927 Thompson	1931 Thompson	1931 Cermak
Czechs	41	16	84
Poles	46	30	70
Lithuanians	43	38	62
Yugoslavs	64	36	64
Italians	58	53	47
Germans	63	42	58
Swedes	62	47	53
Jews	61	39	61
Blacks	93	84	16
Old stock	45	39	61
CHICAGO TOTAL	54	42	58

was certainly assisted by the Democratic resurgence of 1928 and 1932; but he also made a major contribution to maintaining and expanding that resurgence, and played no small role—both as a candidate and as a party leader—in facilitating the Democratic success in Chicago for all levels of voting during the next decade.

Both the sources and effects of Cermak's candidacy can be rendered a bit clearer by once again using measures of association. Table 4.4 provides correlation coefficients between the mayoral elections of the period and between mayoral and presidential elections for Chicago ethnic group voting. These statistics do suggest the changing sources of Democratic support under Cermak's leadership. Note that the lowest correlation in Part A is between Cermak's successful campaign in 1931 and the other Democratic mayoral victory of the period, 1923. This suggests that Cermak's coalition was somewhat different, as indeed it was. It also suggests, in reverse, the effect of Thompson, since 1923 was the only one of these mayoralties when he did not run.

Part B, which gives the relationships between mayoral and presidential elections, also offers confirmation of this idea. The 1931 mayoralty correlates most significantly with the Smith and Roosevelt presidential campaigns of 1927 and 1931. This is not only, or even primarily, because of nearness in time (viz., the correlations for 1919 and 1927); rather, it reflects the developing mass and ethnic base of the Democratic party in Cermak's time, wherein the elections of 1928, 1930, 1931, and 1932 really built the Democratic party's new and enduring successful coalition.

TABLE 4.4
Coefficients of Correlation for Mayoral Elections,
1919-1931
(Percentage Democratic of the Vote of Nine Chicago Ethnic Groups)

Part A. Mayoral Elections

	1919	1923	1927	1931
1919	——	.75	.87	.72
1923		——	.64	.35
1927			——	.89
1931				——

Part B. Mayoral with Presidential Elections

		Presidential		
Mayoral	1920	1924	1928	1932
1919	.90	.90	.91	.82
1923	.86	.91	.74	.53
1927	.84	.85	.90	.92
1931	.59	.60	.79	.91

Finally, in Table 4.5, I have redivided the nine ethnic groups into four socioeconomic classes, to look more directly at the effects of class position on ethnic voting in local elections. This casts considerable additional light on the questions of the real strength of Big Bill Thompson and why that strength did not have long-term viability.

Table 4.5 suggests that the real crux of Thompson's strength among Chicago's immigrant masses was not ethnic, but socioeconomic. Except for his first mayoralty, when he came within two percentage points of winning them, he was stronger among the lower-lower class than any other (and the Democrats fared best among this class in 1923, when Thompson did not run). Before 1931 he did well also among the middle-middle class, but this was only because of that group's general Republicanism, as can be well seen in the column on the 1928 Republican primary. This group voted overwhelmingly against Thompson in the primaries but up until 1931 went along with him in the general elections out of Republican loyalty. This turned around dramatically in 1931, for reasons that we have seen; and even Thompson's lower-lower class appeal declined in that year.

TABLE 4.5
Vote of Nine Ethnic Groups Subsumed into Four
Socioeconomic Classes, 1919-1931

	ELECTION Percentage Democratic of Two-Party Vote				
Class	1919, Mayor	1923, Mayor	1927, Mayor	1931, Mayor	1928 Primary Percentage pro-Thompson*
Lower-lower	51	78	33	44	79
Upper-lower	55	67	44	58	58
Lower-middle	56	66	47	66	40
Middle-middle	34	38	38	55	29

*For definition of pro-Thompson vote in 1928 Republican primary, see note to Table 4.2.

The problem, for Thompson, was dual. Most importantly, he was appealing to Chicago's masses on the wrong basis—a socioeconomic appeal was just weaker than an ethnic one, in the long run, and he did not realize this. His long-run unsatisfactoriness, compared with the Democrats, on such ethnic issues as Prohibition, immigrant defense, and nativism, produced a steadily increasing cultural basis for these groups to desert him. Secondly, even his class appeal was weak—he did not really get to the mass of the urban working class which was either in or about to enter the upper-lower and lower-middle classes. And his flamboyance and alleged dishonesty alienated the traditionally Republican middle class, not only among the ethnics, but among the old stock as well.

Cermak's Democrats, on the other hand—and by inversion of the above—were building a much stronger and more reliable base. Because Cermak constructed an appeal to the ethnics on an ethnic base, he was able to minimize the importance of class for the lower three groups. And, for that matter, the Democrats' alternative to Thompson's nativism in 1931 was not lost on middle-class Jews, Swedes, and Germans either. Other middle-class groups came over for essentially anti-Thompson reasons, to be sure, and not all of these stayed with the Democrats—for local or national elections—afterwards. But some of them did; and the lower- and working-class ethnic voters stayed with the Democrats for good.

Thus the picture provided by voting statistics suggests the strength on which Anton Cermak's political machine had come to be based by the time he was elected to the mayoralty.

Another indication of Cermak's political strategy can be seen in one anomaly in the returns. Cermak's running mates for city clerk and a vacancy on the municipal court also won; but his other running mate, for city treasurer, did not. This was most unusual for Chicago politics, where the clerk and treasurer are part of a ticket with the mayor. But the Republican candidate for treasurer was the only member of that ticket who came from the Charles S. Deneen faction in the Republican party; and this has led some students to conclude that Cermak made a deal with Deneen for an exchange of mutual—albeit quiet—support. The hypothesis is reasonable, and if it is true it was a good deal for Cermak. His power was enhanced, and it really did nothing for Deneen or his organization in the long run: Chicago has not gone Republican since.

So far as Cermak was concerned, his own election to the mayoralty was only an important step in his control of the Democratic organization. And as an entirely ethnic politician, one of his first steps after the election was to try to bring in the two groups which had not supported him. An Italian Democratic commiteeman soon appeared in the most Italian of the city's wards, and there was an increase in the number of Italians on the Democratic ticket in 1932. The continuing battle against organized crime also served to free Italian voters from Republican obligations. And the effects of all this were apparent as early as 1932.

Blacks also were introduced to Cermak's carrot and stick. As soon as he took office, he fired over two thousand temporary employees—many of them blacks who had been hired by the Thompson administration. He also cracked down on Black Belt crime—most practitioners of which had been of necessity allied to the local Republican party. As the *Chicago Defender* put it, "The entire city is closed up like a drum. The lid went on five minutes after it was certain Mayor Thompson had lost." Cermak told the bosses of policy gambling in the black wards that they had better change their politics if they wanted to stay in business. And he began the more constructive task of building a black Democratic political organization, under black leadership. While this had only begun at the time of Cermak's death, it was the inauguration of a highly successful campaign: before the end of the decade this most Republican of groups was firmly enmeshed in the Democratic coalition.

Anton Cermak died in early 1933, from complications following his wounding in an assassination attempt that was probably meant for Franklin D. Roosevelt. Thus his career ended just as it had reached its peak. But his machine, or organization, although it came back under Irish control, continued as long-term testimony to what he had built.

Cermak, as a boss, had some similarities to Charlie Murphy. But he was also different—a function of his own background as much as anything else. As an immigrant from eastern Europe, he was more aware than most of the changing nature of the mass base of urban politics and of the things in which this new urban mass was really interested. He is more comparable to Fiorello La Guardia of New York than to perhaps any other urban politician of his day. Their origins were similar, and their careers were both steeped in the knowledge that ethnicity was crucial in American urban life and politics. This was the whole crux of Cermak's career, and his success. And the fact that his Irish successors followed the course he had laid down, with exactitude, is testimony to how clearly he had shown the way.

Thompson, on the other hand, was a rather distinct phenomenon in urban politics. He was exciting, flamboyant, and not unconcerned with the plight of the urban masses. But he saw them only in general, rather than culturally specific terms; and he was not of them, as was Cermak. Thus his success had to be temporary, as indeed it was; and he built nothing. With his loss of the 1931 election, both he and his organization disappeared as viable factors in Chicago politics.

Cermak's approach was ideal for its time—one of rapid immigration to the United States and to the industrial city; and one where the urban masses were unassimilated and culturally particularistic. Sensing this, he was able to build a machine on a base both deep and broad. His successors, in Chicago and elsewhere, would be able to be equally successful only if they were as able to anticipate the development of urban mass culture as perceptively as had Cermak himself.

5

RICHARD J. DALEY:
THE LAST BOSS?

Anton Cermak had built Chicago's first real political machine through two developments. First, he had melded a conglomerate urban population of varying cultural orientations and aims into a functional entity. And second, he had built a tightly structured, highly disciplined political organization, which was susceptible to efficient centralized direction. The line between party boss and humble precinct worker had been made direct, if hierarchical. And these two accomplishments explain both the success and the longevity of the Chicago Democratic machine.

Under Cermak the offices of party leader and mayor were in the same hands.* This was very important, since the mayor's office in Chicago is not legally very strong. What really gives the mayor his strength over the city council, and government generally, is his being the individual leader of the party. It is a situation rather like that in the Soviet Union, where the party chairmanship and premiership are sometimes in the hands of one man, sometimes not. And, to carry the parallel further, it can be said that on the whole it is the party leadership position which has the greater strength, when the two are in separate hands—at least that has been the case in Chicago since Cermak really created the city's modern Democratic Party.

Cermak's successor as mayor, Ed Kelly, was a powerful and popular mayor; he was elected in his own right three times—1935, 1939, and 1943. But he never controlled the party as Cermak had. Pat Nash, an old Cermak

---

*Unlike Daley after him, Cermak did give up the official chairmanship of the County Central Committee after he was elected mayor. But he did not really give up his control: the chairmanship went to the loyal Pat Nash, and Cermak remained a member of the committee and its treasurer as well.

ally, served as party chairman until his death in 1943. And while Kelly was nominally chairman after that, he did not have even enough control to prevent the party leaders from dumping him in 1947.

Traditional problems of graft and scandal, plus the debilitating forces of time, had persuaded the party leadership, and especially the new chairman, Jacob Arvey (Chicago's only Jewish "boss"—and never a complete one), that a new face, and a more respectable one, was needed. Thus the eight years (1947-55) of Martin Kennelly, an amiable, moderately competent administrator who never established his own control of the party.

After the death of Cermak, his organization continued triumphant, electing one Democratic mayor after another, and creating also a very successful Democratic voting record for local, state, and national elections. But the direction of that organization, and the role of the mayor therein, tended to separate; rule became more collegial. This was not necessarily bad, as the party's success suggested; but it seemed always likely that another Cermak might arise who could merge the two positions once again and rise to greater individual power in the city than any one man had possessed since 1933.

This, in 1955, is what Richard J. Daley accomplished when he took over the party chairmanship and the mayoralty—both of which offices he held for over twenty years. In the process Daley became famous and notorious and was widely heralded as the "last boss." In an age when the old political machine seemed to be disappearing—in New York, in Boston, everywhere—it flourished under Daley in Chicago. What this says about Daley, and about Chicago—as well as about the future of the urban political organization—is a topic of both intellectual and practical interest, and is the subject of this chapter.

While Chicago has changed in a number of ways since the days of Big Bill Thompson, one important consistency—which was crucial to Tony Cermak and remained so to Richard J. Daley—is the availability of patronage. Unlike other American cities, which in the Progressive Era and afterwards underwent great diminution in the number of jobs available by appointment to the public payroll, Chicago continues to offer huge opportunities in this area. From positions of real authority and influence down to trash collectors and indescribably unreal clerical and manual laborers, the party in control of Chicago has perhaps thirty thousand jobs at its disposal; to this can be added an even greater number of state and county jobs, and many thousands more from the contractors and other employers who seek the organization's largesse.

The rise of civil service has not interfered too much with the operation of Chicago's patronage. First, it does not apply to all jobs; second, there were, by the mid-twentieth century, enough striving party loyalists at every level of education, etc., that some deserving worker could usually be found among the top scorers from which officeholders were to be picked; and third, barring everything else, it is not that difficult for a well-entrenched party to get around, or over, the civil service laws when it wishes to do so.

Thus the Chicago party, more than perhaps any other, continues to have a guaranteed loyal coterie of stalwarts, whose very livings and chances of economic and status mobility exist within the party's largesse. For this reason, if no other, one has a strong explanation of the continuation of Chicago's Democratic machine: so long as there are poor and underemployed people in the city—and this has been a constant in modern American urban history—and there are jobs available for them through the party, there exists a hierarchy of very willing laborers, whose own voting, and familial, ethnic, and social influence on other's voting, will play a crucial role in the party's success.

Indeed, once in power, a party can find the civil service system beneficial, since it tends to preclude the other party—if it takes office—from entirely undoing the first party's patronage base. The Chicago Democrats have not been out of power in the city since Cermak; but this principle has been of some applicability in county and state politics.

Moreover, the nationalization of the party's traditional welfare activities since the time of the New Deal has not had the debilitating influence on party that many at first expected. This is chiefly because of the lingering effects of American federalism and popular fear of national government: the welfare and other provisions of Social Security are a curious mélange of federal and state funding and administration, and the latter especially is under local control. Thus while social welfare payments may derive ultimately from the federal government, they are dispensed by the county government; and federal controls are simply not very great. Especially when a party—as in Chicago—tends to control city and county government (and often state as well), it is more than possible to use the federal welfare program as an additional party service and weapon. This has been the case. As the welfare system grows, it requires more employees, who are under local control; and the welfare check itself is a powerful weapon in the hands of local politicians who are willing to make an issue of it; in Chicago they are. This is at least part of the explanation of one of the most puzzling aspects of Daley's strength: the overwhelming support of his machine by Chicago's poor blacks, who were served less well by his machine than any other group.

The nature of Chicago's population—of the bosses' constituency—had changed since Cermak's day, as it had in most American cities during this time. Indeed, such change was considerable even during the years of

Daley's mayoralty. And it is testimony to Daley's ability that he was able to keep his machine intact despite such demographic change.

Some indications of Chicago's demographic change between Cermak's day and Daley's appear in Table 5.1, which compares the city's composition in 1930 and 1970. Notable here is the lack of any real change in total

TABLE 5.1
Demographic Characteristics of Chicago Population

	1930	1970
Total population	3,376,438	3,362,947
Percentage foreign born	25	11
Percentage second generation	39	19
Percentage black	7	33
Percentage Polish	12	6
Percentage German	11	3
Percentage Italian	5	3
Percentage Spanish-speaking	——	7
All government workers as percentage of employed over age 16	N.A.	13
Local government workers as percentage of employed over age 16	N.A.	8

Source: Fifteenth and Nineteenth Censuses: *Population.*

city population, but considerable change in the constituent elements of that total. Daley, unlike Cermak, was confronted not so much with an immigrant city as a "minority" one: one-third black (and growing steadily), along with a large Spanish-speaking (mainly Puerto Rican, with measurable Mexican and other components) group as well. The total white foreign stock (immigrants and their children) declined from almost two-thirds of the population in 1930 to less than one-third in 1970.

This decline of the immigrants and their children was important, since we have seen that this group was the crux of the rise of Cermak's Democratic party in Chicago; and was, more basically, the crucible in which the modern political machine was created generally. The group's decline in Chicago reflects two forces. First, with the passage of time, the immigrant generation began to die off, their places taken by the third generation, which is more assimilated and is counted by the census as part of the general white population. And second, there was a great deal of geographic mobility among the first and especially the second generations. In 1898, for example, almost half the Germans and Irish, 60 percent of the Poles, 85 percent of the Italians, and over 70 percent of the Jews, lived within three miles of the center of the city. By 1920 this declined to about 10 percent for Germans and Irish, 38 percent for the Poles, 25 percent for the Italians, and about 30 percent for the Jews. And by 1960, less than ten percent of any of these groups (except the Italians, at 13 percent) lived within three miles of the city center. And for each of the groups, 20 percent or more lived ten or more miles from the center of the city, many outside its corporate limits. This suggests a movement from the center of ethnic organization and ethnic force, and thus, a measure of assimilation.

The city's black population, too, spread widely, partly as a function of the success of some of its members, and partly due to the group's overall great increase in size. Thus, whereas 24 percent of the blacks lived within three miles of the city center in 1920, only 13 percent did in 1960. For most blacks this meant an extension of the ghetto rather than an escape from it, which distinguishes their experience considerably from that of the second- and third-generation whites.

Significantly, 40 percent of the Mexicans and 50 percent of the Puerto Ricans did live in the central ring of the city in 1960, as they, with the remaining blacks, moved into the areas formerly populated by the European immigrants.

The considerable decline in the overall and relative numbers of white European immigrants and their children, and the geographic dispersal of most of those who did remain, created a considerably different problem for Daley than had existed for Cermak. Although he might be able to appeal to many of these people on cultural and economic grounds, the appeal would have to be less direct, and was less controllable. The white ethnic communities were no longer as defined by organizational networks as they had been before. Moreover, Daley would have to deal with blacks as the most important single population group in Chicago, and deal with them during a time of rapid growth and change within the black community. It is for this reason that I shall deal with Daley's politics among the blacks as a separate topic, recognizing its centrality to the success of any Chicago political organization.

Richard Joseph Daley and the Bridgeport neighborhood where he was born, grew up, and lived until his death, were inextricably tied to one another. It is a cold, concrete, very urban neighborhood, quite contained and relatively unchanging. It was largely Irish at the beginning of the twentieth century, and the Irish continued to live there, joined over the course of the years by eastern European immigrants who shared their Roman Catholicism and their provinciality. It is a warm and secure place for those who are part of it, and a forbidding, even dangerous place for those who are not—especially if they seem somehow threatening to its cultural stability. Thus in more recent years it is a white island, surrounded by but entirely immune to the South Side black ghetto.

That Richard J. Daley lived only one block from where he was born was primarily neither political public relations nor fear of loss of supporters; he was simply more comfortable there, in an increasingly alien city. He was born in 1902 to a working-class family (his father was a sheet metal worker), the grandson of Irish immigrants. He was an only child, unusual for Irish Catholics at the time, and thus had relatively greater attention, security, and comfort than most of his class at the time. Indeed, young Richard was almost a bit of a prig, too nicely dressed, too well behaved; but somehow he managed to get along with his peers all the same. Some would say he was born to politics.

He applied himself to his none-too-demanding studies in the local Roman Catholic schools, and to a Roman Catholic commercial high school, acquiring skills that were unusual for a politician. Work as a secretary was not a standard road to bossism, but it was hardly inappropriate, for it put Daley in a position where more than one superior would find him indispensable.

Moreover, he did in some important respects follow the path of other bosses. He was very active in athletics and social activities, becoming a passable softball player and joining the Hamburg Social and Athletic Club —part sports group, part gang, part acculturative vehicle to the adult community. Thus, like Murphy, Thompson, and others, he insinuated himself into, and rose to leadership of, a social organization which gave him the base for entry into elective politics. With his fellow Hamburgers, he seems to have taken part in the 1919 race riot in Chicago; then, as later, opposition to blacks alienated very few voters in Bridgeport.

Daley got his first public job (going on the public payroll was as natural in Bridgeport as going to mass) during the Dever administration in the 1920s, as a clerk at city hall. This was in recognition of his loyal precinct work in Bridgeport, which he continued, while at the same time attending De Paul Law School at night. He was also, in 1924, elected president of the Hamburgers, a position he would hold for fifteen years, and use, as other bosses had before him, as a key to his rise to power.

Daley's biographers have tended to ascribe much of his success to luck, to having been allied to people who made the right choices or who died at the right times. Certainly there is some truth in this. His alderman, "Big Joe" McDonough, decided to ally with Cermak rather than his rivals in the 1920s, which led to McDonough's becoming county treasurer when Cermak was elected mayor in 1931. Daley went along as Big Joe's secretary, but it was Daley's own efforts and talents that made him indispensable to McDonough, and he took good advantage of his opportunity. McDonough was lazy and let Daley virtually run the treasurer's office for him, during which time the latter learned a lot about government and taxes, and about the inner operation of the political system.

Daley held that job until McDonough died in 1934; and with some good fortune—a couple of fortuitous deaths especially—he entered the lower house of the state legislature in 1936. Two years later he moved on to the state senate, where he remained for another eight years, combining loyal service to the Chicago organization with intelligent and competent legislative service for the state. He gave up his senate seat in 1946 to run for the position of Cook County sheriff at the request of party leaders. Here he suffered the only electoral defeat of his career, but even that was not without benefit, since the sheriff's office in Cook County has rarely avoided corruption, and has even more rarely been a springboard to further political success. Moreover, during most of the time he had been in the legislature, he had also served as the appointed comptroller of Cook County, and so in 1946 lost only one of his two public positions and only one of his two public paychecks. And his law firm, which had his name but rarely his presence, produced additional income, with Daley's loyal party service a not inconsiderable factor therein.

Most important for the future, Daley had been careful enough to maintain good relations with almost all Democrats. Thus the dumping of Mayor Kelly and the rise of Arvey to power did not dim his rising star. Indeed, in 1947 he fought a bitter and successful battle to become the Democratic committeeman of his ward, the Eleventh, and thus he became a member of the ruling Cook County Democratic Central Committee. He was now an important and powerful man in Chicago Democratic politics, but still one of many. He had the advantage of being the leader of one of the city's most reliable wards; he had status in the tribal structure of the Catholic Irish; and he had outlived or beaten most of his enemies and made lots of allies. But from there to the party leadership and/or the mayoralty was still a very large step, and it took him almost ten years.

Daley worked well with the Arvey organization, accepted Arvey's slating of Paul Douglas and Adlai Stevenson in 1948, and delivered his ward for the ticket. This led to his appointment by Governor Stevenson, at Arvey's behest, as state revenue director in 1949. His combination of being a loyal party man, a politician of thus-far untarnished reputation, and pretty much of an expert in matters of government and of finance, made him an attractive choice for this post, or any other for that matter, by the end of the 1940s.

His interests were not in Springfield, however, and he quit that job in

1950 to run in a special election for county clerk, the incumbent having died. The clerkship is a fairly high office in Chicago politics, and became even higher in 1950, since Daley won in what was a disastrous year for the local Democrats and for Arvey as their leader. He was now not just an important figure in the party, but one of its city and county leaders. Like Murphy and others before him, he had spent years in cultivating friends and allies, had remained true to them and to his word, and had played the machine's game rather better than most of the other people around.

One of his most productive alliances had been with the black congressman and South Side leader William Dawson, and that relationship was very useful in 1953, when Daley achieved the fruition of a life's labor and became chairman of the Cook County Democratic Central Committee, the most powerful political position in Chicago. It was even more powerful than usual at that time since the incumbent mayor, Kennelly, was pretty much a political outsider, and thus less powerful than his immediate predecessors.

Daley's position as party leader was reinforced by the party's success in 1954. His ally Dan Ryan was elected to the powerful presidency of the County Board, and Daley himself was reelected county clerk. The party was in his hands, and he used this power to achieve the one public office he had been seeking for a long time, the mayoralty. Kennelly wanted a third term, and Benjamin Adamowski—an ambitious and competent politician with very strong Polish support, who had served in the state legislature with Daley—also was a major contender for the office. But Daley had the party, and the central committee voted 49 to 1 in favor of the slate-making committee's recommendation of Chairman Daley. The primary remained, to be sure, but even an incumbent mayor had little chance of a primary victory without formal party support. The organization that Cermak had built and within which Daley had risen to power seemed stronger than any one man, especially if he was as external to it as the incumbent mayor.

The outcome of the primary was interesting. Daley received 49 percent of the vote, Kennelly 35 percent, and Adamowski 16 percent. Daley had a majority in twenty-three of the fifty wards, and a plurality in only four more: either the organization had a ward or it didn't. Daley swept the black vote, and most of the working-class and ethnic wards, often by huge margins; he was strong where the organization was strong. Kennelly had his main strength in the more middle-class areas along the borders of the city; and Adamowski ran strongly mainly among the Poles. (See Table 5.2.)

Daley was not, before 1955, a household word in Chicago. His was one among a small number of well-known political names, but one receiving increasing media coverage from the time he became party chairman. Thus

TABLE 5.2
Daley Vote in Six Mayoral Campaigns, 1955-1975, and 1955 Primary
(Percentages)

Ward	1955	1959	1963	1967	1971	1975	1955 Primary
1	89	87	74	91	81	91	86
2	80	86	84	87	69	86	70
3	76	84	87	89	81	91	87
4	67	84	84	88	77	86	65
5	40	75	76	83	45	60	54
6	62	82	76	82	61	84	67
7	35	61	45	71	64	80	29
8	41	66	54	76	58	85	38
9	44	59	42	67	69	86	38
10	57	70	45	71	74	86	42
11	81	87	72	89	91	95	75
12	58	76	45	70	76	85	30
13	53	66	37	64	71	84	38
14	80	88	59	82	83	88	59
15	56	66	42	67	73	85	39
16	63	79	65	81	73	91	52
17	54	80	76	85	68	86	56
18	51	65	49	72	75	86	38
19	41	60	42	68	69	78	27
20	73	83	82	83	70	87	86
21	70	83	51	70	60	85	57
22	73	79	59	79	81	87	57
23	61	72	32	53	68	80	50
24	92	96	95	94	89	93	78
25	81	91	73	85	87	92	73
26	75	87	69	86	84	90	45
27	88	91	87	95	87	94	86
28	80	78	67	84	74	91	69
29	78	90	87	93	82	93	72
30	59	74	55	75	70	74	49
31	70	85	66	84	88	90	56
32	59	82	54	75	80	85	23
33	46	68	45	65	69	75	25
34	46	67	42	66	69	88	32
35	45	61	34	60	65	69	19
36	46	62	41	68	71	77	26
37	46	65	52	75	74	84	36
38	44	59	35	65	71	73	30
39	42	61	46	71	67	72	36
40	43	71	63	77	61	69	38
41	32	44	27	58	62	69	24
42	64	80	74	82	63	76	78
43	54	74	59	71	49	58	53
44	41	70	56	75	57	70	41
45	43	60	31	58	67	68	41
46	49	69	57	74	60	73	52
47	38	57	43	63	62	63	38
48	43	66	55	70	57	65	41
49	38	69	56	75	58	72	25
50	37	65	60	77	60	75	23
Chicago Total	55	71	56	74	69	75	49

his 1955 primary victory was largely an organizational rather than a personal one. He could take great satisfaction, however, in having been for some time an important member of that organization, to say nothing of now being its public as well as actual leader. He may well not have even dreamed, in 1955, of how long his party leadership, and his holding of mayoral office, would last. But that tenure was based to a considerable degree on his own efforts and success.

Richard J. Daley was the leader of the Cook County Democratic party for twenty-three years and was mayor of the city of Chicago for over twenty. He was not only elected mayor six times, but directed an almost endless series of successful local, state, and national campaigns, wherein Chicago was about as reliably and consistently Democratic as any place in the United States. The deference shown him by presidents and would-be presidents was in no way illogical, and he became a politician of real national power and importance. On the whole, he had operated on the broader sphere just as he did locally, with little concern for issues or much more for individuals—except in the important aspect of supporting those who were loyal to himself—but rather as a partisan leader who equated the success of the organization, the party, with political success generally. If this was the measure of his noninvolvement in the larger matters of the day, it was at the same time the measure of his success and his power.

I want to look at the development of his own campaigns, as a way of focussing on the development of his organization, and on that organization's response to the local issues and concerns of Chicago during his reign. Table 5.2 gives Daley's percentage of the two-party vote in his six mayoral campaigns and the 1955 primary, for Chicago's fifty wards, and the city as a whole.

The first campaign was the most difficult. Daley's primary victory over the not unpopular—and generally considered honest—Mayor Kennelly inevitably led to division within the party and to general charges of "bossism." Kennelly and Adamowski both refused to support their party's nominee, remaining neutral. Other Democrats, especially Assessor Frank Keenan, supported his opponent. And his Republican opponent, Robert E. Merriam, was young, bright, liberal, well connected and well supported, and ran probably the best campaign that Daley ever confronted.

Daley was never an effective speaker, and the presence of television—a force our earlier bosses never had to contend with—did create problems for him. But he had defeated Kennelly, whose television personality was good, and thus had reason to believe that organization was more effective than "presence." Beyond organizational work, Daley campaigned on limited themes, primarily among Democrats only. He told the Democratic women that women should have more public positions, he worked hard among the Poles and other ethnic groups, and he stressed to groups like the International Brotherhood of Electrical Workers that he wanted to keep the "thinking and philosophy of the Democratic Party" in control of Chicago.

When accused of bossism, Daley pledged that he would resign from the party chairmanship if elected, a promise he later simply ignored. And he matched Merriam generally in the vigor and activity of his campaigning. He matched him as well in allegations, responding to Merriam's charges of corruption and a "wide-open city" with his own, indirect, publicity of Merriam's being divorced, or left wing, or being remarried to a part-Negro woman—the particular allegation matched to the neighborhood where it would do the most good.

But the key element was the organization, down to the individual precinct leaders and their canvassing and promising. The organization shepherded voters in to register or to reregister if they were among those who had been purged from the rolls due to Republican bookkeeping and publicity. And the organization marched them to the polls on election day.

Like his famous father in the 'teens and twenties, Merriam railed against political corruption and the lack of law and order which the Democratic machine represented. During March, a large-scale investigation of "ghost voters" was undertaken, amidst much news of vote scandals. The inquiry was directed by County Judge Otto Kerner, who was a party man. The role of organized crime was also publicized, but fairly well neutralized by Daley, when he pledged a series of public hearings on crime if elected.

Most striking was Daley's brilliant triumph over a potentially very dangerous event. Alderman Benjamin M. Becker, the party's candidate for city clerk (mayor, city clerk, and city treasurer run as the only three citywide candidates in mayoralties and are almost always elected together), was cited by the Chicago Bar Association for misconduct (fee-splitting, alleged payoffs, etc.) and had to be dumped. But Daley shrewdly selected Morris B. Sachs, a popular Chicago retailer and television amateur hour sponsor and host, who had run for the position on Kennelly's ticket in the primaries. Moreover, Daley switched his own city treasurer candidate, John C. Marcin, to the clerk's position, so that the respectable Sachs could be slated as treasurer and make the public confident of the proper supervision of its monies.

Given all his problems, Daley's 55 percent of the vote over Merriam was a good showing. He did well in the more interior working-class and ethnic wards, and very well among the blacks. But the conflict with both

Kennelly and Adamowski had hurt, and some work would have to be done before 1959.

Indeed, 1956 made this all the clearer. In this first general election since Daley assumed the mayoralty, the Chicago Democrats did poorly in national and local contests. More disturbing than the reelection of Eisenhower, however, was the election of Adamowski, now a Republican, as state's attorney for Cook County, a position wherein he could oversee, and potentially hurt, the Democratic organization.

But Daley was not idle. Preparations for 1959 had begun on election day 1955. The organization was purged, worked on, tuned to great efficiency. And he began his successful process of winning over the social and economic elite of Chicago with his support of business and his ambitious building program. The construction of O'Hare International Airport, the expressway system, redevelopment of the area around the University of Chicago—signs were omnipresent (each of them emblazoned "Richard J. Daley, Mayor") that the city was vigorous and economically healthy. And during the campaign it was announced that Chicago's property tax assessments were being cut by 8 percent at the same time those in suburban Cook County were rising.

Thus even the *Chicago Tribune* felt in 1959 that his record "deserves respectful consideration"; and the "Nonpartisan Committee for the Reelection of Mayor Daley" and the "All Chicago Committee for Mayor Daley" included such names as William Patterson, president of United Air Lines and member of the board of governors of the United Republican Fund; Clair Roddewig, president of the Association of Western Railroads; Chancellor Lawrence A. Kimpton of the University of Chicago; and many, many more, a veritable Who's Who of Chicago.

Combining this middle- and upper-class support, and money, with the organizational base among the blacks and the white ethnics (he would campaign among the Swedes, Greeks, Italians, and Croatians, among others, and his ticket included one Jew and one Slav), Daley confronted the election—there was no primary contest—with confidence. The Republicans were in disarray, lacking funds and candidates. Timothy Sheehan took the Republican nomination that no one wanted and was beaten by the largest mayoral majority in Chicago history except for Kelly's in 1935: 71 percent to 29. Daley carried forty-nine of the fifty wards, missing only the Forty-first, on the far northwest side; and in all but two wards he did better—usually considerably so—than he had in 1955.

Turnout did decline in 1959; it was 60 percent of those registered, as compared with 69 percent in 1955. (This would continue to be a characteristic of his elections.) But it was a stellar performance by any count; the Daley machine was as deeply insinuated in Chicago politics as any in the city's history.

During his second term Daley became an acknowledged Democratic leader of national importance. And his Irish Catholicism as well as his party allegiance oriented him to Kennedy in 1960. The machine's alleged vote stealing in the 1960 campaign was just Daley's way of not hedging any bets: he wanted to be sure that Illinois went Democratic, and he wanted to remove Adamowski from the state attorney's office. He was successful in both, and the allegations of vote fraud were shrugged off as well, not only by Daley but by his supporters—from lowest class to highest, from the South Side ghetto to the rarified air of North Shore suburbia.

The mayor confronted his third mayoral campaign with equanimity, shattered a bit by the lingering effects of the famous "Burglars in Blue" scandal, which had surfaced during the 1960 election year. A captured burglar, Richard Morrison, became talkative and implicated a number of Summerdale District police officers as his accomplices. This did lead to a great deal of publicity, as well as successful prosecution of Morrison and the accused officers, which lasted through the 1963 mayoralty. Once again, however, Daley was able to turn danger into triumph; he pledged to remove politics from the police department and, after a national search had been conducted, brought in the highly respected Orlando W. Wilson as police commissioner.

Try as they might, Daley's opponents were not able to turn the issue to their advantage. Alderman Leon Despres, the independent-minded representative of the University of Chicago area, writing at the time in the *Nation*, bemoaned both the corruption of Daley's Chicago and the machine's lack of interest in and support of national liberalism. But amidst his many criticisms, Despres acknowledged that "school administration is very good, and the city's finances are handled by a distinguished comptroller, streets are cleaned and repaired, garbage is collected, the water and sewage systems do their job, and assorted public works flourish." What Despres did not say, and apparently did not realize, was that these were the things most Chicago voters were concerned about, not the national and ideological issues that so excited intellectuals.

Adamowski, trying to ride the prestige he had gained as exposer of the police scandal, took the Republican mayoral nomination in 1963. He was well known, now had a reputation for opposition to the machine, and had a good base among Chicago's Poles. But the police issue had been blunted by Daley's response, and it was very difficult to generate much interest in the campaign.

Daley's sources of support were pretty much the same as in 1959, with the exception of the Poles. John C. Marcin, campaigning for reelection as city clerk (and generally claimed by both Czechs and Poles, which made him doubly attractive) stressed in a speech the recognition given ethnic and racial minorities by Daley's Democrats; and Daley personally carried his campaign into the Black Belt, stressing what he had done for the people there. President Kennedy came to Chicago, to speak in Daley's behalf, and to join him in the dedication of O'Hare Airport.

Business-class support continued strong. Daley's man as new president of the County Board had carefully appointed leading business and professional figures (often suburban residents who worked in the city) to various boards and commissions, as had Daley in the city, leading the *Tribune* to applaud the mayor's performance. It would have endorsed him, the paper said, were Chicago politics nonpartisan and unconnected with national parties; instead, it endorsed neither candidate, but did say that Adamowski's "capacity and temperament fall short."

Adamowski, searching for an issue that would reach the front pages, raised the issue of birth control—alleging that Daley favored it. Daley denied this, and also that he had authorized the welfare department to provide birth control devices. It was hard to persuade Catholic Chicagoans that Daley, who attended mass every morning, was anything other than a loyal Catholic. In a last desperate move, Adamowski openly came out against open housing, catering to white fears of black incursions. This Daley could not match, even if he wanted to, for reasons of national Democratic policy; but he equivocated nicely enough, and it was too late for Adamowski anyway.

Daley and his running mates won, but his 56 percent was well below his 1959 performance. Turnout was higher than in 1959, continuing the trend of a negative relationship between size of Daley's percentage and size of turnout. Daley's percentage declined a bit almost everywhere in the city, but his main losses were in some—by no means all—middle-class or Republican areas (e.g., wards Seven and Forty-seven) and among the Poles (e.g., wards Nine, Thirty-three, and Forty-one). That the mayor trailed his running mates for the first and only time suggests that Adamowski's personal appeal to some groups, rather than any general alienation from the machine, was the key.

That the mayor was indeed in good shape became clear four years later, in 1967. It seemed that everyone was for Daley, every newspaper in the city, business and professional groups, ethnic organizations, etc. His opponent, John L. Waner, a businessman of Polish extraction, impressed no one. And even the beginnings of Daley's conflict with Martin Luther King during the 1967 campaign did not slow the momentum.

The mayor led his ticket, reached a new high of 74 percent of the vote, and maintained his overwhelming control of the city council. About 155,000 fewer people voted in 1967 than in 1963, a turnout rate of 64 percent; the machine's supporters were there on election day, and its detractors had been persuaded to stay home.

The machine did suffer the next year, in the violent riots and police violence attendant upon the 1968 Democratic National Convention and the ensuing Democratic defeat at both national and state levels. But the damage can easily be overestimated. Tom Wicker, writing in the *New York Times Magazine* one year later, concluded that "all America [was] radicalized" by the events in Chicago in 1968, and that Humphrey lost the election because he had not stood up to Daley. And it is indeed true that Daley's actions were vicious and insensitive. But the same newspaper's public opinion poll one day after the "police riot" found overwhelming support of the police position. And a Survey Research Center poll two months later found more people saying the police used too little violence (25 percent) than that they used too much (19 percent). Moreover, support for the police increased with the age of the respondent and decreased with educational level—in both cases suggesting that supporters of the Chicago Democratic organization were among those most likely to approve of Daley's position.

That only one important group was critical of the police—the blacks—suggests the greater problem that the machine was confronting: how to reconcile the increasingly conflicting aims of the white ethnics and the blacks of Chicago. This was becoming increasingly urgent in the late 1960s, with issues like open housing, the presence of Martin Luther King in the city, and control of the police. I will look more directly at this problem below.

The resiliency of the machine was clear enough by the 1970 off-year elections, when Daley recouped his 1968 losses and the machine's vote led to a Democratic sweep of county and state offices, sending Adlai Stevenson, Jr., to the United States Senate (thus removing a potentially powerful Daley rival from the local scene). Even the state senate went Democratic for the first time in thirty-seven years. The stage was set for Daley's fifth campaign in 1971.

Richard E. Friedman, former head of the Better Government Association, took the Republican nomination against Daley, but there was little evidence that he had even the support of the kind of people who were active in that association. Once again, every daily newspaper in the city endorsed the mayor. With Daley, on the Democratic ticket, were the now-perennial John C. Marcin for clerk and, for the first time, a black, Joseph Bertrand, for treasurer.

The mayor campaigned vigorously, once more leaving nothing to chance. On the same day he inaugurated construction of a United Steelworkers housing complex he also addressed the Junior Chamber of Commerce, where he was given a plaque as "Chicago's No. 1 Volunteer"; he went on from there to address another middle-class group on pollution and to note in passing that Chicago was the only large American city to have an AA bond rating. He took up the issue of ill treatment in nursing homes, having initiated well-publicized law suits against some of them; and he responded to Friedman's taunts about his income with just enough information (his federal 1040 form) to blunt the issue.

Holding the entire coalition together was not too easy, however. At a Polish Democratic meeting the mayor was praised for his opposition to public housing in white neighborhoods, as well as for his famous "shoot to kill" order during the 1968 riots. His remarks ignored both elements for praise; although they were central to his white working-class support, they were dangerous to black support. And he closed his campaign speaking to union and black audiences, focussing on more neutral topics: no one important was against unions, not even his upper-class supporters. But the rift between black and white was becoming increasingly disturbing.

Nonetheless the mayor carried forty-eight of the fifty wards in 1971 (two less than in 1967), and 70 percent of the vote. He led his ticket once again, but did it with the lowest turnout in thirty-six years. It could be argued that this apathy was a two-edged sword, signifying a steady erosion of the organization's base. But that could not be proved until some opposition organization found a way to involve nonvoters.

This was even clearer in 1975, when Daley won his unprecedented sixth term (and the only other five-term winners, Carter H. Harrison I and II, were mayors when the terms were for only two years). Daley's margin of 75 percent was his highest, but it was based on the lowest total vote in over fifty years and probably the lowest turnout rate in the city's history.

Daley ran this campaign amidst a number of real difficulties. For the first time in his career, his health was an important issue. Moreover, new police corruption, and corruption among some of his oldest and strongest allies in politics, hurt him. Even the *Chicago Tribune* and other papers that had become the mayor's most consistent supporters refused to endorse him, although this did not lead to endorsement of his opponent, Republican alderman John J. Hoellen.

The best appraisal of the campaign came from Hoellen himself, who said after the election that "It's hard to be a Republican in Chicago." It is indeed, because the declining base of the Daley organization, as seen in turnout rates, had simply increased the number of nonvoters and had redounded to the advantage of no other party or organization. As Table 5.2 shows, Daley carried every ward in the city in 1975, with no less than 60 percent anywhere, and over 90 percent in eleven (the machine-reliable black and ethnic wards).

Some additional light on this amazingly consistent success can be sought in Table 5.3, which gives the correlation coefficients for the Daley elections. What the table suggests, first, is an overall strong correlation among Daley elections; the sources of his support—and of the organization's support—remained essentially consistent over twenty years. This is as we should expect from our understanding of the development of the Democratic machine and its coalition. This is the crucial factor behind the enduring strength of any political organization, and it was the chief reason for the strength of the Daley machine.

TABLE 5.3
Correlation Coefficients (Pearson's *r*) for Daley Elections,
1955-1975

	1955	1959	1963	1967	1971	1975	Primary 1955
1955	———	.898	.700	.731	.728	.740	.838
1959		———	.842	.840	.565	.636	.795
1963			———	.952	.337	.456	.818
1967				———	.478	.573	.766
1971					———	.813	.412
1975						———	.512
1955 Primary							———

Beyond this, however, there are some interesting variations in the table. Particularly, the last two elections (1971 and 1975) relate less strongly to the earlier heights of Daley's strength in 1959, 1963, and 1967. Their relationships are still significant, but less strong; and, interestingly, they are stronger in relation to the first election (1955), when the party was divided over the dumping of Kennelly and there was a primary contest, than in relation to the subsequent elections. Moreover, 1971 and 1975 show a considerable dropoff in strength in relation to Daley's vote in the 1955 primary.

Some of this is simply the result of time and of changing population in the wards that are my basic units of analysis. The statistic is a function of the movement of each ward in the percentage Democratic relative to all other wards. Thus population changes that resulted in a ward's becoming either more or less Democratic would lower the correlation over time.

Beyond this, however, it is worth asking if there is any substance in the declining level of association seen for 1971 and 1975. For this purpose, we can isolate some distinct types of wards, representing specific population types, to see if there has been any considerable falloff in Democratic vote among them.

In Table 5.4 I have selected three groups of wards and merged their vote (the mean of the percentage Democratic of the several wards in each group) for an overall measure of Democratic voting for blacks, foreign-stock working-class whites, and middle-class whites. And the question, once raised, appears to be answered in the negative. The black vote had

TABLE 5.4
Daley Vote among Selected Groups,
1955–1975 (Percentages)

	Blacks	Foreign stock, working-class white	Middle-class white
1955	82	54	38
1959	89	73	57
1963	88	51	39
1967	91	72	66
1971	80	75	64
1975	91	84	74
1955 Primary	77	38	26

Source: as in Table 5.2 Figures are mean of percentage Democratic for selected wards: blacks, Wards Two, Three, Twenty-four, Twenty-nine; foreign stock working-class white, Wards Thirty-one, Thirty-three, Thirty-four; middle-class white, Wards Thirty-eight, Forty-one, Forty-nine.

remained consistently high (the falloff in 1971 will be considered below), and the working-class and middle-class white vote had both increased quite steadily (the 1963 falloff being explained by the attractiveness of Adamowski to Polish voters). Thus the lower rate of association for the 1971 and 1975 elections in Table 5.3 does seem to have resulted not from a declining party base, but simply from gradual population change, which had led to modest changes in the relative positions of the various wards.

Our table of coefficients, therefore, has suggested the consistency behind the enduring strength of the Daley organization. It has not, conversely, given any evidence of important change in that support over the twenty years of Daley's leadership. More significant in this regard is the declining turnout rate that Daley experienced; this was across the board and did not undercut the Democrats' position.

Richard J. Daley, like William Hale Thompson, bossed Chicago in part because of his ability to hold onto the black vote. Behind this gross similarity, however, there are also differences. Thompson, as a renegade Republican who never controlled all of his party, needed the largely Republican blacks as his major factional support. Daley, on the other hand, a Democrat presiding over a united party, confronted a rapidly growing black population that had been turned Democratic by his predecessors.

With a black population of over one-third of Chicago's total population, one that had undergone important new pressures and leadership since the 1960s, the problem of the local Democratic organization was to avoid losing the political loyalties of this group to any of several alternatives. And as the late 1960s witnessed increasing tension between the major constituents of the Democratic coalition—the blacks and the immigrants and their children—while independent black leaders rose to contest the machine, it was not easy. But the Daley organization did hold onto the overwhelming majority of the black vote. It is therefore worthwhile to look at this aspect of his power more closely.

The shift of the previously overwhelmingly Republican black vote to the Democrats took place in the late 1930s, a result of the organizational drive begun by Cermak and continued by Kelly and Nash, plus the national policy and politics of the New Deal. The shift was also seen in, and to some extent led by, the new generation of black politicians rising at the time. Some, like William Dawson, anticipated the trend and jumped parties just in time to be part of the new movement; others first entered politics in the 1930s and 1940s, when the future was already quite clear. The Democratic organization saw the increasingly important role blacks were going to play numerically, and did work to create a viable organization in the black wards.

Because of the relative poverty and the lack of sophistication of the rising number of blacks in the city, they were susceptible to traditional machine methods of attraction and needed the services which the organization could provide. New Deal welfare programs did not, as I have already suggested, change this, since local government intervened.

Moreover, the Democrats were, by the 1930s, a good deal more responsive to blacks, both nationally and locally, and began to give them an increasing share of nominations and appointments—never proportionately as many as they gave to most other groups, but nonetheless more than the Republicans gave. And those at the bottom of the socioeconomic ladder are most needful of the party in power, so that the blacks and black leaders needed the Democratic organization as much as the organization needed them.

The question was, as the black population of Chicago increased from about 7 percent of the population in 1930 to a third of it under Daley, whether or not there would be anything like equivalent growth in their political and economic power. And the answer is, no—with effects we will look at in Chapter 6.

I want to look first at some of the sources of black support for the Daley organization and then at some of the problems which arose in that support. The most important of those strengths is partisan—the Daley organization is the local Democratic party, and to the extent that party loyalties extend across national, state, and local lines, this was a consistent reason for black loyalty to Daley. Certainly at the national level the Republicans offered little reason for blacks to desert their Democratic loyalties. And, apart from any particular reasons of policy, the very weakness of the local Republicans, and of local third parties, had the same effect.

At the start, Daley's cultivation of Congressman Dawson was very important, since the latter was by far the most important political leader in the old South Side Black Belt and the rapidly expanding West Side ghetto as well. As the *Chicago Defender* pointed out in 1955, the black vote was the key to Daley's primary victory. It was also a Dawson success, both in Daley's victory, and in that of Dawson's own man, Ralph Metcalfe, over incumbent alderman Archibald Carey in the Third Ward. This election also saw the number of black aldermen increase from three to four.

By 1959 the *Defender* could argue that Daley was the best mayor Chicago had ever had, lauding him for his concern with racial problems as well as his general leadership of the city. Daley's opponent, Sheehan, was criticized for being a typical Republican, failing to commit himself on issues of integration. This suggests, again, that however inadequate the Daley machine was in meeting the needs of black people, it was nonetheless better than its opponents. Voters can, realistically, choose only between real options, not ideal ones.

In the 1963 and 1967 elections, black support remained very high at all levels. The *Defender* consistently pictured Daley as an outstanding leader who really sympathized with black problems. The local and national Democratic party's alliance with organized labor was also useful in getting consistent support from groups like the Joint Council of Negro Trade Unionists. And black business groups responded like their white counterparts in supporting the most "building" mayor in the city's history.

The organization was slowly but steadily responsive to questions of black representation. The number of black aldermen increased (to 14, by 1971). In 1971 a black was slated for citywide office (treasurer), the first time in history. The *Defender* in that year noted the large number of black judges, officeholders, and administrators that had come into being under Daley. Black ministers also supported him strongly in 1971, despite the rising conflict over civil rights that had marked his fourth term.

Thus the Daley organization was sufficiently responsive to black social, political, and economic ambitions to forestall its being undercut by Republican or black rivals. It was a minimal approach, but a successful one. In 1975, for example, when a "Committee to Elect a Black Mayor" fell apart, the *Defender* noted with only moderate regret that "the time is not feasible for the election of a Black Mayor." Moreover, the paper said, despite his inadequacy on police control and housing discrimination, Daley "has done a creditable job of running the city," and deserved reelection. This was not only the point of view of the black middle class, but also of the black politicians, and it explains the continuation through his sixth term of Daley's hold on black voters.

If we look more carefully at some of the conflicts which Daley had with the blacks of Chicago, we may at the same time see further indications of the extent and consistency of his success. Such conflict did exist, as was perhaps inevitable, given the tremendous changes that took place among American blacks during the years that Daley was mayor.

In Chicago those conflicts revolved around two major problems: First, the question of whether or not the Daley machine was sufficiently responsive to the political, economic, and racial desires of the city's black population. And second, the question of power—not so much the substance of rule, but its form, the hands which were to control the destiny of the city generally and its black areas specifically. Both of these questions were divisive, but the latter related most directly to the survival of the machine itself.

One early source of conflict came from the rapid increase in size of the black community and its geographic spread, which led to a more rapid increase in the number of black wards and precincts than in that of black ward and precinct leaders and aldermen. The Seventeenth Ward on the South Side, for example, had been about 50 percent black in 1959 but rose to 90 percent by 1963. The machine supported its incumbent white alderman, despite some organized black insistence that a black man replace him. And Charles Chew, a black with support from a number of black leaders, entered the 1963 primary as an Independent Democrat and defeated the white incumbent.

Chew supported Daley's reelection in 1963 but remained somewhat outside the organization and a potential source of opposition for a while. Moreover, Daley did not really learn much from the event. True, the number of blacks slated did increase slowly—but too slowly. More important, when Daley sensed a conflict between what working-class whites wanted and what blacks wanted, he would generally choose the former.

The situation shortly became more serious. By the mid-1960s disputes over school segregation and inferior black schools were more and more frequent. In 1964 a famous conflict developed when a couple of young blacks moved down the street from Daley's home; this led to riots and counterdemonstrations for which the mayor hardly concealed his support. The next two years saw Martin Luther King come to Chicago, leading marches and protests, rent strikes, and other formal opposition to the status quo. Daley prevailed, because Chicago segregation was extralegal and time was then on the mayor's side. But it was not a complete victory. He was correct in seeing that too great compliance with black wishes would alienate his white supporters (the National Guard had been needed at one point in 1966), and that the only real threat was the one at the polls. But he was not right in underestimating the depth of the issues and the extent to which they might become irreconcilable. Daley, however, was motivated first by his striving for political power and second by his provincial Irish Catholicism, which led him to a dislike of blacks and lack of sympathy with their goals. If he had to choose, he would choose his own people every time.

That most black politicians, as practical as Daley in their orientation, remained with the organization, was a key factor. The black community could have been led away from the machine in the mid-1960s, but the leadership to do so did not appear. Thus in 1967 only one black, A. A. Rayner, was able to defeat the organization's choice for alderman, in this case in the Sixth Ward. It is noteworthy that both the Sixth Ward and the Seventeenth, where Chew had been successful, were relatively more middle-class black wards, where feelings of group awareness and of deprivation were more likely to exist.

And Daley's 1967 campaign for reelection was as successful among blacks as among the rest of the people. He bent far enough in response to black demands to confuse his opposition in that community; but never so far as to alienate his white working-class supporters. His vote in black wards remained tremendous, and about as much so in the more middle-class ones (e.g., the Sixth, Seventh, and Seventeenth—see Table 5.2) and working-class ones (e.g., Twenty and Five) as in the very poor (Two, Three, and Twenty-four).

In April 1968, as a result of the assassination of Martin Luther King, Chicago experienced violent riots, leading to Daley's famous order to "shoot to kill any arsonist or anyone with a molotov cocktail in his hand because they are potential murderers, and . . . to shoot to maim or cripple anyone looting any stores in our city." His strong reaction to the riots was condemned by black leaders and the liberal press, but widely supported by working class people in Chicago. The gap was becoming clearer.

This approach was reified in Daley's response to the young radicals and the police riot later that year during the Democratic National Convention.

But, as we have already seen, his actions were by no means unwelcome to most white Chicagoans. The City was becoming increasingly polarized, on a basis that was by no means readily reconcilable. Daley would proceed on the logic of his political sagacity and his ethnic provincialism, to the satisfaction of no one group—and to the clear disadvantage of Chicago's blacks. But perhaps this was also about as well as anyone could do.

In one of the few perceptive things ever written on Daley, David Halberstam noted in *Harper's* shortly before the 1968 Democratic convention that the city's blacks were still very weak; their representation in government and finance, for example, was still proportionately much lower than that of any other group. (Moreover, the machine had somehow been able to separate black politicians from their group, a most unusual but crucial development.) Daley's problem was not simply political, but also ideological: he had, Halberstam argued, a rather old fashioned Roman Catholic sense of "individual sin" but no modern sense of "social sin." And he remained a Bridgeport provincial; as one black interviewee put it: "I think one of the real problems he has with Negroes is understanding that the Irish are no longer the out-ethnic group."

All this was true. Daley was provincial, insensitive, and unsympathetic to the plight of urban blacks. What he gave them he gave them for political reasons; and his lack of sympathy and sensitivity made him less of a leader than he might have been. But the defense of expediency is also a real one. Had Daley really tried to deal with black problems, there is good reason to argue that he would have lost not only much of his white ethnic support but his upper-class business support as well. It was a risk he was surely not willing to take.

Some blacks and many white liberals continued critical of the mayor during his fourth term. Even the generally supportive *Defender* noted during the 1971 campaign that there was more criticism of him in the black community than ever before. He had refused to cooperate with the more independent and assertive black organizations like Operation Breadbasket and its controversial leader, Jesse Jackson. His housing plans were widely condemned as political and not really addressed to the problems of segregation. The Independent Voters of Illinois condemned him as "a flagrantly racist mayor," which was an exercise in liberal verbosity: few blacks belonged to the IVI or listened to it. And Jesse Jackson finally decided against a write-in campaign for himself, urging instead that blacks vote for Republican Friedman.

This long-term tension was not without some cumulative effect. Daley's vote did decline in black Chicago in 1971, although a black man was running on the citywide ticket. And the decline was evident in black wards at every socioeconomic and machine-controlled level. The Second Ward, the heart of the old Black Belt and of Dawson's organization, declined in Democratic voting by 21 percentage points from 1967 levels; and the Seventeenth fell off by only one point less. Of the thirteen wards that might be considered black in 1971 (Wards 2, 3, 4, 5, 6, 7, 15, 17, 20, 22, 24, 27, and 29), all but two showed declines in the Democratic vote for mayor. On the other hand, all but one of these wards (the Fifth, influenced also by a large, liberal, University of Chicago vote) did go Democratic, and with majorities of 60 to 89 percent. Thus if we can argue that the events of the 1960s did lead to a gradual undercutting of the organization's black support, we must also realize that this was only partial. It suggests a basic problem that Daley did have by the end of the 1960s, but not a problem that was in any way overwhelming at the time.

The dropoff turned out to be temporary. The organization's black support in Daley's 1975 campaign was as high as it had ever been; all the black wards went Democratic, by margins that were much higher than those of 1971, and in more than half of them even higher than in 1967. But turnout continued to decline. Daley was strong among steadily declining numbers of blacks, and this was ominous, even if not so perceived at the time.

Daley had confronted a primary contest in 1975, wherein he was challenged by both a black state senator, Richard Newhouse, and a white liberal, Alderman William Singer. Citywide, the challenge was not significant, but in the seventeen largely black wards there were indications of some continuation of black opposition. Daley received 48 percent of the primary vote in those seventeen wards, Newhouse and Singer together the other 52 percent. Variation was considerable from the poorer and more machine-dependent to the more middle-class and independent. Thus Daley won 58 percent of the vote of the West Side's Twenty-fourth Ward, and 55 percent in South Side Ward Three; but he held only 49 percent in the increasingly independent Second, and 44 percent in the more middle-class Ward Six.

This discrepancy between a real primary challenge for the first time since 1955 and an overwhelming general election victory points to the continuing importance of state and national politics. The Daley machine, after all, was part of the national Democratic party, which was always a major source of its strength. And its relationship to blacks was always tempered by the fact that third parties are notoriously unsuccessful in the United States, especially in a city like Chicago, where the party serves so many purposes. The conflicts seen in 1971 did not disappear in 1975, then, but were focussed in the primary, and after that the general appeal of the Democratic party and the obviousness of Daley's impending victory neutralized the opposition.

But the relationship between Daley's Democratic organization and the blacks, however strong it was, continued to be tenuous. The problem was not so much the relative insensitivity of Daley and the other Irish rulers of Chicago's politics, but rather the quite real conflicts of interest between constituent elements of the Chicago Democratic coalition. Successful majority voting coalitions have always consisted to some degree of mutually conflicting interests; the difference here is one of degree, but of a very great degree.

For the Democratic organization created by Cermak and honed by Daley to persist into the 1980s, it would have to find a way to pacify black demands (including, most probably, a black mayor) while holding onto white working-class support and white business support, which have been equally important to its previous success. This would not be easy.

In considering how, precisely, Daley managed to maintain the Democratic organization in a form and strength relatively unchanged from the time of Cermak, it is important to look directly at his strategy and his tactics. In the process, I shall try to deal with the argument about the "decline of 'bossism.' "

In a 1956 article in the *New York Times Magazine*, Cabell Phillips wrote that new Mayor Daley was "a reformer at heart rather than a boss." He offered no particular proof of this, but had to say it because the thrust of his article was that the old-time boss had disappeared: the decline of patronage, the rise of public welfare, the presence of organized labor, and a more educated and aware electorate—all had contributed to this development. Phillips rather asserted these "facts," treating them as almost common knowledge, than demonstrated them. It was part of his conviction that "American voters . . . have matured to the point where they have taken their political destinies into their own hands."

It was a very wrong-headed approach, not least for its assumption that boss politics was a politics of immaturity, wherein the voters were not choosing objectively from among the alternatives available to them. We might profitably compare the comments, a few years earlier, of a Chicago precinct captain to two scholars investigating urban politics:

I am a lawyer and a prosecuting attorney for the City. I have spent 19 years in precinct work. . . .
I try to establish a relationship of personal obligation with my people, playing cards, talking, and helping them with their problems. . . .
Actually I consider myself a social worker for my precinct. I help my people get relief and driveway permits. I help them on unfair parking fines and property assessments. The last is most effective in my neighborhood [middle class].

The only return I ask is that they register and vote. If they have their own opinions on certain top offices, I just ask them to vote my way on lower offices where they usually have no preferences anyway.

I never take leaflets or mention issues or conduct rallies in my precinct. After all, this is a question of personal friendship between me and my neighbors. . . .

I can control my primary vote for sure because I can make the party regulars come out. I don't encourage a high vote here, just a sure vote. In the general election there is much more independent voting, and I can't be sure of control.

It is instructive to compare this precinct captain's role and that of George Washington Plunkitt in Tammany's New York in the late nineteenth century. There are differences, to be sure; both the politician and his public are more secure, more sophisticated, more aware. But their relationship remained essentially the same, and the basis of that relationship in the local political arena remained the same. The nature of the party's support had not changed essentially, despite the New Deal, the AFL, and the creation of a massive middle class. And this suggests not that Phillips's generalizations about Daley and Chicago were overoptimistic, because what is good or bad in urban politics is arguable; rather, it suggests how wrong Phillips was, and others after him.

What kept Daley and his organization in power was essentially the natural conservatism of the professional politician—his reluctance to change anything he does not have to change. And the Daley organization of the 1970s was as much like the Cermak organization of the 1930s as it could possibly be. Moreover, Daley, as the boss, was as much like Cermak as he could possibly be. This was the measure of his strength; perhaps in the future it will be considered the measure of his, or his successors', weakness.

I noted at the start of this chapter the continuing role of patronage in the Chicago Democratic organization. More and more of these jobs are other than unskilled labor—as in the case of the above precinct worker whose patronage job is as public prosecutor—but that makes their effect no different. Sophisticated and educated people need jobs as badly as others, and they do not always find the process of getting a job any easier. So the tens of thousands of jobs at all levels which the machine has access to directly or indirectly continue to produce loyal party workers and loyal voters.

Daley always understood the centrality of patronage to party strength and single-mindedly sought to maintain it. Thus he successfully avoided some of the most threatening aspects of the civil service laws, sometimes by such powerful devices as not scheduling examinations for long periods, or making them hard to find, or hiring "temporary" employees (who are exempt from civil service regulations) on a permanent basis. It was one of the reasons, also, why he opposed aspects of the civil rights movement— less because of the threatened rise of black people than the danger the movement implied for party control.

Likewise, with a sort of reverse patronage, he was loyal to those he appointed. People were kept in their jobs as long as there was no scandal associated with their tenure; competence was rarely insisted upon. He also remembered their names and maintained some personal contact. And like other successful bosses before him, he was loyal to his friends so long as they remained loyal to him. (The number of Bridgeport people in city government is very great indeed.) Old Hamburg Club pal Robert Quinn was made fire commissioner despite obvious questions of his competence; and the mayor never had a more loyal political supporter.

The mayor was aided by the nature of his own ambitions: he sought power, not wealth. Thus his own political career was untouched by personal scandal. At the same time, like Murphy and others, he did not expect other people to maintain a similar probity. So long as they avoided scandal and did not hurt the party, they were free to make some money for themsevles. He supported county treasurer Herbert Paschen for governor until scandal attached to Paschen's use of discretionary funds became well known, and then Daley dumped him. As forgiving as he could be, he could also be apoplectic when a machine politician engaged in actions that threatened the party.

Daley was always a party man, by conviction and by practical logic. And as he used appointive patronage, he also used nominations to office. Ethnic representation continued to be basic; and if blacks, for example, did not have the proportion of representation that the Poles or Irish had, theirs nonetheless steadily increased—enough to avert major defections from the party. Within the party Daley exhibited a real knack for co-opting or otherwise undercutting his opposition. Thus in 1955 he turned scandal to advantage when he added Morris B. Sachs to his ticket. And in 1970, when Senator Dirksen died, Daley was able to persuade State Treasurer Adlai Stevenson, Jr., to run for Dirksen's seat, thus slating an attractive and eventually successful Democrat for the previously Republican senatorship and removing from local affairs one of the mayor's potentially most powerful opponents. Daley used his control of the slating committee well, moving more reliable candidates to more powerful positions, and less reliable ones to positions that might have civic power but were always politically less threatening.

It is control of the party that was most important. In 1955 he reneged on his pledge to resign as party chairman if elected mayor; it was logical that he do so. It was through his control of the party, not his elective office, that he gained complete control of the city council—always having at least forty of the fifty votes, sometimes more. Thus the mayor, not the council, decided the budget; the mayor, not the council, really decided on the legislation that ran the city.

Likewise, his control was extended to the Cook County Board via his party chairmanship (he was head of the *county* Democratic party), giving him control as well over the great budget and power that county commissioners command. So long as the Democratic party was successful at the polls, the mayor ruled; thus success at the polls was crucial.

The primary, on the other hand, was not. Since the party slate-making committee did recommend candidates for the primaries, those candidates started out with such an edge that it was extremely difficult for other Democrats to beat them. And it has been very rarely—for offices ranging from ward level to national—that a Chicago candidate other than the duly designated one has received a Democratic nomination. This obviously made it illogical for any aspiring Democratic politician in Cook County not to make his peace with Chairman Daley.

Party unity, moreover, was a universal watchword to Daley. He made his peace with downstate Democrats, controlling what he could, giving in when he had to. And he was ever loyal to the national party as well. Kennedy's election was indeed due in no small part to Mayor Daley, not so much for the votes he may have stolen as for the 89 percent turnout he delivered. The mayor worked for Humphrey in 1968, although he didn't like him; and even after his delegates had been unseated in the 1972 Democratic National Convention (a cruel blow to one who understandably saw himself as one of the party's greatest stalwarts), he worked for McGovern, whom he detested. Chicago went Democratic in 1968 and again in 1972. Small wonder, then, that Daley insisted on party loyalty from those under him; he did practice what he preached. And he could be vicious indeed to those who failed to follow this cardinal rule of politics.

His great power in Chicago also gave him a margin of control over the local Republican party as well. Illinois law favors partisanship: until 1980 the state assembly districts, for example, each had three representatives, and each voter had three votes to distribute. Thus an accommodation had often existed when the party in power had slated two candidates and the party out of power one: a little gravy for everyone. Moreover, the Democrats in power generally allotted some patronage to the Republicans, to keep the party alive and a bit dependent. This was not without advantage: in 1961, for example, although the Illinois House had a Republican majority of one, it elected a Democratic speaker, because of Daley's ability to wheel and deal with Chicago Republicans. Thus the local Republican party, weak as it has been, has been generally resistant to major legal changes in the party system.

Daley's political acumen was perhaps nowhere better demonstrated than in his ability to turn adversity into advantage. He not only over-came major scandals and other challenges to his control, but very often turned them around so that he emerged the hero of the piece. This was seen as early as the 1955 campaign, when he did not really suffer for having placed Becker on his ticket; rather, he was generally praised for having replaced Becker with Sachs. Likewise, in the famous "burglars in blue" scandal in 1960, Daley was able to emerge as the "reformer" who removed the police department from politics (temporarily) and defended the inde-pendence of the new police commissioner, O. W. Wilson. He was similarly lauded for freeing the city's welfare department from politics—a develop-ment, like that in the police department, that did not really happen: the welfare check remained under some machine control, as did the police department once Wilson was gone.

Probably the foremost demonstration of this phenomenon, however, can be seen in his sixth election (1975), because here, for the first time, scandal reached right into his inner organization. Indeed, the fifth term had seen numerous troubles, not least of them Daley's first serious extended illnesses in his public career: some wondered whether the mayor, now over seventy, could still handle the job. The years 1971–74 had given him sufficient reason to be ill.

In December 1971, Otto Kerner (at the time a judge on the U.S. Court of Appeals; former governor of Illinois, chairman of the National Advisory Commission on Civil Disorders; son-in-law of Tony Cermak; and shining light of respectability in the Chicago machine) was indicted; in February 1973 he was found guilty; and in July 1974 went to prison for tax evasion and perjury charges arising from his allegedly having profited from his position as governor in collusion with racetrack interests. In September 1972, County Clerk Edward J. Barrett, an institution of sorts in the ma-chine and local politics, was indicted on charges of soliciting a $187,000 bribe for the purchase of voting machines; he was convicted in March 1973. New police scandals emerged in the fall of that year; the "depoliticization" of the department had indeed been temporary. Matthew Danaher, Daley's neighbor and closest confidant, whose job was circuit court clerk, was in-dicted in April 1974 on charges resulting from a $400,000 real estate scheme. One month later, Daley's floor leader in the city council and very close associate and personal friend, Thomas E. Keane, was indicted for conspiracy and mail fraud, also over questionable real estate transactions; he was convicted in October. The mayor's long-term press secretary, Earl

Bush, was also forced to resign under conflict of interest charges, which came to trial in 1974. And similar charges even came against the mayor's own family: his son was charged with having received favorable treatment in selling insurance to the city.

Scandal and corruption had been alleged and proved among his closest political friends and aids—in his personal political family, as it were. Never had scandal gotten so close to Daley before. Moreover, there was an attractive first-term Democratic governor, Daniel Walker, who had defeated Daley's own candidate in the 1972 primary (a most unusual circumstance) and who continued openly to oppose him. Alderman William Singer, who had played a role in unseating the Daley delegates at the 1972 Democratic National Convention, announced his plans to contest the mayor in the 1975 primary. Daley had two strokes in 1974; small wonder.

Yet, as we have seen, Daley beat Singer, and Newhouse, in the 1975 primary; and he slaughtered Republican Hoellen in the general election. The charges of corruption never touched him personally, though a great deal of energy was expended trying to make them do so. What he could not turn to his advantage he managed to override, or ride out. His control of the party, and the party's support by the electorate, overcame probably the greatest challenge he had faced since 1955.

One thing he could bank on in 1975, which I have already noted as being central to his control, and new to "bossism," was his large-scale business leadership support. He had wooed the business community from the start, in his great building program, in getting Democratic national conventions in 1956 and 1968, in providing good police protection for private property, and in fostering an overall environment conducive to economic growth. The contractors, the banks, the downtown businesses, were pleased—not only economically, but also in terms of their sense of civic responsibility: the city appeared clean, its books were balanced, its credit rating was good, and the number of nonpolitical special commissions was legion. And this Chicago Democratic mayor was applauded and supported by the city's four essentially Republican newspapers as no Democrat had ever been before. When Richard Friedman, of the Better Government Association, ran against him in 1971, he had found almost all of his associates on the other side.

Daley worked hard to maintain this element of support; it seemed that he had an emotional need for it as well as a political one. At times, this required that he ride roughshod over more traditional Democratic supporters, as when he chose a central location for the new campus of the University of Illinois, which required the destruction of an old, well-established inner-city community and of the venerable Hull House as well. But the urban Italians, however much they protested, did not seem all that likely to bolt the party; and in the final analysis, they did not. Other kinds of urban renewal likewise displaced the urban poor, but the political effects of all this were on balance beneficial to the machine. Not only did the business community, the upper class, and "society" applaud him and support him; not only did the industrialists and retailers and union presidents to whom he deferred, defer back to him in response; but the building and the contracts also greatly increased the patronage—via private jobs—available to the machine. Sometimes, indeed, it could provide jobs to the very people the projects were displacing. It is a complicated business to evaluate; but it was a key aspect of a political machine that was still strong when Daley died in 1976.

The resemblance between Tweed—or better, Murphy—and Daley is striking, and will be developed somewhat further in the Epilogue. The basic goals and means of urban machines have remained pretty much the same. In Daley's case, one can say in his defense that the boss was out in the public eye; his positions and leadership were known and subjected to the plebiscitary scrutiny of the electorate time and again. And on at least six occasions, the people of Chicago declared quite decisively that, given the alternatives, they would willingly accept this boss and this machine to direct their city.

6

BLACK CITIES,
WHITE MACHINES

In the immediate aftermath of Richard J. Daley's death in December 1976, it appeared that the machine continued in control. Even though Daley had made most major decisions himself and had not designated a successor, the excellence of the machine's organization created an inertial force for stability. It was a brief period of stability, however, for reasons comparable to those operating in many American cities at the time. We will probe these reasons in some detail, as a case study of the effects of black population dominance and political maturity.

The almost inevitable challenge came—ominously, from a black—in a time of some confusion and in a city whose politics was always shrouded by legal and constitutional ambiguity. Alderman Wilson Frost argued that his position as president pro tem of the city council made him the interim mayor. It was an exciting challenge, but a futile one. Frost had been given his position as a racial sop at a time when the mayor ruled and official leadership of the council meant little. Machine leaders and the city's Corporation Counsel disabused him of the notion, undoing both his try for the mayoralty and his council leadership position.

The city council, under full machine dominance, made Alderman Michael Bilandic, from Daley's home Eleventh Ward, the acting mayor, pending a special election. And Alderman Edward Vrdolyak replaced Frost as president pro tem. The machine's strength was seen also in the transition of the chairmanship of the Cook County Democratic Central Committee, the other post that had cemented Daley's power. County Board president George W. Dunne's elevation to the job was an organization choice of an organization man.

Bilandic was a Croatian-American, the first non-Irish mayor since

Cermak, and as such a kind of compromise. The Poles and the blacks both wanted the job and would have felt ignored, particularly if another Irishman had gotten it. So their discontent, which was patent, was muted to some degree, while the Irish still controlled the party.

The organization remained in control, Bilandic having promised that he would not be a candiate in the 1977 special election. Moreover, it was the city council, led by people like Vrdolyak and Edward Burke, rather than the mayor, that now shared political control with the party chairman.

Thus, when Bilandic changed his mind and decided to run for the remaining two years of Daley's term in the spring election, this was not really a threat to the machine. The machine supported him, since he was reliable and, it appeared, controllable. Moreover, Bilandic was a compromise, ethnically speaking, in an increasingly charged post-Daley atmosphere. Alderman Roman Pucinski, a machine man, entered the primary as a Polish alternative—dangerous only in that he was bucking the decision of his own organization. And the specter of black opposition also became concrete, in the person of State Senator Harold Washington.

Black groups had been working since Daley's death on the possibility of making their first real try for power. They were not united, however, and Washington was a controversial, largely self-promoted choice, not least because of a 1972 conviction for not filing income tax returns. The confusion among blacks was seen in Washington's first entering the campaign, then dropping out, and finally entering once again. Other blacks flirted with the idea or were flirted with by various black organizations. And while some influential black groups, like Jesse Jackson's Operation Push, ultimately supported Washington, there was by no means unanimity among the Chicago black power structure on the wisdom of this candidate and this year for their quest for power.

Bilandic won easily enough, sharing the white vote with Pucinski and defeating Washington handily among blacks. He was also way ahead among the city's increasing number of Hispanic voters. However, as in the last few Daley elections, the machine's strength here can easily be overestimated, since what Bilandic received was a large majority from a relatively small number of voters. Over 70 percent of blacks and Hispanics of voting age did not vote in the 1977 mayoralty; the time bomb of black political power was still there, but it had not yet found the fuse of group organization and popular enthusiasm that would get it ticking.

Michael Bilandic, and the machine that carefully watched him, were presiding over a city very different from that which had elected Tony Cermak in 1931 and Richard Daley in 1955. Its population was now almost 40 percent black and 12 percent Hisplanic. If any movement among blacks could overcome the traditional problem of low black registration and turnout, it would be in a position to frustrate the machine for the first time since it had arisen under Cermak in the 1920s. The cruciality of black support to the machine by the 1970s made this obvious, and it would probably have emerged in any event, but the confused politics of the mayoralties of Bilandic and his successor accelerated the process.

Bilandic's mayoralty started out smoothly enough, once it was clear that Bilandic accepted the real distribution of power. His relations with machine leaders were good, and his public image was also positive—a middle-class, apparently reasonably honest, machine mayor. His greatest strength, as far as machine leaders like Vrdolyak, Burke, and Dunne were concerned, was that he did not threaten their control of politics and patronage, whereas any of numerous other aspirants to his job might. Also, his ethnic background maintained a compromise of sorts, keeping the blacks away and at the same time placating the Eastern European working-class whites who made the machine work. Moreover, his persona and policies continued to attract the business support that had been so important to the machine in the later Daley years.

Bilandic was not a strong leader, however, in a city that had come to view the mayoralty as a position of strength. Thus, while the machine was apparently content to reslate Bilandic for a full term in the 1979 mayoralty, others viewed his weakness as a vehicle for circumventing the machine, or even defeating it.

Moreover, no one anticipated eighty-seven inches of snow in the winter of 1978-79, the greatest accumulation in the city's history. Week after week the build-up remained and conditions got worse, snarling traffic and disrupting lives for about two months. It was a formidable disaster, offering an opportunity to a mayor who wanted to prove himself, but Bilandic failed to handle it. His image deteriorated badly; he began to appear like a bungler, and there was strong public anger at his inadequacy. This was exacerbated by the inevitable allegations of corruption, revolving primarily around a lucrative contract for a report on the snow problem being given to a Bilandic crony who produced nothing of value.

In effect, nature simply provided a catalyst, making hopes for a way to break the machine seem not so fanciful any longer. Both blacks and ambitious whites took advantage of the situation, but none more successfully than Jane Byrne, a most unlikely force even in a city not unaccustomed to unlikely political careers.

Jane Byrne came from the solid middle-class "lace curtain" Irish of Chicago—not rich, but comfortable and very respectable. She was educated at Barat College, an exclusive Roman Catholic women's school, and made her debut in the equally Catholic Presentation Ball. She was widowed young, however, with a small child to support, and from a beginning as a Kennedy volunteer in 1960, she became a paid public servant in the plethora of programs created by Lyndon Johnson's War on Poverty. Along the way, she caught Richard J. Daley's eye and became a favorite, for reasons no one has really determined.

Byrne became a public figure of sorts when Daley made her Commissioner of Consumer Sales, Weights, and Measures in 1968. She made the office visible, and did a good job, with no scandal attached to her administration. At the same time, she became increasingly active in the machine, to the point, in 1975, that Daley made her his co-chairman of the Cook County Democratic Central Committee. To be sure, this was a nominal position, with her senior clearly in charge, but nonetheless it expressed her unique relationship with Daley and made her a person of consequence.

George Dunne dropped Byrne from the co-chairmanship right after Daley's funeral, but her ambition had been kindled, and she received a great deal of publicity in a battle with Bilandic over alleged collusion and corruption with taxicab companies. In late 1977 she was fired from her commissioner's job, but it was too late. She had become a popular champion of sorts—in the machine but not of it, by no means an outsider but apparently independent and honest, a defender of the consumer.

This widespread public sympathy was all Jane Byrne needed, and she jumped into the battle against Bilandic's 1979 renomination. The snow helped enormously, as did the lingering taxicab scandal. Moreover, Byrne filled a vacuum, wherein no one else seemed really in a position to contest the Democratic primary. Hers was not an antimachine campaign; indeed, she worked hard to suggest that she, rather than Bilandic, was the real heir to the politics and leadership of Richard J. Daley. The central committee's refusal to endorse her, she argued, showed how far the machine had wandered from loyalty to the former mayor.

Byrne's strength lay in her being the only viable alternative, both for the city's liberals and the antimachine blacks, who, at the moment, were simply too disorganized to mount their own campaign. It was, however, the snow, and the expanding public perception of Bilandic as a bungler, that made the whole thing possible.

Byrne won the primary, carrying twenty-nine of the city's fifty wards. The two candidates split the white ethnic vote, Bilandic carrying the southwest side and Byrne the northwest. Byrne beat him handily in the more liberal lakefront wards, where the machine's image had always been negative. Bilandic won the Hispanic vote handily, but less than 20 percent of the city's Hispanics actually voted. And, most importantly, Byrne outpolled Bilandic about 3 to 2 among blacks, while black turnout increased 7 percent over what it had been in recent elections.

The fact that two-thirds of Chicago's eligible blacks still did not vote at all suggests that Byrne was hardly an exciting prospect to those voters or their leaders. Nonetheless, it was a significant measure of the cumulative effect of black alienation from the machine. Not only did it give Jane Byrne the nomination; it also suggested that the time was riper than ever before for the rise of a black leader who could truly unleash the power that black voters controlled in Chicago.

As always, the primary was the real election in Chicago. Byrne swamped Republican Wallace Johnson in the general election and entered the mayoralty with great popular backing. Her position with the party leadership was ambiguous, however, and she by no means controlled it or the city council.

At first, Byrne as mayor seemed to fulfill the reformers' hopes. She stayed somewhat apart from machine leaders and seemed reformist relative to patronage as well. In fact, she wanted to take control of patronage in order to dominate the machine, at the same time reforming it (for example, firing large numbers of do-nothing payrollers) so as to retain her non-partisan support.

She did make the necessary compromises. When State Senator Richard M. Daley, the former mayor's son, sought the party's nomination for the politically powerful office of State's Attorney in 1980, Byrne recognized this as a real threat to her re-election. She made peace with her machine enemies through their mutual support of Edward Burke--one of the "evil cabal" she had excoriated in her campaign—for the nomination. It was a sign that she had developed some real strength but also that she probably needed the party regulars more than they needed her. Daley's victory in the spring 1980 primary suggested just how deeply in disarray the once monolithic organization had become. Byrne was not, to leaders like Burke and Vrdolyak, really one of them, even when she cooperated. And her being a woman made it even less likely that they would ever accept her; they were, after all, very traditional, even tribal, in their political values.

Her compromises were well-publicized and diminished some of the middle-class and minority support she had garnered as a battler against the machine. More to the point, she proved a poor mayor, and within a year of her inauguration, her administration was in a shambles.

For a while, it seemed that Byrne would continue Daley's good relationship with the city's business elite. She exposed "hidden" budgetary deficits and promised to cut costs. She did drop 1,500 payrollers in her 1979 budget, took a hard stand with public employee unions, and avoided a general tax increase. That and a balanced budget gave her the image of a fiscal conservative in the business community.

But Standard & Poor's, in a much-publicized action, dropped the city's bond rating from AA to A+. The Board of Education was apparently on the verge of bankruptcy, for which the mayor was at least partially blamed. And labor problems worsened.

Under Daley, city workers did not have collective bargaining agreements, but their administratively set wages were established under "prevailing wage" guidelines that left them relatively well paid. Unions were placated by having control of hiring practices, and business groups by the labor peace and economic growth that attended the process. It was a sometimes wasteful situation, but it pleased many people. However, some city workers who were not in the crafts and building trades, including the fire and police departments, felt left out and underpaid. Byrne's effort to regularize the city payroll included a willingness to accept collective bargaining agreements in place of the prevailing wage agreements. But this threatened the craft unions, in terms of both lost wages and the possibility of their losing power to newer noncraft unions like the American Federation of State, County, and Municipal Employees.

By the end of 1979, Byrne was in trouble. She had weathered a Chicago Transit Authority strike in December 1979 fairly well, posing as a defender of the commuter against greedy workers. But a teacher's walkout and strike were more complex. And in February 1980 the firefighters went out; their strike was long and costly, and very bitter. The mayor did not seem to be in control, and she was widely regarded as one of the villains of the piece.

Politically, Byrne was also stumbling. She had endorsed President Carter for re-election very early, in the fall of 1979. Then, fearing to alienate the Irish leaders of the machine, who were anti-Carter, she flip-flopped to support Edward M. Kennedy. This made her look foolish and made the spring 1980 primaries very important to her position. When both Daley and Carter won in March, Byrne seemed to be out of control. She had to go along with party leaders who wanted to replace George Dunne with Edward Vrdolyak as chairman, but the end result was that the ward bosses were once again firmly in control.

Byrne's position never improved after the spring of 1980. Her own controversial personality—combative, impulsive, and vindictive—didn't help. She was distrusted by party leaders, had a poor image in the press, and her middle-class and minority support steadily dissipated. Everyone seemed to be just waiting for the 1983 campaign, not least black leaders who felt that their time, at last, had come.

Indeed, Byrne's clumsiness on racial issues was ultimately crucial to the development of the city's first real flexing of black political muscle. She and the machine, finally, thought they could prevail among blacks on the basis of traditional manipulation and appeals, but time had run out on such an approach. The mayor opposed busing, while admitting that the schools were segregated. And she consistently opposed a scattered site plan for public housing, reflecting working-class white opposition to the presence of public housing, and blacks, in their neighborhoods.

In late 1979, when a new superintendent of schools was required, she ignored strong black pressure for promoting a black deputy superintendent, and put in a white. Two years later, she did appoint an outside black woman to the post, but only after an organizational change had removed control of the budget from the superintendent's hands to those of a separate—and white-controlled—body.

Also, in 1981, she moved to replace two blacks on the Board of Education with two white women, both with anti-integration backgrounds. She did the same with the Chicago Housing Authority, to create a white majority on that body, even though more than 80 percent of the residents of CHA projects were black. This move was bitterly criticized in the black community, and by a number of previously machine-loyal black aldermen. Indeed, Allan Streeter, a black alderman appointed to fill a vacancy by Byrne, broke with her over the Board of Education appointments, leading Byrne and the machine to try to dump him in the special election. Streeter suddenly became a black hero, and won the election. Now it was clear that the machine could be beaten, and black organizations were emboldened relative to the 1983 mayoralty.

Byrne's efforts to placate blacks were clumsy and out of date. When she and her husband moved into the Cabrini-Green public housing project for three weeks, vowing to stay there until it was cleaned up, she got some good publicity. But black leaders were no longer so naive, nor so easily satisfied. Likewise, her much-publicized distribution of food baskets to the black poor smacked of the nineteenth century—they were not a viable device in the 1980s.

Black organizations boycotted the mayor's ChicagoFest urban festival in 1982. They worked instead on a black voter registration drive that resulted in 87 percent of Chicago's eligible blacks being registered by the 1983 primary—an increase of sixteen percentage points over 1975, and five points higher than white registration for 1983.

The machine tried to neutralize this increase in a traditional way, via redistricting. It managed to reduce the number of black-majority wards from nineteen to seventeen and to dissipate Hispanic concentration as well. The action would be overturned by the federal courts later, as a violation of the voting rights act, but it did last through the 1983 elections. However, it just became more grist for the organizational mill of Chicago's blacks. Also, it ignored population dynamics, which meant that the changes would only be temporary in any case.

In November 1982, both Richard M. Daley and Harold Washington (now a congressman) declared for the Democratic mayoral nomination. Neither appeared before the Democratic slatemaking committee, which quickly endorsed Byrne. But former party chairman George Dunne and twelve other ward committeemen refused to support Byrne, reflecting, most of all, Daley's support. The machine was clearly in trouble.

Mayor Byrne tried to focus her campaign on all groups: white ethnics, blacks, white lakeshore liberals, and Hispanics. With white ethnics, her problem, obviously, was Daley, whose strength on the southwest side—his father's power base—was formidable. And, really for the first time, black support was very weak; the machine's traditional strength here was by no means gone, but it was less than at any time since the rise of Cermak.

Daley tried to attract black support, but this was hard to do when his main strength was among the white working class. He never committed himself to any of the issues that black organizations had raised. And while he had the support of the city's two major newspapers, this did not really resolve the major weaknesses of his campaign.

Washington, for his part, had a number of weaknesses. He was not well known generally, nor was he truly a leader of Chicago blacks. His conviction and jailing for not filing income tax returns made it easy enough for the city's white power structure to write him off. His campaign, moreover, was poorly organized and financed. But he did well in four televised debates, which showed him to be bright and articulate. And, more important, he was the only game in town as far as black leaders were concerned. This was the year, finally, to try, and Washington was the only black in the right position at the right time.

The outcome of the Chicago mayoral primary of 1983 reflected both the inevitable result of long-term forces and a variety of short-term ones that were distinct to its particular time. Ward results are shown in Table 6.1. Such an outcome was bound to occur in Chicago, but it might well not have come in 1983 had Richard J. Daley not died when he did, and Jane Byrne not emerged in the wake of the machine's post-Daley confusion.

Jane Byrne and Richard M. Daley split the white vote almost evenly, with Byrne a bit stronger on the northwest side and Daley much stronger on the southwest. Byrne also beat Daley in the wealthy and relatively liberal lakeshore wards, and she won the Hispanic vote as well—although Hispanic turnout remained very low (24 percent), and thus unimportant.

Harold Washington, however, carried twenty wards, of which nineteen had black majorities. He had over 80 percent of the black vote, and an unprecedented 64 percent of eligible blacks did vote, exactly the same percentage as among whites. Thus it was a racial victory, made possible by the division within the Chicago Democratic Party. Washington beat Byrne by only two percentage points, as Table 6.1 indicates; nonetheless, it was a major victory for the city's blacks, and the first concrete political demonstration in Chicago of the voting power blacks now had in more and more of the nation's cities.

Since the 1930s, the Democratic primary in Chicago *was* the election; by the time of Richard J. Daley, the Republicans' main problem was in finding someone willing to be humbled in order to maintain the appearance of a two-party system in the city. And Harold Washington had every expectation that this would be the case again in 1983. However bitter the primary campaign may have been, Washington assumed that tradition would prevail and that the party would coalesce around him. Certainly, nothing in his background or ideology made him antipathetic to the machine; all he really wanted was its recognition of his own place, personally, and that of blacks generally.

This was not to be, however; the machine's tribal and traditionally antiblack sentiments were too strong. Moreover, the danger of Washington and his supporters, as outsiders, was equally as threatening. Control is the key element in any machine, and, in Chicago, blacks were not only racially repugnant to the old guard, they were also a threat to the political control of those who had been running things for fifty years. And as it turned out, the fear that the machine leaders had of Washington was another sign of the machine's closeness to its voting base—the white working-class ethnics of Chicago did not want a black mayor. Almost from the moment the primary ended, a groundswell of popular anti-Washington sentiment burgeoned on the northwest and southwest sides of the city.

The Republicans had also conducted a primary in 1983, participated in by fewer than fifteen thousand voters, and with only a single candidate, Bernard E. Epton. Like most Republican candidates in the city's recent history, Epton was independently wealthy and relatively liberal. He had served in the state assembly for fourteen years, elected as the Republican representative of the Democratic and liberal Hyde Park (University of Chicago) area. This was possible because of the Illinois lower house's unusual system of having three representatives from each district, with interparty agreement that the minority party in each district gets one of the three seats.

Epton lost his assembly seat in 1980, when the nature of representation was reformed to single-member districts. Thus, he was looking for new opportunities. As a relatively liberal Republican, he was a reasonable choice

TABLE 6.1
Voting Data—Chicago, 1983

Ward	Dominant Ethnicity	Primary—Percentage of Vote			General Election—Percentage	
		Washington	Byrne	Daley	Washington Vote	Turnout
1	Mixed	42	41	17	63	78
2	Black	80	16	4	98	80
3	Black	84	13	3	99	78
4	Black	78	13	9	93	80
5	Black	77	13	10	91	83
6	Black	87	10	3	99	84
7	Black	65	22	13	82	78
8	Black	86	9	5	99	83
9	Black	80	15	5	94	83
10	Mixed	24	54	22	34	86
11	White ethnic	13	9	78	26	86
12	White ethnic	8	33	59	15	84
13	White ethnic	1	46	53	4	91
14	White ethnic	8	47	45	16	87
15	Black	48	28	24	61	84
16	Black	77	19	4	99	82
17	Black	84	13	3	99	83
18	White ethnic	36	23	41	44	87
19	White ethnic	12	25	63	20	85
20	Black	84	13	3	99	79
21	Black	88	9	3	99	85
22	Mixed	20	35	45	52	70
23	White ethnic	1	36	63	4	90
24	Black	79	18	3	99	81
25	Mixed	24	45	31	49	73
26	Mixed	9	50	41	46	74
27	Black	72	23	5	93	78
28	Black	81	15	4	99	79
29	Black	76	18	6	93	80
30	White ethnic	2	58	40	13	83
31	Mixed	17	53	30	61	75
32	White ethnic	15	39	46	44	76
33	White ethnic	8	61	31	38	77
34	Black	87	10	3	99	84
35	White ethnic	4	52	44	16	81
36	White ethnic	1	55	44	5	87
37	Black	58	27	15	77	81
38	White ethnic	1	53	46	6	87
39	White ethnic	3	55	42	12	84
40	White ethnic	5	48	47	17	82
41	White ethnic	2	52	46	7	84
42	Lakefront middle class	28	38	34	46	81
43	Lakefront middle class	15	48	37	36	81
44	Lakefront middle class	17	48	35	39	79
45	White ethnic	1	47	52	7	87
46	Lakefront middle class	27	42	31	47	78
47	White ethnic	5	55	40	18	81
48	Lakefront middle class	26	41	33	44	76
49	Lakefront middle class	22	45	33	43	77
50	White ethnic	6	51	43	18	82
Total		36	34	30	51.8	82

for that party's mayoral nomination. And as a relatively undistinguished public figure, his background was quite consistent with that of most of his predecessors. Only fate, in the person of Harold Washington's nomination, made Epton's bid for the mayoralty anything other than one more chapter in a running Chicago joke.

The 1983 mayoral campaign was mainly, indeed almost exclusively, racial in nature. The responsibility for this is arguable; the candidates, the machine, and the media, among others, have all been accused at one time or another. All of them played a role, to be sure, but, ultimately, the racial focus was a true grassroots issue. Tens, perhaps hundreds, of thousands of white Chicagoans were absolutely opposed to a black mayor, and perhaps especially to Harold Washington. Their feelings about this, as they saw them, were entirely reasonable: a way of life was endangered. Similarly, tens of thousands of Chicago blacks were excited, politically, as they had never been before, and they supported Harold Washington as exclusively on the basis of race as whites opposed him on that basis.

The machine itself was deeply divided. Edward Vrdolyak was able to get a Cook County Democratic Central Committee endorsement of Washington's candidacy only by avoiding a role call vote at its meeting. Ten committeemen boycotted the meeting entirely, and another twelve sent deputies rather than attending personally. Ultimately, only about half a dozen Democratic ward committeemen supported Washington, and eight openly opposed him; the rest just hid. Equally significant, the real heart of the party, the precinct workers, were overwhelmingly anti-Washington and began supporting Epton from the moment of his nomination.

All over the city, large white ethnic crowds turned out in a demonstration of great enthusiasm for Epton. He had little—as a Republican, a liberal, a Jew—to offer them, but he was the great white hope of 1983, and that, as it turned out, was all he needed.

Jane Byrne sought to take advantage of the situation by offering herself as a write-in alternative in mid-March. But write-in voting in Chicago is extremely complex, and her chances were nil. So the machine turned her down. Also, the national Democratic Party was very critical; Edward Kennedy, for example, who had supported her in the primary, came out for Washington and castigated Byrne for her action. After about a week, the former mayor dropped out.

Epton and Washington both abjured the issue of race early in the campaign, for example in their one televised debate on March 21. Epton focused on the questionability of Washington from an ethical perspective—his jail sentence for not filing income tax forms, his suspension from the right to practice law, and so on. And Washington tried to adopt the mantle of reform—pledging to work for a change in the law so as to end the patronage system that had characterized Chicago politics from time immemorial.

But race would not be denied. From every quarter, it was constantly reiterated. The campaign was nasty, as well, particularly on the southwest and northwest sides. Racial epithets were constantly yelled out at Epton rallies, and a wide variety of racist brochures were circulated in those areas. It was the "nigger" Washington they feared, and few had much reluctance about putting it in those terms. Epton could hardly fail to realize that it was race which had made him, quite unexpectedly, a viable candidate for the mayoralty. He might deny that the slogan, "Epton for Mayor—Before It's Too Late" referred to race, but everyone else took it for that, and nothing more.

The Washington campaign was not well run, and his efforts to appeal to whites had little strength. It *was* a black campaign; that was its strength and its weakness. But the mobilization of black support exceeded, by far, anything Chicago had ever seen before, and it accounted for the margin of Washington's victory. A generation of machine neglect, both political and in terms of issues, came to a head. It was inevitable, by the time of Daley, that this revolution would take place somewhere along the line; and the history of Chicago politics since Daley's death made 1983 the year of the inevitable.

The outcome was the closest since before the rise of the Chicago Democrats, Washington defeating his rival with 51.8 percent of the vote in an election with almost 1.3 million voters. (If one includes the forty thousand voters who took ballots but did not make any mayoral choice, Washington's share of the vote declines to only 50.3 percent.) Table 6.1 shows, by ward, Washington's percentage of the vote and the unusual turnout rate of the election. Blacks turned out at a rate of 73 percent, almost 6 points higher than whites—a first in Chicago, by a long shot. Washington got virtually the entire black vote, plus about a 4-to-1 margin among Hispanics (only 24 percent of whom bothered to vote, however). Epton swept the white ethnic wards by almost as much and had a strong majority in the lakefront wards, but it was not quite enough. If Chicago mayoral elections were nonpartisan in nature, denying Washington the residual power of a Democratic label, he would have lost. But Chicago had a black mayor.

The election of Harold Washington created a stalemate in Chicago politics and a lack of a focus of power. The machine had suffered an obviously crushing blow, losing control of the mayoralty for the first time since Cermak defeated Thompson in 1931. Without the mayor's office, the political beast had lost one of its two heads—the other, obviously, being control of the party. But old guard leaders like Vrdolyak and Burke would not give in; they were ready neither to lose their own personal power nor to defer to a black, even if he would respect the machine.

Washington, for his part, was frustrated because the Chicago mayor's office is not, constitutionally, very powerful. It, too, requires the second head, and the conjunction of legal and party control was what had made the Chicago Democrats so powerful for more than fifty years. Washington's coattails were long enough to pull a number of nonmachine black city councilmen into office with him, but not long enough to secure control. The party regulars continued to control the city council, making it difficult for Washington to govern, to say nothing of influencing the party.

Thus Washington's first term has been marked by indecision and confusion, with the reins of government split between two sets of hands, and those of party inaccessible to him. Unfortunately, it has not been a leadership problem only, since the people of Chicago remain as bitterly divided over issues of race as they were during the campaign.

The ultimate effect of all this on the Chicago machine is not yet clear. The machine may well bounce back in 1987, but the steadily growing black population will make this difficult to accomplish, even if white turnout is huge and efforts are made to stuff the ballot boxes—a not-unknown practice in Chicago's history, but one that was not widely used in 1983.

The machine may well find that its only real chance to hold onto power is to give a truly significant role in its leadership to blacks. Harold Washington is probably amenable to a reconciliation; moreover, there are many other ambitious black politicians who would like to replace him. The tribal provincialism of Chicago's Irish and Slavic machine leaders will make the pill of permanent black power difficult to swallow, however. Only their even greater desire not to lose power completely may persuade them that they have no alternative.

Blacks were long denied their proportional share of power in Chicago, more than was the case for other ethnic groups in the city's history. But two factors, the long-term effect of the civil rights movement and black population growth, made it inevitable that the machine could not extend that denial into perpetuity. Even Richard J. Daley, had he lived, would have been confronted with this reality. However unhappily, he either would have bent to it or would have lost control.

Machines, as we have seen, survive by being flexible. They must, first, co-opt the populations of their cities. This is just what Charlie Murphy and Tony Cermak understood and excelled at—moving from the Irish and the Germans, to the Jews and the Poles, and so on. The situation is no different in this respect now—only the groups, black and Hispanic in startlingly increasing numbers. If race is to be the measure that undercuts this traditional machine approach, even the Chicago machine will die.

Second, machines have had to adapt to changing needs, particularly the demographic changes that meant serving middle-class electorates rather than lower-class ones. Changing racial values and interests are also among those dynamic need considerations, and the machine has to recognize them, as well. The Chicago Democratic machine outlived most of its contemporaries because it responded relatively well to both of these realities, within a hospitable legal environment. If it does not continue to respond, it will survive no longer.

Harold Washington's defeat of the Chicago machine is particularly relevant to the understanding of contemporary American urban politics because it was by no means unique. Throughout the country, in both machine and nonmachine cities, the twin dynamics of the civil rights revolution and black population growth have challenged the political status quo. And, as in Chicago, the struggle has tended to center on mayoral elections.

As early as 1967, for example, Carl Stokes was elected mayor of Cleveland, Ohio, and Richard G. Hatcher won the same office in Gary, Indiana. In Stokes's case, his very narrow victory came in a city that was only one-third black. Hatcher, on the other hand, became the first black mayor of a predominantly black city, in a campagin that was as bitter and racist as that in Chicago sixteen years later.

Tom Bradley lost a racially charged campaign for mayor of Los Angeles in 1969, but bounced back four years later to win, with extensive white support in a city where blacks were a decided minority. Coleman Young was elected in Detroit, which was about 50 percent black, in the same year. Bradley's campaign went well beyond the issue of race, despite his opponent's efforts to make race the issue. Young, on the other hand, won on an almost straight racial vote in a city whose ethnic makeup was comparable to that of Chicago. Similarly, Bradley won in a city with no real machine tradition in the twentieth century, whereas Young defeated an entrenched Democratic organization.

In that same banner year of 1973, Maynard Jackson was elected mayor of Atlanta, in an outstanding testimonial to the effects of the Voting Rights Act of 1965. He became the first black mayor of a major southern city, starting a trend that has continued into numerous cities, large and small, throughout the south. Even Birmingham, Alabama, the city of Bull Connor and "massive resistance" to the civil rights movement, gained a black mayor with Richard Eddington.

By the 1980s the trend, if not yet a flood, was nonetheless remarkable. In cities from Mount Vernon, New York, to Plainfield and Camden, New

Jersey, to New London, Connecticut, plus myriad smaller towns in between and down into the south, blacks won mayoralties. In 1982, a black Republican was able to force a white Democrat into a runoff in Atlantic City, New Jersey, when he kept the latter from gaining a majority in the non-partisan primary. Blacks crossed party lines to support one of their own.

One month after Harold Washington defeated Bernard Epton, Wilson Goode won the Democratic mayoral primary in Philadelphia, defeating controversial mayor and former police commissioner Frank Rizzo. Goode won 97 percent of the black vote, but also 23 percent of the white vote, in a largely middle-class reaction against Rizzo's contentious personality, racism, and flawed administration. Goode went on to win the general election that fall, bringing another of the country's cities with a tradition of machine strength under black mayoral control.

Even Boston, as machine-driven a city as Chicago, with an equivalent tradition of segregation and racism, was not immune. Despite the city's population being only about one-fifth black, Melvin King ran a good race against the eventual white winner, Raymond Flynn, winning 35 percent of the total vote. Never had Boston's Irish come quite so close to displacement.

In fact, by the end of 1983, eleven major American cities (with populations exceeding 200,000) had black mayors, four of them in the south. The effects of this, in both machine and nonmachine contexts, were obvious. Black interests, both parochial and general, are now very much the stuff of urban politics and can no longer be denied.

This development is not all that different from what we have seen in earlier chapters of this book. Blacks are replacing the Irish, Italians, and others in an almost natural progression. It is distinct in that race has been a greater barrier than religious and national ethnicity, causing blacks to wait longer than other urban groups.

Black urban political power will not remain quite so monolithic over time. Rising class differences and individual personal ambitions among blacks, for example, will lead to increasing intragroup rivalry. Moreover, the dynamic of progression of ethnic groups has not stopped. In many cities Hispanics are increasing their numbers even faster than blacks. Hispanic politicians will continue to be influenced by black progress to follow a similar path. And in some cities other groups, such as oriental immigrants, will also enter the competition. The process continues.

EPILOGUE:
OF BOSSES AND BOSSING

As one looks back upon the development of urban political machines and upon the career of Richard J. Daley as the "last of the bosses," one is tempted to argue that the question generally asked should not be, "Why has the machine survived only in a few places?" but rather, "Why has it not survived elsewhere?" The reasons for this are only partly clear, but they provide a reasonable focus for some summary thoughts about the relationship of the political machine to its electoral base.

In looking at the careers of the men considered in this book, we see a natural progression or development among them; they have a good deal in common. The challenges differed from time to time and from place to place, but their relationships with the electorate remained fairly consistent. None of these bosses seems in any way extraordinary. They were highly competent, well-trained in a practical sense for their particular kind of work, and able to maintain focus on their major goal—which in the case of all but perhaps Tweed was the same: power. This, plus the professional politician's understanding of the need to compromise, to give in where there is no possibility of overriding, was central to their success. In Daley's later years, and since his death, the Chicago machine tried to ignore this need, denying to blacks the share of power their numbers demanded; and they did so at great cost.

One reason the machine survived in Chicago while it declined in most other places is the legal milieu in which Chicago exists. New York and other states gradually changed their laws governing civil service, partisan elections, the power of political parties, primaries, and so on (non-machine cities usually experienced these changes very early, during the Progressive Era). But Illinois was very slow to make changes of this kind. Cumulative voting for the lower house of the state legislature, for example, prevailed until very recently, despite frequent attacks from those who wanted to diminish the power of party. Little change in the patronage system, or in other built-in advantages to the existing parties, came about over the years. This legal structure does not guarantee that politics in Chicago will maintain the form that existed under Daley and his predecessors, but it does make that form possible, whereas it no longer is in most American cities.

The partisan, extralocal aspect of the urban political machine's strength has also been crucial. Daley, for example, was the local leader of that political party to which most ordinary Chicagoans were loyal—in formal membership or just in voting proclivity. This has not always been true for urban machines, but it has been for those that lasted any length of time. Other things being equal, or even nearly equal, this provides a real edge. It is also a phenomenon that is to some degree outside the machine's and the boss's control; in this regard, then, luck does play a role. The Philadelphia Republican machine, for example, had a long and successful life, which failed, in large part, because by the 1930s it was allied to the wrong side of the political ledger.

Patronage, and organization itself, were always central to machine success, because they related directly to a hold on the mass base of the machine and were a key element in its structure and maintenance. The Daley machine, for example, or that of Murphy in New York, were among the major employers of their regions. And if "reform" over the years removed some jobs from machine control, the tremendous increase in all governmental bureaucracies more than compensated for the loss, especially in cities like Chicago, with their supportive statutory environment. As Table 5.1 indicates, among all employed Chicagoans above the age of sixteen in 1970, 13 percent worked for some governmental agency and 8 percent worked for local government. This means that tens of thousands of families, from the very humble to the upper reaches of the middle class, are directly or indirectly beholden to the machine for their material support. And they influence others, since it is in their interest to do so.

The machine has existed because it has been able to respond quickly and directly to the needs of the very large numbers of dependent or semi-dependent people to be found in the modern American city. Changes in law and in the distribution of wealth have only partly affected this phenomenon. New dependent peoples have replaced others; and new kinds of dependency have been created by the very system designed to end the old ones. As long as the country maintains a division of powers between national and local governments, with the latter serving as an intervening administrative entity between the former and the masses, there remains the possibility for the city and county to continue providing the kinds of services which Plunkitt described so well at the turn of the century, as well as newer ones that characterize a middle-class society.

One important expansion Daley made in the support of the machine can be described as vertical rather than horizontal. The traditional mass base of the machine was supplemented by his successful wooing of the city's—and the suburbs'—financial, economic, and social elite. This was not the first time business leaders and machine politicians had cooperated, but under Daley that cooperation was institutionalized. In accomplishing this, it can be argued, the machine was trying, increasingly, to serve mutually conflicting interests, and thus had to slight the needs of its mass base. This is to some degree true, as those who have lost their homes to urban renewal, their jobs to postindustrialization, or their physical well-being to hits on the head by police would testify. But I think this also relates to changes in the nature of the city; it was as important for Daley to add the support of these elite groups as it was for Kelly to add the blacks, or Murphy the Jews. Machines were in the past able to work with mutually antipathetic cultural groups, and it is not necessarily any harder to do the same with economic and social ones.

Indeed, there were indications that for Daley, as for Thompson and others, holding together the machine's disparate mass elements was difficult primarily owing to social and power conflict within the working class itself, and especially across racial lines. That the Daley machine won its victories with a negative relationship to voter turnout, and that turnout generally declined so much, were the unhealthiest omens—for machine politics—of all. We might say of all urban machines, and certainly of the Chicago machine, that over time victory came not because the machine was so popular but because there were no viable alternatives to mold a firmer voter coalition. In Chicago, for example, the Republicans were long frustrated because they were, quite simply, Republicans, and accordingly for decades had little ideological or practical appeal to the urban masses. Third parties have been too poor and weak (here, New York, since the 1930s, has been different, and the Democratic machine has declined accordingly) to offer a real option. So those who have not liked the machine have very often just stayed at home, as was long the case with Chicago's blacks; sometimes they stayed at home in such numbers that, together, they could have elected a mayor.

Machine-run cities have not avoided the deep social and racial tensions of modern America, but neither have they experienced them to a disproportionately high degree. Mayor Daley, for example, could well be accused of what I have suggested may be the major failing of "bossism": it is a political situation that is innately conservative and defensive and that tends, by its very nature, to avoid controversy and division. Thus it does not provide much in the way of leadership or planning for the future. As-sociated with this has been the tribal nature of the largely Irish leadership of most machines. They have been leery of the leadership aspirations of all outgroups—Jews, Italians, the various Slavic groups, for example—from the late nineteenth century to the present. Blacks and Hispanics are just two additional, perhaps even more alien, rivals whose group identities and political interests were to be feared and resisted at the same time as they were being co-opted into support of the machine. This is hard to do, and has been one of the greatest tests of urban political organizations since the rise of American cities.

The tendency to put off the resolution of real social and economic issues and to ignore the aspirations of newer groups was as true of Daley as it was of Tweed and Murphy. Daley did not really try to find new paths of racial accommodation, of easing the economic and social plight of the urban poor, of halting the deterioration of the public school system or the "white flight" to the suburbs, of making the city more livable psycholog-ically and emotionally as well as physically. Nor was he really receptive to allotting more than the minimum necessary power inside the machine to non-Irish groups. These phenomena have been characteristic of machine rule. They are also what led to the post-Daley politics of Chicago, and may be what will turn it and other cities into racial fortresses before the end of this century. But Daley and other bosses did not do demonstrably worse in these respects than mayors and political organizations referred to in less pejorative terms. We should be aware of the weaknesses of bossism, but we should also be aware that alternative political forms have not done much better.

In a way, one can argue that the *system* itself is perhaps overstressed. That, for example, Chicago, has a highly partisan, very structured political system, whereas Los Angeles has very much the opposite and is physically also a very different city, should not cloak the fact that their problems and failings are much more alike than they are different. The city as a political unit deals, within its statutory and other abilities, with the social, ethnic, economic, and other forces of its times. The form of its government is not unimportant, nor are the quality and commitment of the people who govern. But the problems themselves, and the social and cultural nexus, are really the crux of it all. These are often general and national problems: in part they are attitudinal and essentially private problems whose ultimate solution cannot come from any kind of legislation or other government action.

We are properly concerned with trying to understand which form of government—urban, national, or other—is most likely to deal creatively, efficiently, and honestly with a society's problems. In these pages I have tried to suggest the nature, and the strengths and weaknesses, of one general urban approach that has been around for over a century. This form, by whatever name we choose to call it, has performed some essential services in a distinctive way. Its relative value is in the final analysis subject to personal evaluation. But we must beware, in our judgmental process, of focusing too narrowly on form or, for that matter, of relying too heavily on government at all—especially in the sense that government can operate on a plane beyond what citizens themselves believe and desire.

Democratic government—partisan or nonpartisan, amateur or professional, idealistic or cynical—is a reflection of its society; it can be nothing else. When one lives with the advantages of a democratic polity, however imperfect it may be, one must realize that one lives under a system that, through representation, does require us to deal ourselves with our problems as a society. The trouble, indeed, is not with the governors, but with the governed, whom they represent only too well.

FOR FURTHER READING

For a general understanding of the boss and the machine, the works cited in Chapter 1 are all worthwhile. They are leading examples of various popular and scholarly appraisals and interpretations.

Several books of readings have appeared in recent years, reflecting an increased interest in bossism that is due largely to an increased interest in urban history generally. Bruce M. Stave and Sondra Astor Stave, ed., *Urban Bosses, Machines, and Progressive Reformers*, 2d. rev. ed. (Malabar, Fla., 1984) is a good collection on both the machines and their opponents. Blaine A. Brownell and Warren E. Stickle, eds., *Bosses and Reformers: Urban Politics in America, 1880-1920* (New York, 1973) is good on the earlier years; and Alexander B. Callow, Jr., ed., *The City Boss in America* (New York, 1976) is also worthwhile.

On Tweed, the most recent work is Leo Hershkowitz, *Tweed's New York: Another Look* (Garden City, N.Y., 1977), which essays a major reinterpretation upgrading Tweed and downplaying the less savory aspects of the Ring. He is only partially successful, and should be balanced by Alexander B. Callow, Jr., *The Tweed Ring* (New York, 1966), and Seymour Mandelbaum, *Boss Tweed's New York* (New York, 1965). John W. Pratt's article, "Boss Tweed's Public Welfare Program" (*New York Historical Society Quarterly*, 1961) is also useful; and Jerome Mushkat, *Tammany: The Evolution of a Political Machine, 1789-1865* (Syracuse, 1971) explains Tammany's early years.

Less has been written recently about Murphy. Nancy Joan Weiss, *Charles Francis Murphy, 1858-1924: Respectability and Responsibility in Tammany Politics* (Northhampton, Mass., 1968), is informative but asks the wrong questions. Gustavus Myers's classic, *The History of Tammany Hall*, 2d. ed. (New York, 1971), provides an alternative view and deals with Tweed as well.

Chicago and its politicans have been written about more than any other city. My *A House for All Peoples: Ethnic Politics in Chicago, 1880-1936* (Lexington, Ky., 1971) deals with both Thompson and Cermak; and my

The New Deal and American Politics: A Study in Political Change (New York, 1978) has some relevant material on the 1930s. Cermak is also well handled by Alex Gottfried, in *Boss Cermak of Chicago: A Study of Political Leadership* (Seattle, 1962).

Thompson has been written about primarily by journalists, whose works are always interesting if sometimes shallow: Lloyd Wendt and Herman Kogan, *Big Bill of Chicago* (Indianapolis, 1953); John Bright, *Hizzoner Big Bill Thompson* (New York, 1930); Lloyd Lewis and Henry J. Smith, *Chicago: The History of Its Reputation* (New York, 1929); and William H. Stuart, *The Twenty Incredible Years* (Chicago, 1935).

Mayor Daley has received increasing popular and scholarly attention. Two biographies are by journalists who covered him for years: Mike Royko, *Boss: Richard J. Daley of Chicago* (New York, 1971), and Len O'Connor, *Clout: Mayor Daley and His City* (Chicago, 1975); both are informative, but the former is too affected by the author's animus against the mayor. David Halberstam's article "Daley of Chicago" (*Harper's Magazine*, 1968) is suggestive; and Bill Gleason's *Daley of Chicago: The Man, the Mayor, and the Limits of Conventional Politics* (New York, 1970) is a lesser work. Milton Rakove's *Don't Make No Waves, Don't Back No Losers: An Insider's Analysis of the Daley Machine* (Bloomington, 1979) is also worth reading.

The Daley succession and the rise of Harold Washington have already produced some good books: Samuel K. Gove and Louis H. Masotti, eds., *After Daley: Chicago Politics in Transition* (Urbana, Ill., 1982), has a number of interesting articles, and Bill and Lori Granger have produced *Fighting Jane Byrne and the Chicago Machine* (New York, 1980). Paul Kleppner's *Chicago Divided: The Making of a Black Mayor* (DeKalb, Ill., 1985) is a good study of the 1983 primary and general election in Chicago, and Melvin G. Holli and Paul M. Green, eds., *The Making of the Mayor: Chicago, 1983* (Grand Rapids, Mich., 1984), contains a number of articles on the same topic.

Finally, there are a number of interesting interpretations of machine politics in places not dealt with in this book. Some of the more useful ones are: Melvin G. Holli, *Reform in Detroit: Hazen S. Pingree and Urban Politics* (New York, 1969); Zane L. Miller, *Boss Cox's Cincinati: Urban Politics in the Progressive Era* (New York, 1968); Lyle Dorsett, *The Pendergast Machine* (New York, 1968), and *FDR and the City Bosses* (Port Washington, N.Y., 1977); Richard J. Connors, *A Cycle of Power: The Career of Jersey City Mayor Frank Hague* (Metuchen, N.J., 1971); Joel A. Tarr, *A Study in Boss Politics: William A. Lorimer of Chicago* (Urbana, Ill., 1971); and William D. Miller, *Mr. Crump of Memphis* (Baton Rouge, 1964).

INDEX

Lightning Source UK Ltd.
Milton Keynes UK
UKHW010822301020
372497UK00001B/42